Focolare

Focolare

Living a Spirituality of Unity
in the United States

Thomas Masters and Amy Uelmen

NEW CITY PRESS
Hyde Park, NY

Published in the United States by New City Press
202 Comforter Blvd., Hyde Park, NY 12538
www.newcitypress.com
© 2011 Thomas Masters and Amy Uelmen

Cover design by Durva Correia

Library of Congress Cataloging-in-Publication Data

Masters, Thomas.
  Focolare : living a spirituality of unity in the United States / Thomas
Masters and Amy Uelmen.
     p. cm.
  Includes bibliographical references (p.   ).
  ISBN 978-1-56548-374-3 (pbk. : alk. paper)
  1. Focolare Movement. 2. Christian life—United States. I. Uelmen, Amy.
II. Title.
  BX809.F6M37 2011
  267'.182—dc22   2010053819

Printed in the United States of America

For Terry Gunn

Born, Hastings, New Zealand, 1947
Born to Eternal Life, Mariapolis Luminosa,
Hyde Park, New York, 2010

His passion and gift for bringing a spirituality
of unity to English-speaking peoples
was a shining light for all of us.

Contents

Part III

The Focolare Spirituality and Contemporary Culture in the United States

Authors' Preface

On September 14, 1961 the Focolare was established in North America. Giovanna Vernuccio and Serenella (Sharry) Silvi moved into a tiny apartment on Mulberry Street in lower Manhattan, the first women's Focolare house; Antonio Petrilli resided temporarily at the YMCA on 47th Street. After Joseph Patron, Silvio Daneo, Rita Muccio and Anna Pigoni joined them a few months later, they moved into two small houses in Queens. This tiny group of *focolarini** could hardly foresee what would unfold, but in their hearts they carried an immense treasure: the capacity to generate the presence of Christ in the community, wherever "two or more" are united in his name, in his love (see Mt 18:20).

In 1964 Focolare founder Chiara Lubich visited the still-small community in America. Reflecting on this experience, co-founder Pasquale Foresi noted that they had seen many beautiful things in New York, but none could compare with the little houses where the *focolarini* lived with "Jesus in their midst."[1]

This book can only begin to present what that tiny community has become. It acknowledges — directly or indirectly — all who have given of themselves so that thousands across North America could experience the transforming gift of a spirituality of unity.

Focolare: Living a Spirituality of Unity in the United States provides a glimpse of the Movement's animating spirit and the impact of its principles upon American life and culture. It identifies and responds to questions that have emerged as the Focolare has grown in size and depth, and identifies key points for reflecting on the intersection of faith and culture. We hope that this presentation of the Focolare's experience might open a discussion that extends as well to the experience of other faith communities in the United States.

This book has been generated through cooperation, dialogue, and feedback from Focolare members in North America and in its international headquarters in Rocca di Papa, Rome. A similar spirit

---

* This Italian term is the familiar appellation for those who have made a formal commitment to the Movement as part of a Focolare community house. This word, which might be translated "carriers of fire," has no exact English equivalent. The singular would be "*focolarino*" (male) or "*focolarina*" (female).

has informed the process for selecting the personal examples we have included. These do not constitute a "scientific" sample, nor have we subjected them to a rigorous research method. They have been chosen because of their usefulness in representing the scope of the Focolare in the United States, as well as in illustrating and advancing the themes we consider important.

When she died in March 2008, Chiara Lubich left a spiritual and cultural legacy, including the official General Statutes, a comprehensive archive of her private and published writings, as well as multi-media versions of her public talks and informal conversations.[2] The Movement's inheritance also includes the witness and example of those who shared in her experience from the beginning, and who brought the Focolare lifestyle throughout the world. They communicated the charism of unity to thousands, transforming their lives and relationships, and renewing the social and ecclesial contexts where they live and work. This book touches only the surface of this legacy.

Our own personal origins, education, history, and culture bring a particular focus to this account. We cannot help but discern themes and pose questions from our North American point of view. One of the gifts of a spirituality of unity, however, is its capacity to recognize the distinct beauty of every perspective and to comprehend how diverse cultures express it in unique yet harmonious ways. We aim to help readers from any background appreciate the Focolare Movement in the United States, as well as reflect upon and value their own experience of spirituality and community.

Thomas Masters and Amy Uelmen

Introduction:
"I Want What You Have"

What does it mean to live a spirituality of unity? The best answer lies not in detailed explanation, but in experience. These vignettes present moments in the lives of three young women and three young men who put a spirituality of unity into effect in what they do and say.

Rebecca

"One morning I was out jogging with a close friend from college. She was struggling, searching for something deeper in her life. All of a sudden she burst into tears. I was at a loss for words, because this was my friend who seemed to have everything — she was bright, beautiful, and talented. She said, 'Rebecca, I want what you have.' I understood that she wanted to know the love of God that I had been blessed to understand."

What did Rebecca have? In a word, she "had" a spiritual core to her life — a spirituality of unity, a path that led her to discover the love of God, and with the support of others, live every aspect of her life according to this discovery. Her parents first learned about the Focolare Movement in 1986, from an interview they saw on EWTN.[1]

Her mother then invited someone from the Movement to their home to learn more, and a few years later a Focolare community house opened nearby in Columbus, Ohio. From her early childhood on, Rebecca reflects, "I understood that life was meant to be a response to God's love. The more I grow in the Focolare spirituality, the deeper I understand the depth and simplicity of God's love, and that this love can be shared with others."

At the age of eight, Rebecca traveled to Rome to attend an international conference for elementary school children. It was an important part of what she describes as "becoming a global person": "The children spoke different languages and dressed in their traditional attire, but we could understand one another. This sparked in me the desire to live for unity, to learn about different cultures and do something to alleviate the suffering of many people in our world, both on a local and global level."

As a young adult this vision has spurred her to serve as a volunteer for humanitarian efforts in Sierra Leone, Africa. "The choice to go there was difficult because of financial and personal burdens, but I felt

God was calling me to go ahead, and I was confident I would receive the practical support I needed. The Focolare has opened my eyes to the truth of the Church's calling to love. Other young people who also know the Focolare are always there to encourage me to do my best in order to accomplish God's plan of love for me."

• • •

Nick

Nick, who grew up near Baltimore, Maryland, recently completed a master's degree in international affairs. He reflects on living a spirituality of unity in a competitive graduate school environment. "Trying to form relationships by loving other people seemed to be the opposite of what you were supposed to do. But it really worked. I remember one day during lunch, one of my friends noticed how people would keep coming over to join us. She said, 'Nick, you're always so happy and I saw that people are really attracted to that.' I think she was trying to say that when you try to love people, they love you back in return.

"This way of living also helped me in conversations with people who have different political perspectives. If I love them, recognizing their valid points and entering into their mode of thinking, they become open and they reciprocate by trying to understand what I am saying. Some have called me their best friend even though we have little in common.

"I see the impact also with my cousins, who do not go to church. We all have strong personalities and have butted heads. Our relationships had really deteriorated because we were making comparisons about who was successful and who would be left behind. Then it dawned on me that I needed to change. I tried to love my oldest cousin, encouraging her, and pointing out all the great things that she was doing. At first she was suspicious, but at a certain point she realized I was sincere and was so touched she could hardly express herself. At her wedding last April, she invited me to do a reading.

"You have to make yourself vulnerable and you could get hurt, but in the end, the results are amazing. And people say, 'You're so peaceful. How do you do that?'"

• • •

Elizabeth

Elizabeth first met the Focolare when a group of young people held a "sports for peace" weekend at her parish school in a small Indiana town. "At the time I was a total athlete, really into my sport, swimming. I had always felt nurtured by my family in terms of faith, but I had never been able to connect with other teenagers in order to live my faith in a practical way. When these teens who knew the Focolare came to my school, I was immediately struck by the fact that even though we were doing a simple activity, sports, the interactions had a new element. Another big thing that attracted me was that there was a real mix of cultures. Growing up in rural Indiana, this was incredibly striking. I felt that I had the whole world in my backyard, and everyone was interacting with readiness to love, without judgment. I immediately felt that I could be myself with these people, and I wanted to continue to hang out with them in other settings."

• • •

Keith

Keith grew up in an all-black New York City neighborhood. "I met the Focolare through my aunt and my mother when I was in elementary school. Someone from the community would often come to pick me up for meetings, which were held in another part of the city. It was not easy to explain to my friends in the neighborhood who these people were, mostly from a European background, where we were going and what we did. Sometimes, so as not to be teased or ridiculed, I would duck in the car until we drove past my friends, reaching the end of the block. But it was something that I wanted to do, something special, something that I needed and felt drawn to. We would do things that I also did at home with my friends, playing sports and games, but it was a different atmosphere, because we were trying to love one another."

• • •

Naomi

The Focolare's "little city" in Hyde Park, New York, Mariapolis Luminosa (see pp. 107–108),[2] offers week-long summer programs of formation for teenagers in applying a spirituality of unity to their daily lives. Sixteen-year-old Naomi from Chicago described the impact this had on her.

"Before I left for Luminosa, I was your typical teenager. I basically focused on school, friends, shopping and having fun. I found it hard to think of others. All that changed. I think God planned for me to go there because he wanted me to change. I had a lot of fun, and I really didn't notice anything different in myself — that is, until I returned home.

"One experience still amazes me. The morning after I returned, I packed what ended up being nine bags of belongings to give to charity — it was something done at the spur of the moment, but also from my heart. And rather than packing things I did not want, I found things that I still wanted but did not need because I knew someone would value it a lot more than I would. Why should I have a teddy bear sitting under my bed, when a girl somewhere would actually play with it? What about that sweater I wear once a year? The whole process actually ended up taking three days — I had so many things I didn't even know I had! Within the hour, after I finished packing things to give away, the phone rang: it was a local charity. They hadn't phoned in months, and they were asking if we had anything to give! It was a small but profound miracle for me — and I'm sure it was God.

"Now everything has changed, from the very minute I wake up. I make my bed every day. I try to prepare at least one meal a day. I listen to my eight-year-old brother with love, no matter how much he rambles on about Hot Wheels or Spongebob. I load or unload the dishwasher. I try to spend time with my mom at the dinner table. I realize that dinner can also be a time to love, and that time with family is invaluable.

"At school I try to smile at everyone who looks my way, because I hope it can make someone else's day better — I didn't go through braces for nothing! I must admit, I am still working on my insecurities about being 'cool,' but for the most part I am carefree, because I know that God will take care of me.

"I am not buying from the 'cool shops' that charge $100 for a top — which is ridiculous in the first place! Instead, I go with friends so we can motivate each other to shop at more affordable and age-appropriate stores that still have nice clothing. And I have toned down my makeup. I used to have bags and bags of makeup, but now I only use maybe three things. I know the cosmetics will not make me pretty, because I know in my heart I am pretty just the way God has made me.

"I really have been transformed! I honestly do everything for God; everything in my day is an effort to make him happy. Apparently my mom still wonders what happened to me."

• • •

David

David, who lives in upstate New York, first encountered the Focolare at age seventeen, when he traveled to Toronto with a group of young people for the 2002 World Youth Day with Pope John Paul II. "From the first moment that our bus began moving until I was back home a week later, I was utterly enveloped by the atmosphere that I found among the members of Focolare on that trip. In particular, I was astonished by the care one of the other young men showed me. My comfort and my needs seemed to be the only thing that mattered to him. As I observed him rolling up my sleeping bag in the pouring rain, and standing in line for an hour to surprise me with lunch, I felt as if I were experiencing the charity of the early Christians."

Before that trip, David had a fixed opinion concerning religious practices. "My experience had been eminently traditional: our devotional life was grounded in practices such as Eucharistic adoration, novenas, and May crownings; the visible representatives of the Church were habited sisters and priests in Roman collars; and, most especially, we felt a great pride at belonging to the one, true Church and consequently felt a great urgency to convert those who had the misfortune to be in error. In the Focolare I saw none of the devotions that I had associated with trustworthy Catholic groups. I met 'consecrated lay people,' and the humble openness to dialogue with the non-Catholic world that I witnessed made me uncomfortable. In short, the contrast between the style of Catholicism that I had always known and the *modus operandi* of the Movement was just too overwhelming, and it produced in me a suspicion that any real commitment to the Focolare would require a compromise of the faith that I had come to love so dearly.

"Over the next few years, as my relationship with the Focolare deepened, I began to reconsider my thinking about faith and its real-life implementation. My effort to live its spirituality in daily life shed a brand new light on some important questions: Is it more important to be on the right side of every issue or to be living the universal call to holiness? Is it more appropriate to see others as opponents to be persuaded, or to love them as if they were Jesus? Perhaps I had been absolutizing certain devotional practices rather than placing them at the service of the true centerpiece of the gospel, love of God and neighbor. As I began to immerse myself in this spirituality of unity, I ended up with different answers to these questions than what I had previously found acceptable."

In his sophomore year of college David had a roommate who he describes as "an intelligent young man who made it clear that he did not agree with my faith commitment. Realizing that it would be impossible to talk to him about God, I saw in this situation an opportunity to experiment with the new wisdom I had been gaining. I set to work asking him about economics (he had a passion for the subject), cleaning our apartment (without his help), and listening as he talked about his life, his views on politics, and his relationship with his girlfriend. One afternoon, towards the end of the year, something totally unexpected happened: he told me he wanted to return to the Church, and that he wanted me to be his Confirmation sponsor."

David goes on to describe the impact of such experiences for his own vocation. "In the context of this rediscovery of my faith, I began to hear the voice of the Holy Spirit calling me. I am now in formation to become a diocesan priest. I am convinced that I would not be in the seminary today without my encounter with the Focolare."

• • •

The Focolare Movement includes people of all ages and walks of life. Some, like Rebecca, have encountered its spirituality through their families, when they were small children. Others have been attracted by friends or colleagues who live its spirituality of unity in school, church or work environments and have asked to learn more. Some, like David, find the perceived contrast with more "traditional" forms of religious life and devotion to be jarring or overwhelming, at least initially.

In light of such varied responses to the Movement's ideas and approach, this book has a two-fold aim. First, in response to those who might be interested in learning more — "I want what you have" — it provides an initial explanation of what people have found in the Focolare and why they find it attractive. Second, for those unfamiliar with its ideas, structure or history, this book offers an open and accessible explanation of the Movement's motivations, methodology and ongoing work.

In Part I, Chapter One provides background on the Movement's founder, Chiara Lubich, its origins in northern Italy during World War II, and a sketch of its history and development. In Part II, Chapters Two, Three, and Four describe how the Focolare spirituality is lived in daily life, the structures that sustain its members in their commitments, the various vocational paths that its members follow, and the shape it gives to their social and cultural projects. Chapter Five discusses the Focolare's relationship with the Catholic Church, including the history of its approval, its interaction with diocesan and parish structures, and its work for Christian unity.

Part III addresses how the Focolare's ideas, structures and ways of communicating have addressed cultural themes in the United States. It examines what we have identified as four core quests in American culture: the search for happiness and personal identity (Chapter Six); the quest for freedom (Chapter Seven); the search for community in a pluralistic society (Chapter Eight); and the search for the common good in a polarized political culture (Chapter Nine).

The six experiences above suggest that the Movement is best understood not through its mission statements or organizational principles, but by the examples of those who live its spirituality. Beginning with the life of Chiara Lubich and those who first joined her, followed by the example of American boys and girls, men and women, families and faith communities, this book recounts the shared experience of how their lives have been transformed by the light of God's love, and the "adventure" that follows. Each adventure, like each individual, is profoundly unique, yet profoundly alike.

The two founding stories, that of the Focolare and that of the United States, contain intriguingly similar statements of principles. In a Trent bomb shelter in 1944, Chiara and the other six young women who had gathered with her recognized the unique purpose of their lives when they read a passage in John's Gospel: "That they may all be one" (17:21). A little more than 150 years prior, in 1782, the founders of the United States commissioned the Great Seal, which bears a Latin inscription: "*E pluribus unum*" ("Out of many, one"). The two phrases, one a reflection of the divine mandate and the other a reflection of a political will, address a fundamental tension — acknowledging diversity, yet aspiring toward unity. This book intends to show how two forces often misperceived as being at odds with one another — unity and diversity — can summon forth in individuals and in communities their authentic design.

Part I

Origins and Brief History of the Focolare Movement

I
Chiara Lubich:
A Life for Unity

Her *New York Times* obituary described her as "one of the most influential women in the Roman Catholic Church."[1] Chiara Lubich brought gifts to the world that have transformed not only the lives of Catholics, but also those of Christians from more than 350 churches and ecclesial communities, Jews, Muslims, Buddhists, Hindus, Sikhs, and thousands who do not consider themselves members of any particular religious denomination but who share the Focolare ideal of a life based on love.

The Beginnings in Trent

Born on January 22, 1920 into a working-class family in Trent, northern Italy, Chiara was the second of four children.* From her mother, a traditional devout Roman Catholic, she absorbed a deep religious sensitivity. She was particularly close to her father, a Socialist, whom she described as "large of heart" and broad of mind.[2] In the economic turmoil of the late 1920s, her father lost his job, forcing the family into poverty. She worked her way through school, eventually taking a job as an elementary school teacher.[3]

Because Trent provided a strategic passage through the Dolomite Mountains, the Allies bombed the city heavily during World War II. As the violence of war stripped away their possessions, relationships, and hopes, Chiara and other young women her age, many of them Third Order Franciscans like her, confronted an inescapable question: was there an ideal worth living for, that no bomb could destroy? In response, a discovery opened before them — this ideal was God, a God who is love, whose personal love enveloped every aspect of their lives.[4]

---

* Her given name was Sylvia. As a member of the Franciscan Third Order, attracted by the example of St. Clare of Assisi, she took the name "Chiara." Throughout this book, we will use the familiar "Chiara," as do many biographers, interviewers, and political and ecclesiastical authorities.

Again and again the little group had to seek refuge in the bomb shelters; almost by chance they brought along a small book of the gospels, which Catholics of the time generally did not read except during liturgies. Nearly sixty years later, the experience for Chiara is still vivid: "It was as if we had never read, 'Love your neighbor as yourself' — and all of a sudden we understood, ah, it's that old lady who can't run to the shelter; it's the mother struggling with her five crying children — let's help them!"[5] They began to reach out to neighbors all around — frightened children in the shelters, the hungry, the sick and the injured.

They read "Ask and you shall receive" (Lk 11:9). "We asked on behalf of the poor," Chiara recounts, "and each time we were filled with God's gifts: bread, powdered milk, jelly, wood, clothing ... which we took to those who needed [them]."[6] Filled with wonder at God's intervention and the freedom and joy found in a life based on the gospel, they shared their stories with others, and their group expanded.

In January 1944, Chiara and her friends were introduced to the one who would become the central figure in their lives. Chiara had asked a Capuchin priest to bring communion to the home of Doriana Zamboni, who had contracted an infection while they were visiting Androne, an impoverished neighborhood in Trent. As Dori recollected herself afterward, the priest asked Chiara when she thought that Jesus had suffered the most. As was commonly believed at that time, she answered that it might have been in the Garden of Olives. The priest responded, "I believe, rather, it was what He felt on the cross when He cried out, 'My God, my God, why have you forsaken me?'" When the priest left, Chiara turned to her friend and said, "If Jesus' greatest pain was his abandonment by his Father, we will chose him as our Ideal, and that is the way we will follow him." Years later Dori reflected, "From that day on, Chiara spoke to me often, in fact, constantly, of Jesus forsaken. He was *the* living personality in our lives."[7]

Like the Movement itself, the first Focolare house emerged not by design, but as a spontaneous response to particular circumstances. On May 13, 1944, from a wooded hillside where she had taken refuge with her family, Chiara watched as air raids ravaged her neighborhood and destroyed her family home. As she lay awake through the night, looking up into the darkness and watching the stars move across the sky, she realized that she could not join her family in the morning when they would flee into the mountains. She sensed that she had to remain in Trent with the friends who were counting on her, to do something for those who most resembled Jesus forsaken.[8] As she struggled with the consequences of this choice for her family, especially because they had come to rely on her salary to survive, an insight came to her not from the gospels or another religious source, but from the poet Virgil. She recounts, "Almost as if someone suggested it to me ... *Omnia vincit amor*, love conquers all." About four in the morning she dried her tears. She recalls, "From the moment I said that 'yes,' I sensed a new strength."[9]

Soon after, in what she describes as the most painful moment in their separation, she placed her heavy backpack on her mother's stooped shoulders. Her family trudged towards the mountains, and she turned toward the city. Many years later, the scene remained vivid in her memory: "The destruction was total: trees had been uprooted, houses were in ruins, roads were covered with debris. Tears came to my eyes ... and I let them flow." As she wept, a frantic woman sprung out at a street corner, grabbed Chiara, and screamed, "Four of mine have died, do you understand?" She recalls, "As I consoled her I understood that I had to forget about my own grief in order to take on that of the others."[10]

She searched among the ruins for her friends, and was relieved to find them all alive. Since several of their homes had been destroyed or their families had fled into the mountains, they began to live together in a small apartment that came to be known as the "Focolare" (which in Italian means "hearth") because of its warm family atmosphere.

As they continued to take refuge in the shelters, conscious that any moment could be their last, they searched the gospels for words that might express what Jesus expected most of them. When they read, "This is my commandment, that you love one another as I have loved you" (Jn 15:12), they recognized how he had loved — he gave his life. Chiara recalls gathering in a circle and making a pact: "I am ready to give my life for you; I for you, I for you; all for each one."[11]

That pact produced two outcomes. First, it generated new light and energy to understand what loving one another meant. "We are not always asked to die for one another, but we can share everything: our worries, our sorrows, our meager possessions, our spiritual riches."[12] Second, they began to discern an almost tangible living presence of Christ in the community. She notes, "We saw our lives take a qualitative leap forward. Someone came into our group, silently, an invisible Friend, giving us security, a more experiential joy, a new peace, a fullness of life, an inextinguishable light. Jesus was fulfilling his promise to us: 'Where two or three are gathered in my name, I am there among them' (Mt 18:20)."[13]

At another moment, huddled in a cellar, by candlelight they read Jesus' solemn prayer the night before he died: "That they may all be one. As you, Father, are in me and I am in you ..." (Jn 17:21). Chiara describes that moment: "It was not an easy text to start with, but one by one those words seemed to come to life, giving us the conviction that we were born for that page of the gospel."[14] They became focused in their commitment to build unity. As Chiara remembers, "One thing was clear in our hearts: what God wanted for us was unity. We live for the sole aim of being one with him, one with each other, and one with everyone. This marvelous vocation linked us to heaven and immersed us in the one human family. What purpose in life could be greater?"[15]

In comparison to these discoveries all other experiences of daily life faded, so much so that they almost did not realize it when the war finally ended. Within months a community of about 500 — young men and women, married couples, children, the elderly, members of men's and women's religious orders, priests — had begun to order their lives through this new spirituality of unity. Throughout the 1950s, the community spent their summer holidays in the Dolomite Mountains. Each year increasing numbers of friends and others attracted by the atmosphere of unity joined them. By 1951, the "vacation" had become a small "community" (*polis*) of about 250 people of various professions and social backgrounds, a cross-section of society. Potential divisions between social groups and generations receded in the atmosphere of love. In 1957 bishops and other members of the hierarchy began to visit. By the end of the decade, thousands from all over Europe and from every continent were passing through the little summer village, learning how to live a spirituality of unity.[16]

The Encounter with Igino Giordani

In 1948, Chiara met Igino Giordani — writer, journalist, politician, ecumenist, patristics scholar, and father of four. In the 1920s, he had headed the press office of the newly created Popular Party. During the Fascist era, he worked in the Vatican Library, writing one insightful social or religious commentary after another. Through the 1930s, as director of *Fides*, the magazine of the Pontifical Society for the Propagation of the Faith, he became known for his frank, combative style. In June of 1946 he was elected to Parliament and became one of the "Constitutional Fathers" who laid the foundations of the post-war Italian republic.

At that point in his life, this well-known journalist, author, and leader in the reconstruction of Italy received a visit from twenty-eight-year-old Chiara Lubich. She arrived in the company of three Franciscans — a Conventual, a Friar Minor, and a Capuchin. Historically these three groups differed — sometimes quite forcefully — regarding how to live their founder's rule. For Giordani, seeing them together was "already a miracle." When Chiara spoke, he immediately sensed a presence of God. It was, as he noted in his memoirs, the voice he had been waiting for. "She put holiness within reach of everyone. She tore down the grille which separated the world of the laity from the mystical life. She put into the public square the treasures of a castle to which only a few had been admitted. She rendered God near, making people discover Him as father, brother, friend, present to humanity."[17] The encounter left a vivid impact.

> Something happened within me. Those cultural components that had remained disconnected from one another began to come to life and to move, joining themselves to form a living body through which ran powerful lifeblood: [was it] the same blood that burned within Saint Catherine? Love had penetrated and entered into all of the ideas, drawing them into an orbit of joy. It came about that the idea of God had given place to the love of God, the ideal image to a living God.... So, having discovered Love, I found myself, almost immediately, within the inner dynamic of the Trinity. All of the dogmas and ideas emerged from the shelves of my memory to become living material, blood of my blood. I was moving from a library filled with books toward the Church, inhabited by Christians.[18]

When Giordani (Chiara called him "Foco," meaning fire) "moved" from the library to the Church, his writing style was transformed. Once known as the *martello* (hammer) of the heretics, he had become their *mantello* (mantle); the combative defender of the faith had become a humble prophet of love.[19]

Giordani helped the little group understand that they had a "charism," a gift from God to be shared with others. He opened their eyes to the fact that the universal value of the charism of unity was intended not only for Catholics but for all of humanity. A note written to him by Dori Zamboni, dated April 1949, captures this well:

> Dearest Foco, I wanted to share with you right away my gratitude for your visit and I wanted to let you know the impression it left in my soul. It was as if I was a small child in her mother's arms.... When you came, you took me from her arms and you put me on the floor saying: look how big your mother is! You revealed to me something that I may have known instinctively but your presence made me understand it in all of its fullness.[20]

Some inkling of what was coming to life in Trent had been circulating among important people in Rome, but Giordani's judgment guaranteed that this new-born spirituality could have a true theological and social impact, especially for the laity.[21] Chiara later commented: "Giordani was one of the most precious gifts heaven ever gave to the Focolare Movement."[22]

A Summer of Light: Contemplating the Source of Unity

During the summer of 1949, after months of intense activity in Trent and in Rome, Chiara took a much-needed rest. Someone loaned the group a little cabin in Tonadico, a village in the Dolomite Mountains, where amid a routine of hikes in the mountains, prayer, and day-to-day household chores, they continued to focus on living the gospel by choosing one passage each day as their watchword.

Giordani looked for any excuse to visit. Once, when passing through on his way to the University of Fribourg, he asked Chiara whether he could take a vow of obedience to her — as did the followers of St. Catherine, or as did St. Francis de Sales and St. Jane Frances de Chantal. For Chiara, this proposal seemed too restricted for a spirituality centered on "that they may all be one." But she felt that in some way God might be working through Giordani's request — so she proposed instead that they make a "pact of unity," asking Jesus in the Eucharist, on the basis of the "nothingness of themselves," to bring about the unity he had in mind. They did so, and for Chiara there opened up an extraordinary period of light, which over the course of two months she shared with Giordani and her friends.[23]

Chiara describes what happened: "We experienced — because of a special grace — what it means to be a living cell of the mystical body of Christ: it was to be Jesus, and as such, be in the bosom of the Father. The words, '*Abba*, Father' came to our lips.... So began a special luminous period during which, among other things, it seems that God wanted to make us intuit something about the designs for the Movement" and the importance of many truths of the faith.[24]

These insights eventually were translated into foundational documents for the Focolare's work in dialogue and culture. A passage from that time gives a taste: "We need to allow God to be reborn within us and keep him alive. We need to make him overflow onto others like torrents of Life and resurrect the dead. And keep him alive among us by loving one another.... So everything is renewed, politics and art, school and religion, private life and entertainment. Everything."[25]

At the end of the summer, Chiara hesitated to leave what had been an experience of "paradise." Giordani, however, convinced her to return to the city. He wrote: "Chiara, pardon me if I speak to you as one who doesn't know how to detach himself from the world. You have a family, a family that has things to do in the world, suffering and fighting for the glory of God. You cannot abandon it. Aren't you the one who taught us about that supreme love, Jesus forsaken? Now for him and with him, you need to let go of God for God, of paradise for the earth, where you can help many on their path to heaven. Leave the angels and return to us human beings, out of love for Jesus forsaken."[26]

It was at that point, on September 20, 1949, that Chiara wrote "I have only one Spouse on earth," a meditative poem on the mysterious link between love and suffering whose lyrical, mystical language reflects the power and depth of her experience that summer. It expresses the real motivating force behind a spirituality of unity.

I have only one Spouse on earth: Jesus forsaken.
I have no other God but him.
In him there is the whole of paradise with the Trinity
   and the whole of the earth with humanity.
Therefore what is *his* is mine, and nothing else.
And *his* is universal suffering, and therefore mine.
I will go through the world seeking it in every instant of my life.
What hurts me is *mine*.
Mine the suffering that grazes me in the present.
Mine the suffering of the souls beside me
(that is my Jesus).
Mine all that is not peace, not joy, not beautiful, not lovable, not serene,
in a word, what is not paradise.

Because I too have *my* paradise,
but it is the one in my Spouse's heart.
I know no other.
So it will be for the years I have left: athirst for suffering,
      anguish, despair, separation, exile, forsakenness, torment —
for all that is him,
and he is sin, hell.
In this way
I *will dry up* the waters of tribulation
in many hearts nearby
and, through communion
with my almighty Spouse,
in many far away.
I shall pass as a fire
that consumes all that must fall
and *leaves standing only* the truth.
But it is necessary to be *like* him:
to be him in the present moment of life.[27]

The following day Chiara came down from the little cabin in the Dolomites and returned to the developing life of the Movement in Trent.

The Encounter with Pasquale Foresi

That same year one of Giordani's colleagues from the Parliament, Palmiro Foresi, invited Chiara to Pistoia for a meeting among the elite of Italian Catholic laity. Unable to go herself, she sent her friend, Graziella De Luca. Because of a misunderstanding Graziella arrived a day after the event had taken place. She went instead to Foresi's home, and found no one there but his son, Pasquale, who had recently left the seminary and was beginning to distance himself from the Church. Pasquale had heard the new movement discussed at the dinner table, and as he commented later, "They struck me as deluded." Out of courtesy and hospitality, however, he offered to arrange a meeting for Graziella with Catholic university students.

As they were walking to the campus, he asked her what she and the others were doing, expecting to hear about good works with orphans or the handicapped. "We live according to the model of the Holy Trinity," Graziella replied. Taken completely aback, he glanced around to make sure that no one else had heard, lest the two of them be taken for crazy. From the way she expressed herself, he could tell that these young women were living not just words, but a reality. "As I asked her more questions, I saw that she was speaking of the gospel with the same simplicity that I had found in the gospel itself. This kind of simplicity stood in marked contrast with certain ecclesiastical notions of the time that had provoked my crisis with the Church and had caused me to abandon the idea of becoming a priest." He thought to himself, "If they go ahead like this, they are going to run into trouble."[28]

The next day, when Graziella returned to the Foresi home for lunch, he asked her about their relationship with the Eucharist. She answered, "We go to communion every day; if it were possible we would go twice a day." For Pasquale, her statement wiped away his remaining suspicion. "I saw that just as she spoke about the gospel as something vital and alive, she spoke in the same way about the Church. I realized that the Movement was completely imbedded in the Church, and if the Church was not beautiful, the fault lay not only with the clergy, but with me too, because I had pulled back from living the gospel. I saw that I needed to convert and reinsert myself fully into the life of the Church."[29]

In 1954, Pasquale Foresi became the first *focolarino* to be ordained, opening the way for others to enter the priesthood at the service of the Movement. For many years he served as co-president. Together with Igino Giordani, Chiara considered him a co-founder with several important tasks. He maintained contact between the Movement and Church authorities. He oversaw its "incarnation" in publishing activities and in the development of conference centers and schools of formation. He also made substantial contributions to the Movement's theological studies, and worked closely with Chiara on the drafting and revision of its statutes.[30]

International and Intercultural Reach

From the beginning, Chiara sensed that their way of life would have a broad reach. As early as 1946, Chiara noted:

> Before all else, the soul must always fix its gaze on the one Father of many children. Then it must see all as children of the same Father. In mind and in heart we must always go beyond the bounds imposed on us by human life alone and create the habit of constantly opening ourselves to the reality of being one human family in one Father: God.[31]

In 1945, on the Feast of Christ the King, Chiara and her friends offered this prayer after the liturgy: "You know the way to achieve unity. Here we are. If you so desire, use us."[32] Referring to the psalm response in that day's readings, "Ask of me, and I will make the nations your heritage, and the ends of the earth your possession" (Ps 2:8), they asked, with simplicity, that they somehow reach the "ends of the earth."

Throughout the 1950s many met this new spirituality through personal relationships and the ever-larger summer gatherings in the Dolomites, the "Mariapolis" ("city of Mary"). In 1959, people from twenty-six countries, who spoke nine different languages gathered there. Igino Giordani describes the scene: "All united they consecrated their own countries to God, in order to make of all peoples the one people of God, applying the instruction that Chiara had drawn from the gospel: 'Love the country of the other as you love your own.'"[33]

By the late 1950s, the Movement had spread throughout Italy, and by the early 1960s across Europe. In 1954, Pavel Hnilica, a Jesuit who had been ordained a bishop while in a Czechoslovakian prison, told Chiara about the dramatic situation of the Church behind the Iron Curtain. Because East Germany would welcome medical professionals from other countries, between 1961 and 1962 Chiara sent ten doctors and nurses who were members of the Movement to begin sowing the seeds of this new life in Eastern Europe. Business people from all over the Soviet bloc gathered for an annual commercial fair in Leipzig. At the fair, those whom Chiara sent could communicate with Focolare communities that had sprung up in Hungary, Czechoslovakia, Yugoslavia, Russia, Lithuania and Poland.

During this time the Archbishop of Cracow, Karol Wojtyla, through one of his close friends, came to appreciate how Focolare members put the gospel into action. Wearing a simple shirt and hiker's pants, he attended the small Mariapolis at Zakopane in 1978. After hearing couples share their experiences of family life, he commented, "You have the key for living according to what the Church suggests."[34]

The *focolarini* first visited Recife, Brazil in 1958, where two priests who had attended the Mariapolis the year before had brought a Focolare community to life. The Movement spread quickly throughout Brazil, Argentina, and all of Latin America. The first contacts in Asia were in Manila in 1966. Many missionary priests and sisters helped to pave the way for the Movement's development in Korea, Japan, Hong Kong, Taiwan, and throughout Asia. The Movement reached

Australia in 1967, with subsequent developments in New Zealand and throughout Oceania. Following Chiara's frequent visits to Patriarch Athenagoras in Istanbul, a Focolare house was opened there in 1967. This served as the initial point of reference for contacts in Greece, Lebanon, Egypt, and eventually throughout the Middle East.

In Africa, a local bishop requested help for the Bangwa, a tribe facing extinction due to a 93% infant mortality rate. Focolare doctors and nurses arrived in Fontem, Cameroon, in 1965. This is now the site of a burgeoning village complete with one of the best hospitals of the region, a highly-regarded school, and local industry that renders its inhabitants self-sufficient. Today, the Movement has a strong presence throughout the continent.

In North America, the first Focolare house, a tiny apartment on Mulberry Street in Manhattan, opened in September 1961. Soon, houses opened in Chicago (1964), Boston (1966), and Toronto (1967). By the late 1970s, communities in San Antonio, Texas, and Los Angeles welcomed Focolare houses. Others have followed — Washington, D.C. in 1983; Columbus, Ohio in 1990; and Atlanta, Georgia in 2006. Since 1991 the United States has been organized into four regions — East Coast, Midwest, Southwest and West Coast — each with its own headquarters and Focolare centers.

By the early 21st century, the Focolare Movement had established itself in 182 countries with more than 140,000 core members and over 2 million affiliates, including 30,000 friends of non-Christian faith traditions.[35] This wide-spread "family," which John Paul II described as a "people," works as a body toward the fulfillment of the prayer of Jesus, "That they may all be one."[36] The pope's spontaneous remarks to a 1990 gathering of 10,000 young people of the Focolare express the Movement's ongoing aspiration: "The perspective of a united world is the great expectation of people today ... toward a civilization that is truly expressed in the civilization of love."[37]

"Apostles of Dialogue"

On the Focolare's sixtieth anniversary, December 2003, Pope John Paul II commended its members for their work as *"apostles of dialogue,* the privileged way to promote unity: dialogue within the Church, ecumenical and interreligious dialogue, dialogue with non-believers."[38]

The pope's statement explains how the Focolare's work has taken shape. While remaining faithful to their own spiritual roots, members open themselves, as Chiara has described it, "to the reality of being one human family in one Father: God."[39] As the Movement spread throughout the world, spontaneous contact among neighbors of differing Christian churches helped to sustain ecumenical dialogue. Open, trusting relationships with Buddhist, Hindu, Muslim, or Jewish friends paved the way for inter-faith dialogue.

Within a spirituality of unity, persons love when they "empty" themselves completely in order to "make themselves one" with others, so as to understand the depth of their religious experience. Chiara explains: "When we make ourselves one with the others, they can open up, reveal themselves to us, express and explain themselves, and share something of their being Jewish or Muslim or Buddhist or Christian. Some of their immense, even unexpected richness will shine in us too."[40]

This approach to dialogue has received an extraordinary welcome. Leaders of many religious traditions invited Chiara to share her experience with their communities. Nikkyo Niwano, founder of the Japanese Buddhist renewal movement *Rissho Kosei-kai*, invited her in 1981 to address 10,000 of his followers at their Golden Temple, in Tokyo. She shared the story of the Focolare's birth in the crucible of suffering during World War II, explaining the fundamental points of the way of life that had come from her discovery that God is love. She then told them, "Since in this world of ours, we often meet brothers and sisters of other faiths as well, we are living a marvelous experience. Every human being, made in the image of God, has the possibility of a certain personal relationship with him. Indeed, our human nature itself leads them exactly to this communion."[41]

Imam W. Deen Mohammed invited Chiara to the United States to demonstrate the possibility of unity that transcends boundaries of race and religion. On May 18, 1997 at Malcolm Shabazz Mosque, in Harlem, New York she shared her Christian experience and the Focolare's mission to work for unity. The 3,000 African American Muslims present there responded with cheers and shouts of "God is Great!" Three years later, in Washington, D.C., 6,000 Christians and Muslims gathered to celebrate "Faith Communities Together." In her address, Chiara encouraged them, "May our love continue to bring people together in unity as it has us, Christians and Muslims, today. And wherever we are, may it give life to a new world renewed by love, a world in which all people recognize one another as sisters and brothers of the same Father."[42]

Imam Mohammed responded, "For me all that she said was a prayer, and a call to us not only to be good in our hearts, but to be good in our actions. We thank God again for Chiara and I see her as a leader for all of us, and I mean that. I see her as a leader for all of us."[43]

She was the first Christian woman and lay person ever invited to share her spiritual experience at the *Wat Rampoeng* monastery at Chiang Mai, Thailand. Introducing her to more than 800 Buddhist monks, nuns, and lay people, the Great Teacher Ajhan Thong explained, "The wise person is neither man nor woman. When someone lights a light in the darkness, one does not ask if the one who lit it was a man or a woman. Chiara is here to give us the light she has experienced."[44]

Chiara has received the Templeton Prize for Progress in Religion (1977), the UNESCO Prize for Peace Education (1996), and the Council of Europe's Human Rights Prize (1998); honorary citizenships in Rome and numerous other cities; as well as sixteen honorary doctoral degrees in a variety of disciplines. The citation for the 2001 Defender of Peace Prize, presented by two prestigious Hindu-Gandhian institutions in India, acknowledged her use of "the most powerful human force of love and a strong faith in the unity of all humankind as espoused in the teachings of Jesus Christ," which has enabled her "to play a tireless role in sowing the seeds of peace and love among all peoples."[45]

Carrying the Charism of Unity into the Future

In the autumn of 2004, even as Chiara's health began to decline, she managed to update the General Statutes, initially approved in 1990 by the Pontifical Council for the Laity, so as to reflect the Movement's latest developments. Just a few months before her death, she rejoiced at the news that the Pontifical Congregation for Catholic Education had approved the new Sophia University Institute. This university, an important piece of Chiara's vision, offers interdisciplinary graduate degrees in "Foundations and Perspectives on a Culture of Unity."

She died peacefully on March 14, 2008, at her home in Rocca di Papa, outside Rome. At her funeral, 30,000 gathered in and around the Roman Basilica of St. Paul Outside the Walls. Hundreds of thousands of others worldwide followed the ceremony itself and the preceding interreligious tribute via television, satellite, and Internet. The gathering included representatives of all the major religions and the main Christian churches, who acknowledged the global impact of her life and her spirituality. Vatican Secretary of State, Cardinal Tarcisio

Bertone, the main celebrant of the funeral Mass, summarized what she brought to the Church and to the world:

> She formed individuals who were love itself, who lived the charism of unity and communion with God and with their neighbor; people who spread "love-unity" by making themselves, their homes and their work a "focolare" where divine love burns contagiously and sets ablaze all who are close to it. This is a mission possible [for] everyone because the Gospel is within everyone's reach: bishops and priests, children, young people and adults, consecrated and lay people, married couples, families and communities, all are called to live the ideal of unity: "That they may all be one!" … It is up to us, and especially to her spiritual children, to continue the mission she began.[46]

After a founder's death, religious communities often face a period of crisis and testing. In July 2008, 516 representatives from Focolare communities throughout the world gathered for a general assembly that would elect the new leadership. The initial vote indicated an equal division between two schools of thought: one valued continuity, and the other saw the benefits of change. Above all else, the assembly wished to remain faithful to Chiara's legacy, as expressed in the General Statutes: "Mutual and constant love, which makes unity possible and brings the presence of Jesus among all … is the norm of norms, the premise to every other rule."[47] This helped them to listen, love, and open themselves to what the Holy Spirit was suggesting for the Movement's future. The next vote was near unanimous. The new president was Maria Voce, known within the Focolare community as "Emmaus," a 72-year old lawyer who had worked for many years with Chiara to draft the revised statutes.[48]

In a message read at Chiara's funeral, Pope Benedict XVI gave thanks to God "[F]or the gift given to the Church of this woman of intrepid faith, humble messenger of hope and peace, founder of a vast spiritual family that embraces many fields of evangelization." Chiara herself foretold gratitude to God as her final gesture. She described the encounter with the Lord for which she hoped: "When I arrive to your door and you ask me my name, I will not say my name, I will say my name is 'thank you,' for everything and forever."

Part II

Living a Spirituality of Unity in the United States

2
How Focolare Members Live

A Spirituality of Unity and its Premise

A prominent aspect of the Focolare's spiritual path is its emphasis on relationship. Those who live the Focolare spirituality express it in love of neighbor and love for all humanity. As John Paul II noted during a 1984 visit to the Focolare headquarters in Rome, love is the "inspiring spark" of everything done under the name "Focolare."[1]

Shortly after the Second Vatican Council, reflecting on the future of Christianity, theologian Walter Kasper foresaw that the "fundamental form of the faith" would be "the combined love of God and of one's neighbor" that would express a "new form" of being, understood not so much as "substance which exists in and for itself," but as "love which exists for others." According to Kasper, this future should arrive as a consequence of "a new form of holiness and spirituality." The "greatest lack" in the modern Church, he claimed, was its not yet having found "this charisma, this form of holiness."[2]

What Chiara has written and lived might satisfy Kasper's question whether this gift of a "new form of holiness" has arrived. In her spirituality of unity, love of neighbor is not only a consequence of loving God, but the *indispensable* path to loving God. Love for God *inevitably* leads to love of neighbor, and loving one's neighbor in turn leads to union with God. In 1946 she wrote: "Jesus our model taught us two things alone, and which are one: to be children of only one Father, and to be brothers and sisters to each other."[3] She elaborated on this connection in a meditation from 1949:

> Our inner life is fed by our outer life. The more I enter into the soul of my brother or sister, the more I enter into God within me. The more I enter into God within me, the more I enter into my brother or sister. God-myself-my brother or sister: it is all one world, all one kingdom.[4]

Within this "one kingdom," love of neighbor is not a secondary consequence, but an integral, inescapable, even essential dimension of love for God. In Tokyo, sharing her Christian experience with members of the *Rissho Kosei-kai* she summarized: "The heart of my experience is all here: the more one loves people, the more one finds God; the more one finds God, the more one loves people."[5]

This perspective inverts what can be the usual dynamic of human relationships in which love for others compels gratitude to the one who offers that love. Instead, the neighbors who welcome my love become my benefactors because, as Chiara explains, "they have obtained for us what we were seeking all along" — union with God. Therefore, "we should be grateful to them."[6] This new dynamic imbues all relationships with a sense of reciprocal gratitude. Chiara wrote in 1949: "The person next to me was created as a gift for me and I was created as a gift for the person next to me. On earth all stands in a relationship of love with all: each thing with each thing. We have to be Love, however, to discover the golden thread among all things that exist."[7]

A spirituality of unity takes love of neighbor as the measure of everything in life. Chiara reflects, "The basic commandment is brotherly love. Everything is of value if it expresses sincere fraternal charity. Nothing we do is of value, if there is not the feeling of love for our brothers and sisters in it. For God is a Father and in his heart he has always and only his children."[8] Building relationships of love and unity constitutes the heart, soul, and driving energy of every Focolare community, project or activity. The General Statutes open with this statement: "Mutual and constant love, which makes unity possible and brings the presence of Jesus among all, is for those who are part of the Work of Mary,* the basis for their life under every aspect: it is the norm of norms, the premise to every other rule."[9]

This premise recapitulates the pattern of love in the heart of the Trinity, where the Father, Son and Holy Spirit live a life of total love for one another. Human beings can also live according to this model. As Chiara explains, "The life we must try to imitate is the life of the Holy Trinity, by loving each other, with the grace of God, in the way the persons of the Holy Trinity love one another."[10] Because we are made in the image of God who is Trinity, we experience true fulfillment precisely by living relationships of total openness, gift, and love.[11]

On the cross Jesus cried, "Why have you forsaken me?" His actions at this moment not only provide a key to understanding God's love in moments of suffering, but also model how to be completely open with others. In his response to his experience of forsakenness, Jesus shows, as Chiara describes, "that I am myself, not when I close myself off from the other, but rather when I give myself, when out of love I lose myself

---

* The official name under which the Focolare was approved in 1961 is *Opera di Maria*, Work of Mary.

in the other."[12] Building authentic relationships can generate worry and anxiety. Will others take advantage of me? Will I lose my individuality and personality? What happens when we disagree? The example of Jesus forsaken helps answer such questions.

On numerous occasions, for a wide variety of audiences, Chiara outlined the practical implications of a spirituality of unity in what she terms the "art of loving." In a 1997 address delivered in Paris to UNESCO when she was given its Prize for Peace Education, she summarizes this art:

> We must be the first to love without waiting for the other to love us.
>
> It means loving the other as oneself, because "You and I," Gandhi says, "are but one. I cannot injure you without harming myself."
>
> This also means knowing how to "make yourself one" with others, that is, making your own their burdens, their thoughts, their sufferings, their joys.
>
> Now, when this love is lived by others it becomes reciprocal.[13]

Chiara's personal letters, informal conversations and messages, books, magazine articles, and public talks have helped thousands to discover the essential link between the search for meaning in their lives and building relationships of love with their neighbors. "This is the great attraction of modern times," she writes, "to penetrate to the highest contemplation while mingling with everyone, one person alongside others."[14]

Living a Spirituality of Unity in Daily Life

The common reference for all Focolare members, the "General Statutes," contains the principal points of a spirituality of unity and guidelines for their translation into daily life. The sections below offer only a glimpse of what Chiara explains in much greater depth elsewhere. The first subsection outlines "The Points of a Spirituality of Unity." Next, "Aspects for Ordering Daily Life," describes how a spirituality of unity permeates Focolare members' lived experience, as individuals and as a community. Finally, "'Instruments' for Spiritual Growth and Communication," presents the "tools" used within the smaller units in which Focolare members gather.

1. THE POINTS OF A SPIRITUALITY OF UNITY

When someone asks for an explanation of what the Focolare is all about, in addition to sharing something of one's personal life, members often spontaneously describe what Chiara and her initial group of friends discovered as they gathered in the Trent bomb shelters. Re-telling this story is not only an effort to be historically accurate, or to give credit where credit is due. That initial story also contains the seed of the gift that they too have received, a pattern for living their own lives.

For example, the initial group's experience of being taken up, as Chiara describes, by the "fiery brilliance of an ideal that exceeds all things and contains all things: by the infinite love of God"[15] — is for many their own entry point into living a spirituality of unity. Similarly, Chiara's desire to respond to such love by doing God's will, moment by moment, constitutes the ongoing daily commitment for all who live a spirituality of unity.

From the initial group's experience of putting these insights into practice, Chiara delineates the "points" of the Focolare spirituality. She has provided extensive, often book length analysis of each, and has expanded upon them in her meditations, poems, and answers to spontaneous questions. Further references are included in the bibliographical note. Here we provide only a list of the points in the order that they appear in the 2008 version of the General Statutes.

- Choose God who is Love as the "ideal" of one's life (see Mt 22:37, 1 Jn 4:8, 16–18).
- Love God by doing his will in the concrete circumstances of daily life (Mt 7:21).
- Nourish oneself daily with the Word of God, put it into practice, and communicate the consequences of living in this way.
- Love each neighbor (Mt 22:36–40, Mk 12:28–31).
- Make a particular effort to live with others the New Commandment, "Love one another as I have loved you" (Jn 15: 12–13).
- Nourish oneself as frequently as possible with the Eucharist, the bond of unity with God and with neighbor.
- Through mutual love and through the Eucharist, receive the gift of unity for which Jesus prayed, "That they may all be one" (Jn 17:21).
- In every division or expression of disunity, find the remedy and solution in Jesus who cried, "My God, my God, why have you forsaken me?" and who overcame this trial, "Father, into your hands I commend my spirit" (Lk 23:46).
- Like Mary who lost everything at the foot of the cross, even her Son, be ready to let go of everything and everyone in order to contribute to the unity of people with God and with each other.
- Through an always renewed mutual love, live as fully as possible the reality of the Mystical Body and the Church as communion,

maintaining unity with the pope and the bishops as successors of the Apostles.

~ Entrust oneself to the Holy Spirit, listening to his "voice" within so as to receive the fullness of his gifts.

~ Like Mary, generate the presence of Jesus according to his promise, "Where two or three are gathered in my name, I am there in their midst" (Mt 18:20), as the point of departure, ever-present reality, and ultimate goal of a life of unity.

2. ASPECTS FOR ORDERING DAILY LIFE AND ACTIVITIES

Speaking to young people, Chiara identifies a central human challenge: "We … easily slip into dividing and subdividing our life. We take one aspect of life, become passionate about it, and then this becomes our ideal: soccer, movies, art, science, philosophy, social problems....We become specialists in our little idol, and for this reason we often have trouble understanding our neighbors."[16] In contrast, a person becomes fully human by letting God enter his or her life and "illuminate it in its entirety, like a sun placed in the center," a light that can penetrate and harmonize all of life's particular aspects.[17]

A fulfilled life, then, comes not from maintaining "balance" but from discovering the integrity of the unifying presence of God in every specific aspect. "Like a ray of light that passes through a drop of water and opens out to display a rainbow," Chiara explains, "love, the life of Jesus in us, is manifested in different colors; it is expressed in various ways, each one different from the others."[18]

For Focolare members, the "sun" of the life of God shines through every spiritual and practical aspect of their lives, from cooking, cleaning, working and handling finances, to moments of prayer and liturgy, to how they approach illness and death. Nothing is more or less important, more or less sacred. The Focolare spirituality delineates seven aspects of life, each a way of expressing love:

~ Work and sharing material and spiritual goods
~ Outreach and witness
~ Prayer and spirituality
~ The natural world and health, both physical and spiritual
~ Harmony and beauty of dress, home, and environment
~ Wisdom and study
~ Communication and media.

The sense of integrity, "the wonderful unity" that comes as a result of living all these aspects together, permeates each person's entire existence. Chiara explains:

> Everything was to flow from love, be rooted in love; everything was to be an expression of the life of Jesus in us. And this would make human life attractive, fascinating. Consequently, our lives would not be dull and flat since they would not be made up of bits juxtaposed and disconnected…. No. Now it would always be Jesus who prayed, Jesus who engaged in mission, Jesus who worked, Jesus who ate, Jesus who rested, and so on. Everything would be an expression of him.[19]

Focolare members of every age and state of life strive to live this way. Bessie was ninety-three when she reflected on her approach. "It's not easy. Everything is just wearing out, and even the simplest tasks take a lot longer to get done. But she still aims to live all seven aspects:

1. Sharing Material Goods

I'm constantly eliminating things once thought to be indispensable. Recently, I gave something away that afterward I realized I still needed. Then I thought that the person would make good use of it, and God would take care of me. In fact, a few days later I received from someone else the same item I had given away. Giving as a lifestyle never ages, and the hundredfold (see Mt 19:29) is always new.

2. Outreach

Everyone understands the anxiety of children when they start school and have to make new friends, but no one thinks about how a 90-year-old feels moving into an assisted-living facility. She too has to make new friends, and she can't even go home at the end of the day! I've had to learn to listen to people and figure out how each one wants to be loved.

3. Prayer

As I get older it actually gets easier to spend more time praying. I pray one rosary for my family, another for the Church and the Focolare family here and around the globe, and finally one for all of the problems in the world. I miss going to daily Mass and feel blessed whenever someone comes to take me, or the priest is able to come where I live. You might think that by 93 I would have worked out the kinks in my life, but I find myself making the same mistakes I've been trying to correct my entire life. Thank God I have learned how to start again.

4. Health

Even though it's clear that my holy journey is nearing its completion, it is still wonderful to be able to exercise, to eat properly, and to take all my medications. I have also been helped by John Paul II's "Letter to the Elderly" and by the example of his life. It takes a real act of faith to believe in the value of your life when many around you see things differently.

5. Harmony in Dress and Environment

I don't need many clothes or much furniture, but I try to keep what I have in order. With my eyesight so poor, I'm not sure if the colors match, and I might be tempted to think, "Who cares anyway?" But then I remember that even at 93 I have to try to express the beauty of God in the way I dress and the harmony of my apartment.

6. Wisdom and Studies

I've always loved learning new things, so I study the documents of the Holy Father and watch DVDs on the catechism or other topics. I'll never practice nursing again, but it is part of my vocation to stay on top of the latest advances in my profession. So I keep up to date because something I read or hear might be useful for someone else.

7. Communication

I used to send people cards or telephone them. Times have changed. I needed to learn to drive at 50, and I now have had to learn how to use e-mail. Notwithstanding my eyesight, I watch the news every day and I read every issue of *Living City* from cover to cover. Reading how the world tends toward unity helps me to be hopeful even in the midst of so much tragedy. I really believe in a united world.

Focolare members learn about these seven aspects and help each other to live them in their daily lives. They are a frequent subject of discussion at periodic meetings, schools of formation, and conferences. The aspects also serve as an organizing principle for Focolare gatherings, activities, and outreach events.

3. "Instruments" for Spiritual Growth and Communication

"If our souls were like stars, we would want to form a constellation: every star is more beautiful because it is together with the others, and also all together they are more beautiful because they form a design of light."[20] Chiara used this image to explain to the youngest of the initial group, Silvana Veronesi, their life in the first Focolare house. For the Movement today "every star is more beautiful" because of specific "instruments," practices that foster spiritual growth.

The first and fundamental instrument is recognizing that neighbors are not obstacles to union with God, but the surest path. A strategy to address personal limitations or vices is to shift the focus from self to others. Chiara describes how to do this using a classical image of the spiritual journey — the "mountain" of one's own ego. In dying to self in order to live for others, she explains, "I no longer have the mountain of my ego to move, because I take another route." Why bore through a mass of stone and rocks when there is a ready-made path around the mountain? "I must always take the path around the side, which is to live my neighbor."[21]

Biblical scholar Gerard Rossé describes the difference between a morality focused on meticulous individual effort to observe precepts, and a "Paschal" ethic that allows God to bring about the transformation to new life, as received in baptism. "Freed from the preoccupation with personal salvation, seeing that God has taken each person's existence in hand, communicating the gift of eternal life, the believer can now love authentically and deeply."[22]

In a note from 1949, Chiara uses another image to make the same point. "There are many ways to clean a room. You can tidy it up, bit by bit; you can use a small broom, a bigger one, a big vacuum cleaner, and so on. Or, in order to be in a clean place, you can simply change rooms and it is done. It is the same with sanctifying ourselves. Instead of working so hard, one can immediately move and let Jesus live in us. And this means to live so as to remain within the Other; in our neighbor, for example, who in each and every moment is close to us."[23] Many years later, commenting on this text to a group of Muslims, Chiara observed: "When we live like this, our vices disappear, almost like magic; and our souls are enriched with many virtues without our having gone looking for them."[24]

A second instrument, the "Pact," is a solemn declaration of readiness to live out the new commandment, even to the point of laying down one's life — "Love one another as I have loved you" (Jn 15:12). Often merely being aware of needing to renew the Pact spurs Focolare members to talk through misunderstandings or difficulties so as to insure that relationships remain authentic and sincere.[25]

A third pair of instruments reinforces the commitment to help one another on the journey to sanctity: "communion of soul" and "communion of experiences of the Word of Life." During a communion of soul, each person shares what God is working in his or her life. The model for this practice is Mary, who shared with her cousin Elizabeth what God was working in her.[26] These insights may emerge from prayer, from applying the aspects in everyday life, or from working through some particularly challenging situation. "Communion of experiences" focuses on sharing the results of putting scripture into practice. In this form of sharing, members acknowledge the Word as the real actor in a particular situation, and contemplate the Word's transforming power.[27] Elizabeth describes how young people use these instruments in their gatherings:

> Usually we take turns picking a meditation to read together, often a text from Chiara, and we follow this with "communion of soul." It is simple, but deep. It gives me an opportunity to share in a way that I can't share with those who don't live a spirituality of unity. At the same time, I always come away with an "examination of conscience" that carries me through the week. When I am at work and I encounter a situation similar to what one of the others may have shared, it makes me ask myself whether I could handle the situation in a way that is different from my initial instinct.

Keith admits that this kind of sharing does not come naturally for everyone.

> I was born shy. So I would go to the Focolare youth meetings and would not say a word. That was how I was. So this aspect of communion, sharing your life with others, was tough for me, it was something that I had to learn. I am still very shy. I can easily just be in the crowd and be content listening, but being more aware of that helps me to go outside of myself to offer whatever I have. I notice that some who are not "born shy" also admit that they have something to learn — to go beyond superficial chatter in order to reach for the depth that enables them to share what God is working in their lives.

Another instrument, "one-on-one" conversations, are held with someone mature enough in the Focolare way of life to offer guidance for another's unfolding journey. These serve as spiritual "check-ups." Chiara offers a step-by-step guide for spiritual direction, as well as a template for how a spirituality of unity might inform other kinds of conversations. The one listening should receive fully the reality that the other person is living.

> This is what we must do in our one-on-one conversations: we have to start from our brother's or sister's actual situation — which we will come to understand if we put ourselves in the right attitude — that of loving them with all our heart and mind; and if we are totally empty, as the mystery of Jesus Forsaken teaches us. In this way they can open themselves completely, pouring into our hearts the fullness that they have within, so that what emerges is the Trinitarian relationship that we must establish among us.[28]

For those who are sharing, Jesus forsaken, who emptied himself completely, is the model for what it means to put one's spiritual situation in common with others, with its ups and downs, its battles and victories. This "emptiness" leaves space to receive the help, relief, and encouragement that the Holy Spirit might suggest, bringing peace, serenity, and light for the path forward.[29]

A fourth instrument of a spirituality of unity is the "moment of truth," a practice derived from the reference in Matthew's Gospel to "fraternal correction" (see Mt 18:15–17). Chiara explained to young people, "Among the first Christians, there was the practice of saying to each other what they saw that was beautiful and less beautiful in the others, in order to correct each other, motivated only by charity, because they felt that they were one body. It was like one hand washing the other, or saying to the other, 'how beautiful you are.' "[30] Recalling an African proverb, "Our brother is like an eye in the back of our head," Chiara noted that often others can see what we cannot.[31]

This instrument is practiced in a small group of people who know one another well and who have built a sense of personal trust. One person serves as a moderator, to ensure that what is said comes from mutual love, not personal likes or dislikes. A name is chosen, usually by lot, and then in a spirit of reciprocal help, each person in the group observes a general pattern of behavior or cites examples where improvement is needed, as well as examples that demonstrate positive steps or signs of growth in the spiritual journey. When done in the fullness of charity, the moment of truth generates the joy and freedom to travel together with greater speed and ease.

Amy recalls receiving the moment of truth during her first year of Focolare community life:

> I was working in a large law firm, exhausted from the intense schedule and tied in knots by the tensions and expectations

of this high-powered professional culture. I will never forget the gentle yet firm voice of Roslyn, a married *focolarina* well into her 70s, who summed up how I needed to change with these simple words: "Honey, don't let them tell you who you are. You should be 'fire'!" Seeing my work situation through the eyes of my sisters, especially Roslyn's, burned away much of the fear that had been blocking my freedom to love. I felt that it opened the door to reclaiming my identity not as someone who conforms to professional expectations, but as a person who loves.

Finally, Focolare members engage in particular practices of "penance" that their church suggests for people in their state of life. For example, Roman Catholics fast the requisite time before receiving Communion, observe the Lenten fast, abstain from meat on Good Friday, and so on. In addition, Chiara gave particular value to the "penance" of building and rebuilding unity with neighbors, especially the closest ones. Reflecting on how to live the phrase, "Deny yourself, take up your cross," she explains:

> Where, then, can we find our typical, particular cross? In people, in our brothers and sisters who are disunited from God and from each other. It is, in fact, people, with all of their sense of feeling abandoned, the particular cross that the Lord asks us to carry. By taking this onto our shoulders, day after day, we are able to follow Jesus. Otherwise for us this adventure is closed. And the first brothers or sisters that we need to love in this way, in whom we need to recognize the face of Jesus forsaken, are those closest to us, those who live with us.
>
> God does not ask of us a cruel martyrdom. We do not need to whip ourselves or wear a hair-shirt, do long vigils or fasts or sleep on the ground … but always welcome into our hearts our neighbor or neighbors, with all of their burdens, aridity, trials, limits and defects, and do everything we can to help them find peace, trust, love and ardor.[32]

3
Walking the Path to Unity Together

How People Get Involved

M ost people first encounter the Focolare spirituality through someone who lives it. They experience the personal love of a friend, relative or colleague, or watch their friends approach a problematic situation, and want to understand more about what makes them tick. As Rebecca's college friend put it, "I want what you have."

Others may be touched by the atmosphere of love that they encounter during one of the Focolare's events such as the summer Mariapolis. Katherine, a nurse from New Jersey, describes her experience.

> A friend invited me to the Mariapolis but I decided that I was too busy, I couldn't afford it, and my family needed me at home. My friend smiled calmly and told me that my family would benefit from my going. So I registered. I knew she would not lead me to something bad.
>
> When we got there my friend, who has been part of the Focolare for many years, introduced me to her friends and I decided to put my shyness and concerns aside and go with the flow. My next surprise was the fact that there were no handouts, booklets, reading material or folders. I had been to many conferences in my lifetime, and this was the first one in which all the paper I needed could fit into a little plastic holder worn around my neck.
>
> As I began to relax and give myself to the experience, I saw that people were easy-going, funny, helpful and real. After the first day I felt as though Mary had taken me by the hand and introduced me to her Son. From then on I truly felt the presence of Jesus in our midst. Each experience I had, every person I met, every conversation I had made me feel they were directly meant for me and were what I needed to hear and learn at that moment. At first I was overwhelmed and amazed by this, but later I realized it was because Jesus was there, and he was running the show, loving me and giving me what I needed.

Deborah, a human resources manager from Long Island, had a similar experience: "Something was new. I felt welcomed, loved, accepted and free to share. I was listened to and felt no judgment. Although I had just met these people, they made me feel understood. It was a place where I could be myself and be loved just as I am. I wanted to love others the way I had been loved — unconditionally."

Will, who began meeting with other kids of the Movement in Boston when he was twelve, offers his first impressions. "I was struck by the experiences they shared. One spoke about loving Jesus in his little brother. I had never heard anyone talk about Jesus in another person, and I was surprised and captivated." Some months later he traveled with a large group to the summer Mariapolis. "During that long journey, I was touched by the way they spoke about Jesus in such a familiar and simple way. We kept busy during the trip: playing cards, singing, sharing food, telling jokes, praying the rosary — very normal things. But there was something different; it all seemed to be very sacred. The thought suddenly occurred to me: we were in the presence of God. I had bumped into God almost by accident, and it took me by surprise. He was there among us, and I wanted to stay there for the rest of my life."

Others meet the Focolare through one of Chiara's books, the Focolare magazine, *Living City*, or one of the Movement's websites. One of the sisters in her community brought Mother Rose Schulte a copy of *Living City*, where she read about people putting the gospel into practice. She was touched by the common search, as she describes it, for the "sense of Christ's presence in their lives, a relationship with him. This was the way I wanted to live the gospel, too!" Later, at a meeting for women religious in Chicago she was able to meet such people face to face.

Some meet the spirituality of unity through the "Word of Life," a scripture passage, usually taken from a particular month's Sunday liturgical readings. Small groups often gather to reflect on their efforts to put it into practice. Effie met a couple who organized one such meeting at the Arizona prison where she is serving a sentence. She writes:

> I have begun to understand the ideal of unity that this spirituality embraces. Now, I feel that my life has become firmly anchored in my love for God, and I find it easier to love the people around me, most of whom couldn't care less about anybody. One day, I found my cellmate eating the beef jerky that I was saving for later because snack food in prison is precious. But instead of my usual reaction of anger, I decided to see my cellmate as Jesus eating my food, and I told her that it was all right and that I was giving it to her.

I have begun to see my day-to-day sufferings as the necessary ingredient in my search for perfection in my love for God and my neighbor, and now I feel my burden lightened and my life filled with hope. I find complete joy in my faith in God's love for me.

One of my projects here in prison is to write about my experiences to youth organizations around the country in the hope that young people could learn from them and find the right path.

Effie's experience demonstrates, as do those of Katherine and Deborah, that living a spirituality of unity generates an awareness of how this gift may be shared with others, in ways that are appropriate to each person's network of relationships.

Some people get to know the Focolare as children, and then make a more conscious decision to live its spirituality later in their journey. Monica participated in Focolare activities for children while growing up in Baltimore. She distanced herself from the Movement during her adolescence. "As I got older and busier, I gradually drifted away. Life and all its stresses consumed me. I began searching everywhere for answers to philosophical questions in an attempt to survive in this wilderness. I read books, attended talks, participated in debates and discussions, but still found no answers. I was in a confused place, somewhere between misery and happiness." Then as a young adult she decided to return to a Focolare lifestyle. "While reflecting on my life experiences, I noticed that the times when I was truly happy were when I lived the ideal of unity, when I loved others 100%. In this moment, I felt very loved by God and made a conscious choice to discover God's will for my life. Then I had to put this choice into practice."

Adherents

The largest group of those who live the Focolare spirituality, "adherents," nourish themselves on its ideas and live out its principles. Chiara herself defined them as the most beautiful part of the Focolare. If the Movement can be said to resemble a tree, the adherents are like the leaves, a sign of freshness, growth and life. Although they do not have a formal commitment, their action in their families, churches, schools, and communities carries forward the personal and social renewal that is central to the Focolare spirituality. They often attend the Mariapolis and other Focolare events.

Laurie was raised Catholic, but all her life felt the desire for a deeper spiritual experience. In her words, "I looked to other religions, such as Buddhism, Judaism, and to other Christian traditions for answers. Often, I wasn't even sure what my questions were. I had this gnawing sense that I was missing something about how Jesus' life pertained to my life in the 21st century." She was introduced to the Focolare through some friends she knew in college. They had invited her to various events for many years, and in 2001 she and her family attended a Christmas party in Indianapolis, near their home. The next summer they attended the Mariapolis and, as she states, they "fell in love with the Movement."

> When I met the Movement, I thought, I knew it!! I knew it!! I suddenly realized that the restlessness I felt gnawing at me must have been the Holy Spirit. The Focolare spirituality helped to give dignity and purpose to each and every moment. Each step I take, each breath, each key stroke can have eternal meaning if I do it with love, in the presence of God.
>
> I often wondered why God, who is so great and all loving and created everything, couldn't have come up with a better idea than pain for the people he said he loved so much? Jesus forsaken answered this question for me, and continues to reveal new depths. Jesus forsaken is the great equalizer to pain in the world. While suffering is part of life, I realized that we look at it all wrong. I now see it as critically important to our formation. We think we are born as a finished product, physically and spiritually, but we are not. Suffering is like a chisel in the hands of the artist.

Laurie considers herself a "close adherent." She finds that Focolare principles provide a practical framework for her life.

> I participate in all my children's activities, work full-time as a program chair at a local community college, and am involved in my church, particularly in our choir.
>
> One of our choir members, Mary, is in her late eighties and still accompanies us on piano and organ. She is very close to her son Chris, also a musician, and relies on him for comfort and support. She is usually bright and peaceful, but at one practice seemed sad. As it turned out, the next day Chris was moving a thousand miles away to accept a job offer as an organist. The prospect of not having him

nearby really made her suffer, and I could feel her fear and vulnerability. I silently asked Jesus what I could do for her. Five minutes later the answer came to me. "Tell Mary you will be her 'Chris.'" This is exactly what I did. I told her, "Call me anytime. I will be there for you."

Two days later, when I was at work, she called. I had a student in my office and a pile of work to be sorted. But I had said my yes. Mary could hear that I was out of breath and said "I shouldn't have called!" I told her, "No, this is totally fine, I was running to the phone. Let me answer this student's question, and I will call you right back." When I did so, she was very upset and cried as she told me a number of things. Somehow I found the words to help her put things in perspective. She said I was an angel. I accepted this compliment on behalf of Jesus, because I knew it was not I who had spoken.

My pile of work was still there, but God's gift to me was peace. I wasn't stressed out at all, because I had taken thirty minutes to be there for one of his children.

Laurie's approach to her daily relationships and commitments is multiplied many times over by the thousands of men and women who find a focus for their personal, family, and professional lives in the Focolare spirituality.

Focolarini

Madeline first encountered the Movement in her small central Texas town when a priest visiting their parish read an excerpt from Chiara's commentary on scripture. A few years later she met the women who lived in the Focolare house in San Antonio. She describes her growing attraction to life in a Focolare house.

I had a beautiful family with lots of brothers and sisters to share life's every adventure and parents who have always been a shining example of how to overcome life's trials with faith and simplicity. I had a successful job, a new car, and a beautiful relationship with the guy I felt I would spend the rest of my life with. At the same time, I had a deep sense within me that this could not be everything in life.

I was strongly attracted by a presence that I felt when I was with those who lived in the Focolare house. I would go there as often as I could for meetings or just to wash dishes, or put some shelves in order; anything to be there. Only later did I understand that the basis of this life was the commandment that Jesus called "new" and "mine": love one another as I have loved you. Living these words of the Gospel created an incredible atmosphere of Jesus' very presence in that house.

I was also attracted by how the members of the Movement lived a communion of goods, just like the first Christians. No one asked anything of me, but I began filling the trunk of my car once or twice a month with all that I no longer needed, to bring to the Focolare house.

One day Miriam, a Focolare friend about my age from the Caribbean, confided something about the poverty she lived in her country. I thought, if we are all brothers and sisters of the same Father, she's my sister. I have never known hunger. I usually bought clothes on Mondays. That following Monday instead of buying clothes, I went to the bank and withdrew all that I had and sent it to the Focolare community in her country.

And I still felt urged inside to "give." It was at this point that I began to realize that more than my house, my money, my stuff, God wanted me. Living in a world where everything led me to believe I should be as self-sufficient as possible made it hard for me to grasp what it might mean to give God my life and depend totally on him. But in trying to do what God wanted in each moment, step by step, I found myself in the Focolare.

For the little I have given, God is never outdone in generosity. Like the day that my brother said his first Mass in our tiny home town, he told me that I had been the one who, like a mother, generated his "yes." Or, years later, when I ran into my ex-boyfriend he said that my faithfulness had given him the strength to remain faithful to his own choices in life.

In all of life's circumstances, I have seen that when I am able to step into the present moment and give myself without reserve to the person next to me, accepting them as they are, it is then that every moment can become the most beautiful of my life.

Kevin, the youngest of three children, grew up in Boston. His family had been part of the Focolare for some time, and he enjoyed the company of other young people in the Movement and their activities together. When he was a teenager, he began to sense that there was, as he puts it, "something in this life for me personally." He explains:

> My brothers and I had been adopted. As early as seven years old, I had gnawing questions about my real identity, the meaning of suffering, and how to trust in the love of my parents and relationships with others.
>
> When I was nineteen, at a summer Mariapolis I found the answers to my life's questions. I discovered that God loves me immensely and that every suffering has a purpose in his divine plan of love. At a certain point I went into the chapel and experienced a deep sense that God was calling me to follow him.
>
> But then I began to think, "I haven't lived enough of life yet," and I ended up distancing myself from the Focolare community for about six years. However, I persistently felt an impulse to love others. For example, my brother had a friend who suffered from bipolar disorder who used to telephone daily. When my brother was not home, I would take the call and listen to him for hours. At one point he asked me, "Why do you do this when others avoid me?" I saw the contrast between his darkness and the light that was present in my relationships in the Focolare. I wanted to be that light for him.
>
> Then something happened. I was attending the wedding of my girlfriend's sister when, at the reception, their mother suffered an aneurism and died on the spot. Life seemed so short, and once again I felt the urgency to rediscover the Focolare lifestyle of unity. After completing my college degree, I went to Italy for a course of formation in order to live in a Focolare house.

Madeline and Kevin are *focolarini* — a name by which those who lived in the first Focolare house in Trent were known.[1] Their vocation, a new path in the Church, opened as a result of Chiara's own intuitions and experience.

CHIARA, THE FIRST *FOCOLARINA*

Chiara's first intuitions about this vocation came in 1939, when she was nineteen. With other Catholic students she was attending a conference in Loreto, Italy. There, within the huge fortress-like church, stands the little house where according to tradition the Holy Family had lived. Visiting it provoked in Chiara a deep spiritual experience:

> I found myself alone, plunged into this great mystery. And what was most unusual for me, I shed copious tears … I began to meditate on everything that might have happened within these walls: the annunciation of the Angel to Mary, the family life of Jesus, Mary and Joseph. Whenever there was free time from the congress … I wouldn't miss a chance every day to run back to the "little house." And each time it had the same effect on me, the same deep emotion. It was as if a particular grace of God was enveloping me completely, almost as if the Divine was overwhelming me…. It was all contemplation, prayer, as if in some way I was living with the three persons of the Holy Family.[2]

At the concluding ceremony, young people filled the basilica, including a large number of girls wearing white veils. During the Mass, Chiara sensed that she had found her own vocation in life. "I knew that I had found my 'way.' … Then I had an image of a whole host of white-clad virgins following after me on this way. I didn't know what it meant, but that's what I experienced."[3]

Upon returning to Trent, Chiara told her parish priest that she had found her "way." He asked which of the paths for Catholic women would she follow — marriage, consecrated life in the world, or the convent. He did not know what to make of it when she responded that it was none of these.[4] At that point she continued living with her family and working in Trent.

Four years later, as a gesture of love for her sisters, who did not want to go out into the winter cold, she took it upon herself to fetch milk for the family. As she ran this errand, Chiara felt a clear invitation: "Give yourself to me." The letter she wrote to her parish priest about this experience convinced him that she was ready to consecrate herself to God forever, a step she took on December 7, 1943. As she ran home from the early morning Mass she bought three red carnations with the few pennies in her pocket and placed them in front of her crucifix, the only sign of celebration.[5] She had no further plans or expectations. "I was completely caught up by the fact that I had married God. It was something between him and me. In fact, if anyone had mentioned anything about companions, about a movement, and so on, it would have completely ruined the enchantment."[6]

That Christmas, Chiara considered whether her consecration to God might entail entering a cloister. She was ready to do so, but when she discussed the idea with the priest he exclaimed: "What are you thinking? This is absolutely not the will of God for you." At that moment "a door opened" for Chiara and she "was able to see that what mattered was not what one does in life, but rather doing the will of God."[7] Within months, the war brought about the circumstances that led to opening the first Focolare house. After the chaos wrought by the bombing of May 13, 1944, the Capuchin friars of Trent gave Chiara and her friends a small apartment as a refuge.

"Whoever does not leave father, mother …"

As Chiara's story illustrates, the "yes" of the *focolarini* means leaving everything to follow God's call and being completely available for the work of building the kingdom of God, wherever there might be a need. For those who live in community, "Anyone who does not leave mother, father, fields …" (Mt 4:20–22, Mt 19:29) signifies the readiness to leave country, language, and culture, as well as relinquishing the possibility of marriage and family.

Will, from Boston, describes his experience of living in Focolare houses all over the world.

> My travels have led me to discover that people everywhere, of every culture and creed, are more similar than I ever imagined. In Asia, I taught at an American school for children of corporate executives; in Central America, I taught the children of wealthy families who often had been involved in sociopolitical violence; in Africa I taught Bangwa children in Fontem, Cameroon, at a Focolare-run boarding school. In each of these places I tried to deal with the contrasts between rich and poor, between my negative judgments and my desire to love everyone.
>
> In each place I have discovered that my true happiness lies in trying to fulfill the plan of love that God has for us, and in seeing each person I meet as my brother. For example, in El Salvador, the poor children were developing infections because they had no shoes. The Focolare young people started a project called "Operation Zapatos" (shoes). When the wealthier children of the school where I taught heard about it, they joined in. We soon had a truck-load of new shoes, and the infection rate went down.

In Singapore there is a large multi-religious population, and their lack of knowledge of one another has allowed alienation to fester. Every day on my way to school I would pass a Hindu temple and would simply greet the Hindu holy man at the door. After some months, he invited me in, and our friendship led to a real dialogue of understanding, a bridge between our two faiths.

Focolarini prepare to work in particular professions, but they are ready to take a different job to satisfy the needs of the Movement, or to correspond to the economic circumstances or immigration rules of the country where they are living. Wherever they work, they do so with a spirit of detachment, aware that any job can be done as a service of love.

The *focolarini* live the evangelical counsels — poverty, chastity and obedience — as "supports" to a life of unity and mutual love. The document which describes their rule of life states: "Since charity is the mother of all virtues, [the *focolarino* or *focolarina*] finds that love for all and mutual love are the most effective means for being chaste, poor and obedient" (Art. 94). The Roman Catholic *focolarini* take "private vows." As distinguished from what canon law calls "religious vows," those who take these retain their position within the Church as laity. Generally, first vows follow a two- to three-year period of formation and another two-year period of "probation" during which they live in a Focolare house and participate in all of the aspects of its life. Perpetual vows usually follow seven or eight years after first vows.

"GO, SELL YOUR POSSESSIONS …"

The *focolarini* take fairly literally the gospel admonition, "Go, sell your possessions, and give the money to the poor … then come, follow me" (Mt 19:21). Each Focolare house supplies from its own resources what is needed for basic necessities, measured according to a simple lifestyle. It then shares the remainder in order to meet the necessities of *focolarini* throughout the world, particularly where economic resources are scarce. Like the first Focolare house in Trent, which received abundant "providence" to sustain the community (see pp. 24–25), the *focolarini* continue to be open to God's loving intervention to meet their needs.

Questions about expenditures are often worked out through a "Trinitarian" decision-making style. Joy explains how they decided upon a particular maintenance project:

The Bronx Focolare house has a grassy area where the kids play when they come for their meetings. We realized that given our summer schedules, we ought to put in a sprinkler system to keep the grass green where the children play, but we were not sure whether to spend an additional $1,000 to bore under the sidewalks for sprinklers outside the fence.

As we talked this decision through, our different perspectives surfaced: Should that money be shared for more urgent needs in another part of the world? What would best fit our neighborhood environment? What would best reflect our commitment to have less rather than more, and to remain open to God's intervention?

Trying to welcome one another's ideas, we felt a real sense of freedom. Talking all of this through, we felt enriched by seeing the problem from so many different angles. Our different perspectives helped to generate a deeper love among us, not a sense of division.

In the end we decided together to put the sprinklers only inside the fence. At the moment, the grass looks great!

"How very good and pleasant it is …"

Focolare households hope to make visible a verse from the psalms, "How very good and pleasant it is when kindred live together in unity!" (Ps 133:1). Each makes an effort to keep a warm spirit of "family" at the center of community life and in their personal commitment to live all of the aspects of Focolare life. The extent to which moments of prayer, meals, exercise, cleaning, study, and other tasks are carried out together often depends on the work schedules and commitments of the members of a given household. Many do manage to eat dinner together almost every evening.

A spirit of love and equality leads to sharing in domestic tasks like cooking and cleaning. As Chiara puts it, "The men and women *focolarini*, whatever their profession, should be happy to be seen wearing an apron by anyone, happy to set the table, to clear away the dishes, and so on. This too is part of their vocation."[8] Ethan, who lives in the Focolare house in Chicago, gives an example: "Making coffee for the others is my first 'act of love' of the morning. It is a good exercise to begin the morning by thinking of the others." Chiara adds, "We know of young people who felt the call to give their lives to God after seeing the *focolarini* carrying out these very tasks."[9]

Focolare houses reflect the gospel dynamic of being in the world, yet not of it (see Jn 15:19). Chiara describes them as places where the *focolarini* "are separate from while still immersed in the world ... where they must show daily, through this divine life, that Christ has overcome the world."[10] At the same time, a Focolare's doors are wide open so that the presence of "Jesus in the midst" can illuminate and sustain the surrounding community, and whoever might come into contact with this "hearth."

For this reason, the architectural style of a Focolare house is to be, as the rulebook for the *focolarini* reads, "in harmony with the environment, the characteristics and customs of the people where the Focolare center carries on its primary apostolic activity" (Art. 48). Chiara explains: "Our house will not necessarily be poor or poorer than others. We can live in a palace or in a *mocambo*, in a skyscraper or in a country cottage. We can live anywhere, so long as our surroundings are an expression of love for our brothers and sisters."[11]

Most Focolare houses serve not only as a dwelling place for the *focolarini*, but also as a gathering place for the community as a whole and for smaller meetings. Many houses are furnished so that they can be adapted easily to the needs of children. Toddler handprints on windows and tables are a sign of inclusion, life, and love. Paper flowers, song lyrics and other decorations make an adult-style living room or workspace comfortable for children. In the kitchens, teenagers make their own pizza, or prepare the strawberry jam or cookies for the bake sales through which they fund their trips, activities, or relief efforts.

A similar rationale of openness to the world determines how *focolarini* dress. Chiara was always touched by the way various religious orders witness to the life of the gospel through their habits. The "distinctive sign" for the *focolarini*, however, is not particular garb, but mutual love: "By this everyone will know that you are my disciples, if you have love for one another" (Jn 13:35). Chiara explains, "The *focolarini* are born to love. They remain in the world without being of the world, and their way of dressing must aid them in this task."[12]

Ethan explains:

> The way I dress depends on who I am with. When I am with the smaller children, then I dress so that they are comfortable with me — usually jeans and running shoes. When I go to my job at the university where I work as an executive assistant, I dress in accord with my title and position. This

is a way of making people comfortable, and of showing love for my boss. I try to make sure that the combination is presentable, and depending on the time of year, I might have to spend more time ironing. This, too, is a conscious act of love for the people I will meet during the day, which changes my attitude toward ironing.

Taking as an example the beauty and simplicity of the "lilies of the field" (Mt 6:28–29), Chiara advises moderation, elegance and simplicity that befits "a person who is a temple of the Holy Spirit"; modesty, "because we are children of Mary"; and avoiding expensive jewelry or accessories "because real value lies in the beauty of the person, inflamed with the love of God."[13]

BETWEEN TWO FIRES

Living in a Focolare house is a dynamic process patterned on the life of the Holy Trinity. By growing in unity with others, each *focolarino* or *focolarina* develops his or her own unique identity. Chiara describes their life as being "between two fires." The first "fire" is "intimate union of God" *within one's self* : listening to the voice of conscience that points to God's will, adoring him in the Holy Eucharist, loving him in moments of meditation, embracing him on the cross whenever occasions arise, and living the words of scripture. The second "fire" is that of union with God *outside of self* : with the person who holds responsibility for the community, as well as in "brothers or sisters who must be loved and served constantly in such a way that the brother *par excellence* of all, Jesus, be always among all."[14]

Because a Focolare house usually includes men or women from different countries and cultures, it becomes a school in which the mundane details of life are lessons for learning unconditional love. Differences may create tensions, but so long as both "fires" are burning, such moments lead to a deeper union with God and a more profound presence of Christ in the community. Chiara writes: "When unity becomes difficult, we must not break, but bend, until love makes the miracle of one heart and one soul."[15] Dori Zamboni describes this dynamic in the life of the first Focolare house in Trent: "We were different, we saw things differently. So at times we would get stuck." For this reason, Chiara suggested a "pact of mercy" — "to look at each other as if in that moment we were meeting each other for the first time."[16]

Reflecting on the impact of Jesus in their midst, Chiara shares how the "fire" of the presence of God has led her to entrust everything to God's mercy, and begin again: "I have been helped in this by the community, by Jesus in our midst who has always straightened me out and got me on my feet again."[17] In fact, one of the most beautiful aspects of living in a Focolare house is the constant realization that unity is not within human design or control. It is a "miracle" of God's presence, a gift.

Married Focolarini

Elena and Michael, who live on Long Island, have four grown sons. Elena encountered the Movement at a time when their marriage was on the verge of divorce. Her efforts to heal these wounds helped her discover her vocation to be a married *focolarina*.

> I had always felt frustrated because my husband did not respond to me in the way I expected. Living the Focolare spirituality, I began to understand that at the end of my life God was not going to ask me, "How has Michael loved you" but "How have you loved Michael?" The spirituality helped me to place God first in my life, and has put in perspective the problems in our relationship. I began to love without looking for anything in return. It was a real challenge, it cost me a lot, like a tree being pruned.
>
> There were still many problems in our marriage, disappointments, my failures in loving, but now they had a name — Jesus forsaken — so there was nothing to hold me back anymore. There was no longer a need for self-condemnation, everything was consumed in the mercy of God.
>
> After a few years of living in this way, my husband and children wanted to learn more about the spirituality of unity. I also grew in understanding how God could be everything for me, and I began to feel the vocation to live as a married *focolarina*.
>
> As a married *focolarina* it is not that I have my home with my family and a second home in Focolare. Home for me is Jesus in the midst. If there is Jesus in the midst, I am one with those in my Focolare house whether I am there with them or in my own house. If I do not feel at home this means that I have to love Jesus forsaken and get out of myself to love again.

When I love I am free. I go to the Focolare house to be the first to love. I try not to lean on the others. This does not mean that I go it alone. If I am unable to love Jesus forsaken, then I share that too so that we can love him together.

We share one another's joys, sufferings, failures and conversions. Every prayer, every act of love, can help to build Jesus in the midst. I know that faithfulness is important also to sustain the vocations of the single *focolarine*, because how I live has an impact on Jesus in the midst with them.

"Married *focolarini*" bring a vital and integral part of the human experience to Focolare houses, which are modeled on the family of Nazareth. This vocation presumes full respect for the sanctity of marriage and the intimacy of family life. An early letter from Chiara to her younger sister, who was about to marry, conveys this vision: "There is just one love: love for God. He lives in the hearts of all of his creatures. But you in particular need to see him above all in one heart, that of Paolo, because this is his will for you."[18]

Tom, a married *focolarino* from Brooklyn, offers an example of how he tried to discern God's will for him in a practical circumstance.

> One night my wife Mary, who at the time thought I was too attached to the Focolare, had prepared my favorite meal from scratch: eggplant parmesan. It took her longer than usual and that night I had a meeting at the Focolare. At first I said, "I can't stay to eat right now because I have a meeting." But when I saw her crushed expression, I said to myself, "I must return her act of love. She is Jesus to be loved." And then I sat down and said, "I'm not going. I'd rather stay with you and eat this feast you prepared for me." Mary was visibly moved.

The first married *focolarino*, Igino Giordani — "Foco" — was instrumental in helping Chiara discern God's design for married men and women in Focolare households. Foco had a profound appreciation for the role of consecrated people in the history of the Church. In one discussion, as he was praising the state of chastity with eloquence and respect, Chiara was deeply touched by his humility. One of Giordani's biographers captures the moment: "She replied in her good direct style that what counts is charity and that there were many proud virgins who may well be in hell for their pride."[19]

Chiara then set out to explain how Foco, a married man, could be a *focolarino.*

> Foco, it is love that virginizes. If you are only love, if every-
> thing that you do in your family life is always motivated by
> love, if every act in your marriage and family is love, what are
> you missing? Virginity is not so much "not being" a certain
> thing; it is "being" love. Why couldn't you seal this with a
> vow, a promise through which you will always do everything
> out of love? In this way you are chaste, poor and obedient.[20]

Thus the possibility opened for married people to take part in an integral way within Focolare households. Each person is called to this vocation personally. In a marriage, one spouse may feel the call but not the other. In fact, Foco's wife did not share his choice. When both spouses do feel the call and when circumstances allow, "Focolare families" often offer to move — even to other countries — for short or for extended periods. They help to nourish Focolare communities, especially in places that have need for the particular witness of a couple and a family who live a spirituality of unity.[21]

Volunteers of God

As a teenager growing up in Philadelphia, Kirk had been puzzled by conflicting aspirations. He wanted to marry and raise a family, and at the same time wanted to put his talents to use for God and society, perhaps in a religious community. "I prayed for an answer, and I can still remember how startled I was when it came ten minutes into a talk given by one of the *focolarini.* The vocation of my dreams existed in the Focolare Movement."

The turbulent 1960s, with the assassination of John F. Kennedy, the struggles for civil rights throughout the United States, and the Vietnam War made Peggy, like many of her classmates at Mount Mercy College in Pittsburgh, restless to pursue truth and do what was right. In 1966, she was particularly drawn to the relationship she saw between two women who had visited the campus to talk about a spirituality of unity. As a student studying sociology, she had an interest in social relationships and community organization, but there was something unique in how these women spoke about the possibility of living the life of heaven here on earth. Peggy had always wanted to do something great with her life and she felt within an invitation from God to join them.

She describes how her response affected her personal and professional life:

> As I grew in my relationship with God, with the others who were living the Focolare spirituality and in my profession as a clinical social worker in a large New York City hospital, I saw more clearly my specific place in the Focolare as a Volunteer of God. Working with families of children who were neglected and sometimes abused, who were dealing with life-threatening illnesses and who lived in extreme poverty, often made me feel powerless. The skills I had learned didn't always provide solutions to such overwhelming problems.
>
> And yet, I knew that God loves each person immensely and even through these circumstances he wants to show his love. Having come to recognize the presence of Jesus forsaken in such difficult circumstances, I could maintain a sense of hope and convey this to my patients and their families. They in turn became convinced of this and even in the most difficult situations had the courage to face their challenges and grow as individuals and as families.

Just as the bombardments of World War II created the circumstances for the first Focolare house, the 1956 Hungarian uprising set the stage for a new vocation within the Focolare Movement — the "Volunteers of God." In October of 1956, the world was watching as student protests turned toward full-scale revolution and the Communist government collapsed. Within weeks, the Soviet Army stormed Budapest, and the brutal repression killed more than 2,500 while 200,000 fled, abandoning their hopes for freedom and human rights.

"God, God, God!" Pope Pius XII cried out in a November 10, 1956 radio broadcast. "Let this glorious name, the source of all law, justice and freedom, ring out in our parliaments, in our streets and squares, in our homes and our places of work." The following January, just back from a meeting in Vienna with some of the Hungarian refugees, Chiara published an open and heartfelt appeal:

> A society has succeeded in eradicating the name of God, the reality of God, His providence and His love from the hearts of men. There must be, then, another society able to put him back in the place that is His.... We must build up a body of men and women of all ages, races, conditions,

bound together by the strongest bond that exists: mutual love, that mutual love bequeathed to us as His testament by a God dying in His human nature. That mutual love that is the highest ideal and an invincible force.... That mutual love that means practical deeds, making our brothers the object of all our love for God. What is needed, then, are real disciples of Jesus in the world ... who follow Him voluntarily, driven only by an enlightened love of Him and His Church in this dark hour.... An army of volunteers, because love is voluntary. An army because it means going to war and building a new society, one renewed by the Good News, ever ancient, ever new, a society in which justice and truth shine forth with love.[22]

Not to be confused with "volunteering," in the sense of setting aside some time to help, the "Volunteers of God" constitute another vocation within the Movement. The Volunteers are called to holiness as laity — with all of the dignity that the Second Vatican Council would recognize in this state — precisely through their direct involvement in the things of the world. They come from every social, cultural and professional background, and are committed to living a spirituality of unity in their families and in their positions in society.

In 2006, more than 7,000 Volunteers and 4,000 guests from ninety-two countries converged on Budapest's sports arena to celebrate their unique vocation. During the program, simultaneously translated into twenty-six languages, artists, farmers, health care workers, housewives, bankers, union leaders, educators, lawyers, journalists, filmmakers, computer specialists, government workers and politicians shared their stories of building "a society in which justice and truth shine forth with love."[23]

In her message to them, Chiara noted, "As lay people, you live in the ordinary circumstances of family, work and social life, and this is why you are called to build up God's kingdom in the world, like yeast in a mass of dough.... Yes, it is precisely by immersing yourselves in the affairs of the world that you can reach holiness. You work to bring out the true nature of the world, not only to continue God's creative work, but also for the redemption of all things. Through your efforts and work, you can contribute to bringing about the new heavens and new earth."[24]

The Volunteers do not live together, as do the *focolarini*, but do come together regularly in small groups of men or women to live mutual love to the point of experiencing the presence of Christ in their midst. Zoe, from New Jersey, explains:

Our group includes twelve women from eight different nations and cultures. We are also in different stages and states of life — some are happily married with families, others are single or single parents, widowed or divorced. But these differences do not diminish the unity among us.

We meet faithfully once a week. It is a sacred moment, a special gift. We try to come on time, and limit initial greetings and socializing to fifteen minutes, because we are all there to take full advantage of the precious "grace" of what we need to do during the meeting. We are there to renew the presence of Jesus in our midst, by freely sharing both our deepest sufferings and the joyful moments of everyday living. In this way, we help each other to grow in how we live the Focolare spirituality.

We express ourselves in different ways. It is amazing to see how the quiet introverts come out to share deep moments in their lives. I am more exuberant and like to joke around, but I see when I need to curb this in order to make space for others to share. The more we share, especially in each other's sufferings, the more that presence of Jesus in our midst grows. Once a month we meet for dinner, which is a more social moment, but also strengthens the relationships among us.

After the weekly meeting, one of us sends an email to our group so that we can stay in touch and live the week together, to pray for and help each other, even in simple needs, like a doctor's appointment, or if someone needs help with a family situation. This is the life that sustains the activities and the substantial growth of the larger Focolare community. Without the Focolare houses and these units for smaller meetings, there would be no larger community.

Gen

When she was two years old, Adanna's family emigrated from Nigeria to the United States and settled in Atlanta. Now a teenager and the oldest of five children, she describes the process of making her own decision to live the Focolare spirituality.

My mother was part of the Focolare Movement before I was born, so I've known about it all my life. As I grew older, I drifted away. Then one day I looked at my life and realized that my beliefs had to be something more than just going to church on Sundays; love was more than something I could live out only when I felt like it. As a teenager, I found myself wondering about the world. I asked myself questions that had not been answered for me in religion textbooks or any of the teachings I had ever heard. I asked God for guidance and shortly thereafter I encountered the Focolare Movement again. I realized that if I wanted to see a united world, I had to start by bringing about unity in my daily life.

I used to get angry with my sisters and brother very quickly, and there were countless times when I wanted to refuse to clean up around the house or do any chores. In making the choice to love, I began to be more patient with them, and this was probably something my mother had been waiting for. She began to relate to me on another level, and we became a support for each other in this life of unity. I also started to look at my friends differently, wondering how much I could give to them each day. I feel that my purpose in life is to love God in all I do, so that all of my small acts will contribute to building a love that will finally change the world.

Like those whose stories open this book, Adanna is a "Gen," short for "New Generation," one of the young people of the Focolare. These Gen, generally under age thirty, have not yet made a firm decision for their future, so they remain open to all of the vocations in the Focolare Movement and in the Church.

Children and young people were present in the Focolare community from the beginning, playing and hiking during the summer Mariapolis in the 1950s. Their first little newsletter, *Atom*, included illustrated phrases from the gospel and their own experiences of living them. In it, Chiara explained: "The children are the smallest, but they contain the power of a great revolution."

One evening during the summer of 1962, shortly after the Movement's official approval, Chiara looked up at the Milky Way and sensed that something new would come to life for the younger generations of the Movement. In 1964, Vincenzo Folonari, a young *focolarino* known as "Eletto," drowned while saving one of the young boys he was supervising on a boating trip. Aware of the stunning loss this was for the children, Chiara wrote in her diary, "Let's hope that on the basis of this suffering something might be born for them, for the glory of God, in the heart of the Work of Mary, and for the beauty of the Church. Eletto would have wanted nothing more."[25] Two years later, Pope Paul VI received at an audience 150 children and young people of the Movement.

Against the backdrop of student protests during the late 1960s, Chiara helped this next generation to lay the groundwork for their own "revolution." From the beginning, they understood that their approach was not founded on sentiment, enthusiasm, or activism, but on a genuine, total life commitment. As one of their slogans from that time states, "To change ourselves in order to change the world; to change the world in order to change ourselves."[26]

The editorial of their first newsletter explained the process of what Rebecca referred to on page 13 as "becoming a global person."

> For us, it is not a problem to work and study with young people who are French, German, African, American, Chinese, Australian, Indian. We see our personality can be enriched by the many positive attributes of people from different civilizations, cultures and races. In the same way, if by chance we are rich, we do not think it strange to play with those who are poor, and vice versa. Naturally, all of this happens if we are not tainted by the mentality of an old society that still wants the world disunited. Instead we know that all people are brothers and sisters because they are children of God.... The world of the future will be on our shoulders, and we accept responsibility for it right now.[27]

The Gen learn what it means to become "a global person" at international gatherings and "schools of formation," where they experience first hand how a spirituality of unity helps them bridge ethnic, cultural and linguistic differences. Elizabeth recounts her impression during a week-long conference in 2002, shortly after the 9/11 attacks.

> At the time I was living in Farmington, Michigan, not far from Dearborn, where there is a large Arab population. There was ethnic tension in my high school and in our community at large. When I arrived at the Supercongress with this burden, I found myself in a stadium full of young people from all over the world. I thought to myself, "Oh my gosh, it can be so simple,

it just takes being ready to let go of defensiveness." Then I stayed for a week after the event for a meeting of "formation" for the Gen. We came from all over the world, yet we were able to dialogue about some of these tough problems. It was there that I understood what it means to "empty myself," to receive the other without barriers or preconceived notions. This is something that I was then able to carry into my school environment, and now in the professional environment where I work. What I learned there helps me to make a concerted effort to listen fully, attentively, and actively to the person in front of me, no matter their ethnicity, race, or religion. I realize that I can't build unity with someone until I am ready to let go of everything in order to be one with that person.

As do those in other vocational paths within the Movement, the Gen gather in small groups in order to encourage one another in their efforts to live a spirituality of unity in their daily lives. As Elizabeth explains, "Seeing the example of the other Gen challenges me to say, 'Okay, right now this might not be the easiest thing, and it might not even feel great, but I know deep down in my heart that this is love. It is a choice I need to make if I am to really recognize Jesus in the other person.' Then there's always peace. We often share how certain choices bring us peace."

As Adanna's experience shows, for many Gen the choice to live for unity begins at home. Evelyn, now in college, recounts how she found a way to heal the strained relationship with her father.

As a young person living the Focolare's spirituality of unity, I tried to "be the first to love" and look beyond people's outer shells. But I felt a contradiction inside, because with my family, especially my father, it was very difficult to do this. Every contact with him was frustrating. It seemed as though he didn't care about what I was doing, and when he did, I felt like he didn't understand me. I thought he was a failure. The divide between us was so big that I didn't think I could love him.

I started school in another town and moved out. At first, I felt relieved. I didn't have to worry about my dad or my family problems anymore. But it was those words, "Be the first to love," that helped me change the way I saw my dad. When I would come home from school, I started to join him while he watched his favorite TV program, even if we didn't say much to each other.

Then, several weeks ago, I asked my dad to lunch. When I arranged it over the phone, he couldn't believe I'd go so far out of my way. "You're coming down? Just for me?" he asked. At that lunch, I started to discover my father and see him in a different light. There was definitely a depth and life in him that I had never seen before. I began to understand that this man wasn't "my enemy"; he was probably my greatest advocate and protector. He wasn't the failure that I had labeled him; he was stronger and more heroic than I had ever known. Being the first to love really made me understand my father better and helped me start a new relationship with him.

When the first Gen began to meet together, Chiara advised them to reach out to the most marginalized. "Let us seek out the young people who are poor, the least, those that the world does not hold in esteem, those who do not know joy but rather tears and hunger."[28] In their local environments, Gen continue to follow this advice. Brian, an 18-year-old from Columbus, Ohio, initially started volunteering as a piano teacher for an inner-city after-school program because he needed to fulfill his high school service requirement. But his contact with the suffering of the children kept him involved.

I was about to leave when the director of the program asked if I could go get one of the kids who had taken a crowbar and was beating the tables inside the gym. I was tired and hungry, but I decided to go as an act of love. I was expecting to take the crowbar from the kid and tell him to get out of there, but he was really pounding on this table. So I stood back and asked him kindly to give me the crowbar. He looked really mad so I asked him if he wanted to talk about it. It took a while and I was getting frustrated, but I kept asking him, till he finally put it down and walked towards me.

Then he hugged me and started crying; I had never talked to this kid before so I was taken aback. I asked him to sit down and tell me what had happened. He said that the night before his mother had been taken to the hospital. I realized that even if I wanted to get out of there, I needed to put him first and love him. I sat and talked to him for half an hour. His mom had been beaten by his stepdad almost to the point of death, and the only thing that had stopped him was this kid, who was nine years old. He was very, very unstable about it. He said,

"I've always heard about God but I don't know how to pray to him." I told him, "All you have to do is talk to him and hope for the best."

At that point I looked at him and I knew I had to keep going there to volunteer, to help out these kids, because even if I want to do stuff after school that may be better for me academically, I felt that they needed every role model they can get. I have been volunteering there ever since.

In the early 1970s the branch of the third generation of young people, Gen 3 (ages 9–17), began to take shape. Chiara saw that these young people would carry the message of hope for "the dawn of a world completely renewed."[29] During their 1970 convention, she encouraged them: "In order to build new cities, it's not enough to have technicians, scientists and politicians; we also need people who are wise, we also need saints. Yours, therefore, must be a generation of saints."[30] She entrusted each with a small copy of the gospels with the wish that they live it so well "that whoever sees you can say: there is another small Jesus living today."[31]

Thirteen-year-old Eugene, from Naperville, Illinois, describes what the Gen life means to him. "If I wasn't a Gen I'd definitely be more negative to the world. When you're a Gen it makes you see the good in people, because you're around people who love others and want to create unity. So it's important to me to be a Gen, because it helps me bring out the best in people, and helps me bring out the best unity."

For Eugene, bringing out the "best" has included stopping acts of bullying and moving beyond long-standing rivalries. "In seventh grade, there was this one kid; he was enemies with me since kindergarten. We were really enemies. One time, he was getting picked on in the hallway, and it went on for two days. During the first day, I didn't do anything, he was my enemy after all. But on the second day, it was even meaner, so I told them to stop, and to get away. The other kids just stopped, and walked away. They didn't do anything to him or to me. We're friends now. We're not enemies any more."

Regina, from Maryland, is twelve. She also sees how the Gen way of life gives her the strength to resist peer pressure, and to suggest alternative values to her friends. She describes how she deals with gossip at her school.

It is really hard not to get caught up in it. It is really negative because it is mostly judging other people behind their backs and I am not comfortable with it. Lately, when my friends gossip, I've been trying to say something nice about the person as well, or change the subject, or offer a different point of view. It was good, and I felt like I was really being a true Christian.

But one time, when I had tried to stop my friends from gossiping, one girl got into an argument with me. She told me that she was talking about the things that interested her, and gossip was what she wanted to talk about and that I had no right to tell her what or what not to talk about. That was hard. I felt really discouraged, and I thought will I ever be able to make them understand that what they are doing is not love? But then I understood that this is what it means to go against the current. There will always be opposition, but I just need to stay strong and keep on loving as Jesus did.

In their school environments, the Gen are often catalysts for breaking through the constraints of cliques and the negative dynamics of peer pressure in order to build healthy relationships. Josh, a sophomore in high school, explains, "When I see a kid who looks sad, I leave my friends so I can hang out with him, so he feels better. And when he does feel better I feel closer to him, which is really nice." In one instance, his capacity to befriend "the guy with the real high-pitched voice" who everybody thought was "weird" enabled that boy "to make friends with everybody else on the volleyball team."

Eric, fifteen, explains in a similar fashion how living the Focolare spirituality helped him to break through common high school barriers.

This is my second year of high school and I now feel that I have the hang of things. I play football, and we start camp at the beginning of summer. My neighbor, who is a freshman, is also playing football, so we started to car pool. I sensed that he was nervous, but I didn't think too much of this, expecting him to just blend in with the other freshmen when we got there. After a couple of days I realized he really didn't know that many other freshmen, and if he did they all usually remained silent. Then I thought about the "art of loving" that we live as Gen. How did I feel last year? And how would I like to be treated?

The next day, after we left the car I really tried to stay with him, just talking to him about how everything was going. From then on I loved that same way each day and soon felt much joy in doing this. After a while he seemed to really get more social and talkative not only with me, but this carried over to the other freshmen. And in the end even though some guys that are sophomores now say, "Hey you have to treat them like freshmen," I feel that I was doing the right thing by loving him and other underclassmen, even when the others weren't.

As far back as 1963, Chiara noted this about the youngest children: "For me they are not small. The soul is not small, it is equal, and God is present in the same way, both in children and in adults. God is calling children, too."[32] Groups of younger children began to meet in the early 1970s. In 1988, at the entrance to an assembly for Gen 3, a small boy in his father's arms asked Chiara, "So when will you have a convention for us?" The following June an international meeting for "Gen 4" was held, attended by 800 children, aged four to eight.[33]

"So here's what you do: roll it every morning, and then you know what Jesus wants from you." Davey held a small cube, each side with a simple cartoon-style drawing and a phrase: I'm the first to love / I love everyone / I love Jesus in the other / I share the other's joy or hurt / I love my enemy / We love one another. Davey is explaining his life as a Gen 4. When he gets together with other children his age, they play, share their "acts of love," often aided by the ideas on the cube, and learn more about the life of Jesus.

Six-year-old Bart gives an example: "It was Sunday morning. I rolled my cube and it fell on the side that says, 'I love everyone.' My dad asked me what I wanted for breakfast, and I wanted French toast. Then my little brother woke up and asked for French toast as well. But there was none left! My brother started to cry. He really wanted his French toast. I then told my dad that he could cut my French toast in half and give it to my brother. He stopped crying and gave me a big smile. I was happy too."

Eight-year-old Denise, from suburban Chicago, recounts: "One day my little sister Bella did something that made me mad, and I wanted to get back at her. And that morning I rolled 'love your enemy' so ... I calmed down." Rose, from Houston, expresses the link that the Gen 4 see between their "acts of love" for others and their love for Jesus. "When I went to the store I did something nice. I wanted my favorite snack. So my mom said that she would only buy one small bag of Cheetos to share with my cousin because my mom didn't have much money. I didn't really want to share, but then I knew I would make her happy. So I did! And I said 'for you Jesus.' We both enjoyed them. But you know what? I had something in return! I had more than half a bag left that I was able to save for another day." Like the older Gen, the Gen 4 learn about the Focolare's goal to work for unity early on. Their songs and games help them see the connections between loving and building unity in the world. For example, these are the lyrics to one of their songs: "We want to love, love, love / We want to fill the world with love / We want to love, love, love / So that the world will be one."

The Gen 4 face obstacles that the adults do not anticipate. During a summer Mariapolis, four-year-old Frannie was busy with a poster, writing the names of all the people that she wanted to love. "Can I write my mommy, my daddy, and my brother Eric?" The *focolarina* helping with the group responded, "Of course! And here at the Mariapolis we try to love everybody." Frannie reflected for a moment, and then explained why this might be hard for her: "But I don't know how to write 'everybody.'"

Men and Women Religious

Sr. Marianne, O.P., met the Focolare through a fellow catechism teacher at a Native American reservation near Los Angeles. Intrigued by the idea that families would meet to share how they lived a selected sentence of scripture, she contacted the local Focolare. She discovered a spirituality that helped her, in her words, "to thank God for his immense love by loving the person next to me in every moment."

> I became sensitive to unity, the presence or lack of it, and I began to recognize its fundamental value and importance. As I learned the steps to building unity, I realized it was pure gospel. I also saw suffering in a new way; it could be transformed into love. This revolutionized my life.
>
> I was working with people who lived in Los Angeles' Watts District. Putting into practice the monthly sentence of scripture, I saw how things around me began to change. Neighbors stopped feuding and people began to pick up their garbage. They seemed to take better care of themselves because they saw more of a purpose for their lives.
>
> I began participating in international conferences for consecrated women, sponsored by the Focolare. I noticed how focusing on unity made us better Franciscans, Benedictines, Dominicans, as we applied the gospel to the different expressions of love left by each founder.

Since its beginnings, the Focolare has had contact with a variety of religious communities. Before the Movement began, Chiara taught at an orphanage directed by the Capuchins of Trent and took part in the local Third Order activities. Her spiritual director, Fr. Casimiro Bonetti, was a Capuchin, the order that offered Chiara and her friends the apartment that became the first Focolare house.[34]

Within a few years, the Archbishop of Trent requested that the Focolare be distinguished from the Third Order. While the new group was under his direct guidance, other religious orders, including his own Stigmatine Fathers, had more contact with the Focolare. In 1948, when a Capuchin, a Conventual, and a Friar Minor accompanied Chiara on her first visit with Igino Giordani, the prophetic significance of their unity was not lost on him. In the 1950s, those who met the Focolare while studying in Rome or during the Mariapolis brought the new spirit with them when they were sent throughout the world. In Africa, Asia, North and South America, in the Caribbean and beyond the Iron Curtain, men and women religious played a pivotal role in spreading the Focolare spirituality.

Fr. Joe Scopa, a Scalabrini priest, was particularly instrumental in bringing the Focolare spirituality to various parts of North America. In the 1950s, just after his ordination, he was conducting an adult religious education program in Chicago. As they discussed Matthew's Gospel and tried to apply it to their daily lives, many asked, "Are we actually expected to live this way? This must be just for monks or nuns." Fr. Joe replied, "But Jesus was speaking to the crowds." They rejoined, "Can you tell us where lay people live like this?"

Praying for an answer, Fr. Joe went on a pilgrimage to Scalabrini ministry sites throughout Europe. There, he met a priest who was on his way to the Dolomites for the Mariapolis. Intrigued, Fr. Joe decided to join him. At the Mariapolis he was impressed by how ordinary lay people were living according to the gospel. For example, he was touched to learn that a doctor had given up his bed and slept on a table so that Fr. Joe would be comfortable.

Back at his parish, Fr. Joe shared what he had seen — lay people too could live the gospel. When the *focolarine* reached Chicago in 1964, Fr. Joe arranged for them to meet his parishioners. "The impact of meeting those people," recalls Chicagoan Margie Varassi, one of the first American *focolarine*, "came from the fact that we had already begun trying to put the gospel into practice in our lives."

In 1968, Chiara reflected on the effect of the Focolare spirituality on religious communities: "Their encounter with the Movement and the practice of the spirituality often means for them ... a rediscovery of their rules, and a more conscious love and appreciation for their founders...."

Some orders, because of a more perfect observance of their own rules, have experienced a true renewal … an increase in vocations [and] new developments in their mission."[35]

Sr. Tiziana, president of the Franciscan Sisters of the Poor, lives at the Congregation's headquarters in Brooklyn. Growing up in the Abruzzo region of Italy, she first learned about the Focolare as a teenager, when she heard Chiara speak at the Pescara Eucharistic Congress in 1977. She was fascinated by Chiara's vision of the unity of the human family and of all creation. Love for Jesus forsaken became a "key" for living everyday life. At a certain point she felt him asking her a question: "I was ready to give my life for you. Are you ready to give your life for me?" She said "yes," and a short time later she met the Franciscan Sisters of the Poor, where some of the sisters were already living a spirituality of unity.

> I was attracted by the example of the founder, Mother Francesca, "angel of the streets," who had opened a home for prostitutes, and worked directly with the poor. When she looked into their eyes she would see Jesus. In the congregation I saw women who were fulfilled, in touch with their own humanity. I was also impressed by how their practice of a spirituality of unity was helping them to rediscover the deep roots of Mother Francesca's charism. In living the Word, in a spirit of mutual love, I felt that I could see the beauty of the entire Franciscan vision of the world.

The sense of connection was immediate, and she left her fiancé, family and friends, in order to follow a vocation to religious life. Sustained by the sisters' efforts to live a spirituality of unity, the congregation as a whole experienced a flowering of new vocations, and was able to deepen the relationship between its German and American branches, to help heal a previous split.

In 1969, Pope Paul VI approved a version of the Focolare's General Statutes that included "priests and religious who adhere to the spirit of the Work of Mary." In this approval, Chiara saw confirmed what she had already intuited: "We cannot conceive of a Work of Mary without the religious."[36] In 1987, at a meeting of the Union of Superiors General (Men Religious), Chiara examined how the core characteristics of the Focolare spirituality — unity and Jesus forsaken — had influenced religious congregations. She noted, "What they discovered certainly does not disturb their own spirituality. Just the opposite. The light they have found has revived it and helped them to understand it better."[37]

Sr. Tiziana affirms:

> Real unity does not create confusion or conformity. It is the work of God, so there is distinction, but not separation. I have always experienced that contact with the Focolare spirituality strengthens my own Franciscan vocation and formation. I like how Vale Ronchetti, part of the initial group with Chiara, and a great help to the women religious over the years, puts it: "When seeds are warmed by the sun, the rose blooms as a rose, not a daisy. Focus on keeping Jesus in the midst, and each one will bloom and grow according to the nature of who they are called by God to be."

During a 1996 convocation of women religious, "Embracing New Horizons," Pope John Paul II encouraged them to foster what he perceived to be a healthy synergy for the life of the Church: "The spirituality of unity which the Work of Mary promotes and develops constitutes an essential dimension of Christian life. I encourage you to grow in it, to live it in your communities, and in the different environments in which you work."[38]

Sr. Geraldine reflects on how the Focolare spirituality has helped her to build unity in her community.

> In a religious community, we somehow seem to be able to unite for larger and more serious challenges, but at times the smaller, unforeseen situations of everyday life become obstacles.
>
> For example, I had a falling-out with one of my sisters. Then I read a little card with the six points of the "art of loving" that I keep in a place where I can't avoid seeing it. With renewed determination, I greeted my friend the following morning but got no response. Then we met alone in the elevator and I apologized for what had happened. She responded with a little grunt but no verbal communication. I knew I had forgiven her.
>
> I continued to greet her and after a few days she began to greet me back. I look for opportunities to sit at her table to continue rebuilding our relationship. Little by little we are becoming friends again. The breakdown of our congenial relationship happened suddenly and unexpectedly, but the reconstruction takes more work. The steps may be little, but love does great things.

Sr. Tiziana reflects on how a spirituality of unity has helped her to see the future of their congregation:

> We are small, but we don't worry about that. What matters is that we are working with a charism that is divine, that shows the powerful presence of the Spirit. What matters is to believe in God's love, keep his presence among us, and let him work — you never know what will emerge as a result! Within the congregation, this brings peace, cohesion and unity. If there is any sense of urgency, it is that of remaining in love.

Like the Volunteers of God and the Gen, the men and women religious who live the Focolare spirituality also gather in small groups. They keep in touch through emails and conference calls when it is not possible to meet face-to-face. Sr. Tiziana describes the group of other sisters with whom she meets: "We are five from five very different congregations, different ways of dressing, and different theological currents. To make the pact of mutual love, and to see each other as new, is always a very strong experience for all of us, a fountain of grace that challenges us to keep growing."

Seminarians, Priests, and Bishops

Most Reverend Michael Mulvey, the Bishop of Corpus Christi, Texas, first encountered the Focolare in 1976, just after being ordained a priest. While finishing his degree in spiritual theology at the North American College in Rome, he was invited to a meeting organized by one of the Focolare's centers for spirituality.

> I was struck by the message of living the gospel in daily life. I was also moved by the spirit of fraternity and communion among the priests whom I met at that first encounter. They were from more than sixty nations — one hundred of them were living, working, and praying together. That impressed me deeply.
>
> In 1978, I was serving as an associate pastor. After a tiring Christmas season, I started again the search for a spirituality. A young woman who was visiting the parish and was attending daily Mass radiated a sense of joy and life. It was she who re-introduced me to the Focolare. Our conversation was like a moment of annunciation: "Here is your way to follow."

As I began to explore the spirituality itself and to actually live the gospel, I began to experience a new sense of life within me. I found that the gospel was not just a beautiful theory to talk about, to interpret, to pray over, but it was words that give life. It seemed that word by word, sentence by sentence, parable by parable, the gospel came to life within me. In finding that life, I knew that it was something that I wanted to share. My homilies began to take shape around not just a theory, but an experience of truth and life. I was able to pass that on by bringing the gospel to a point of application in life experiences.

As time went on I found that my ministry took on a certain flavor. I must say that what has given me most life in my ministry is seeing each person I work with, each person I minister to, each community I am sent to shepherd, as a part of that prayer of Jesus, "Father, that they may all be one." Focusing my ministry on the prayer of Jesus for unity and communion among peoples has given me the direction for which I had been searching. I have also found the fruitfulness of living the cross. In the spirituality of the Work of Mary, the cross comes alive as I recognize the forsaken Christ in each difficulty. I have discovered that he is the way to building communion.

The first diocesan priests who met the Movement in the 1940s never thought that one day there would be a particular structure or branch for them. At that time it would have been highly unusual for diocesan priests to be linked to a movement that included lay people and members of religious orders, particularly one led by a woman considered to be the bearer of a charism. Moreover, the Movement's key words — love, unity, and Word of Life — could easily be associated with sentimentality, communism and Protestantism.[39]

After a period of study in the 1950s, the Italian Bishops' Conference issued a directive that its priests must detach themselves from the Movement. On that occasion, Chiara wrote to Fr. Silvano Cola, one of the first diocesan priests to adhere to the Focolare spirituality, "If we die on this side, life will flower on the other. It is all part of a wonderful plan of God, and there is nothing else but to comply completely, right?"[40] At that point, the center in Rome for the diocesan priests and men religious disbanded.

Nothing, however, prohibited them from keeping in touch with one another, sustaining each other in their efforts to live a spirituality of unity. A few months after the Movement's official approval in 1962, the prohibition was lifted and contact was again allowed. In the following years, courses of formation and other meetings for priests resumed. The Second Vatican Council document on priestly ministry, *Presbyterorum ordinis,* reflected a great consonance with a spirituality of unity. An "Association of Priests of the Work of Mary" was provisionally approved. The branches for priests and seminarians are now fully incorporated into the Work of Mary. Their regulation includes a particular focus on fostering a "vital" unity with the pope, their particular bishops, and with their brother priests, as well as creating a spirit of unity with all of the people entrusted to their ministerial care.[41]

Diocesan priests now have a variety of paths for living a spirituality of unity and sustaining each other in their priestly ministry. Some, if diocesan commitments and structures permit it, live together in small communities patterned on the life of Focolare houses, so that Jesus present in their midst can illuminate and sustain every aspect of their vocation and service to the Church. Others live alone or with other priests who do not have a relationship with the Focolare. Like the Volunteers of God, they meet periodically with other priests who share the same commitment to live the spirituality. Similarly, in accord with the heads of their seminaries, like the Gen, seminarians occasionally meet with others in formation to become priests. If they do not live close enough to hold actual meetings, many use conference calls or Internet video meetings to keep in touch.

Many priests have found that such meetings provide a vital balance for their daily lives. Visiting a seminary in Rome in May 2001, Chiara reflected on the value of communal support: "Today priests are often caught up in a sense of activism — and they ruin their health because they work and work, but do not have a sense of peace inside — and then temptations arrive because they are alone. If instead, they were to live in communion, they would experience the atmosphere of a supernatural family. Jesus, the Risen One, is there."[42]

Fr. Steve, pastor of a parish in Delaware, first heard about the Focolare from a parishioner. "I politely listened and then filed it in the place we tend to put 'after Mass' conversations with parishioners." Several years later, serving in a different diocese, he befriended an Italian priest.

> It was then that the word "Focolare" came back into my life. Rather than filing it away, I began to listen actively, to read and, most of all, to experience. At my first Focolare summer gathering, I was able to experience the beauty of a spirituality of unity. Since then, I have found the annual gatherings with

other priests at Mariapolis Luminosa in Hyde Park, New York, have made a big difference in my life.

Members of religious orders have a spirituality based on insights from either their founder or a particular saint. As diocesan priests, we have no specific spirituality but are guided by the Decree on the Ministry and Life of Priests, which calls for us to "preserve and strengthen a necessary oneness with their brothers in the ministry." In the Focolare spirituality I have found a reflection of what my life as a parish priest is all about.

I have grown immensely in my own relationship with God. As a diocesan priest who is part of the Focolare, it helps me to have others with whom I am able to experience Jesus in our midst and to develop a closer relationship with him and his body, the Church. Whether through the weekly Internet conference call with priests throughout the U.S., visits to Mariapolis Luminosa, daily conversations with fellow priests or my interaction with the Focolare in our area and beyond, I know that the entire Movement is supporting me and helping me as I strive through my life to bring about this spirit of mutual love in our parish and diocese.

Fr. Doug, from a small town in Texas, explains how his encounter with the Focolare spirituality as a seminarian helped to foster his vocation to the priesthood.

While my first three years at the seminary were filled with learning, there still seemed to be something missing. I lost the "spark" of a radical choice of God; my desire to put God first in my life had shallow roots. Then a spiritual director there introduced me to the Focolare's monthly commentary on a passage from scripture, and to other seminarians who met to share how they put it into practice. I loved listening to those stories!

That summer, after I completed my college courses, I traveled through Europe and visited Loppiano, the little city of the Focolare in Italy, and I stayed five weeks. While there I heard Chiara Lubich speak about God who is love. I was struck by how obvious this seemed. Why hadn't I recognized this before?

Two years later, I returned to Loppiano to spend eight months learning about and living the Focolare spirituality. During this time, I renewed my choice of God, who expressed the depth of his love when on the cross he felt abandoned by the Father. I wanted to respond especially to him.

Pope John Paul II encouraged the seminarians gathered for their Focolare conference in 1994: "It is good for you to be here, because 'focolare' says a very simple and profound thing. It speaks of being together. The seminarian calling is not a solitary, hermit-like vocation, it is a vocation to live together: to live for others, in the wider family. I think that the Focolare spirituality prepares you well for this calling."[43]

David, currently in formation to be a diocesan priest, affirms the need to move beyond hermit-like tendencies. "I find that the effort to survive the enormous amount of studying and formal formation work asked of the seminarian can present serious temptations to individualism and isolation." He explains how the "Gen seminarians" in his group try to generate a sense of community: "We set weekly times to meet in order to talk openly about what God is doing in our lives. We also try to study together instead of in isolation, and take free weekends to travel or be together rather than catch up on work. In my own journey, I have seen that when I take the time to be there for the others, even in ways that cost me as I try to meet deadlines and manage my own time well, I have been immensely fortified."

In 1975, Klaus Hemmerle, from Germany, and a few other priests who had been living the Focolare spirituality with particular intensity were ordained as bishops. They felt the need for a structure to sustain them in their efforts to live a spirituality of unity in this new service. During their first meeting, they attended a general audience with Pope Paul VI. When they went up to greet him, the pope said, "What an atmosphere! You can feel that there is Jesus in the midst."[44] There are now several hundred bishops who follow the same path.

They began meeting annually in 1977, and their guidelines for participation in the Movement were approved in 1998. Many set aside the time to vacation with other bishops who live a spirituality of unity, living a "Focolare style" community life, including time to cook and clean the house, to rest, and to be refreshed in their own spiritual journey and in their service to the Church.

4
A Spirituality of Unity and the Renewal of Social Life and Culture

Focolare members try to live the spirituality in every aspect of their daily lives, in their families, their communities, and their workplaces. As a consequence, other people are often touched, and join in the effort to let love and unity inform their relationships in a particular environment.

As the Movement has spread and grown, structures for outreach to family, professional, youth and parish life have developed. Similarly, mutual love has taken the form of projects that meet particular social and economic needs. As those in academia and the arts began to share the insights that emerge from applying the Focolare spirituality to their work in these contexts, they began to see the potential for renewing their particular fields, and for a rich interdisciplinary exchange.

This chapter explores each of these projects for social service and cultural renewal. It closes with a brief description of the physical places — the small villages, known as "Mariapolis," or "city of Mary" — that demonstrate how an entire society might be renewed if people were to live mutual love on a constant basis.

Mass Movements

Everything that members of the Focolare Movement do stems from its specific goal, which can be represented with a coin. One side contains the legend, "That they may all be one," signifying the desire to build unity in the world. The other reads, "My God, my God, why have you forsaken me?" signifying the preferential love for all who suffer. Chiara recalled an incident in which one of the men from a religious order was returning to his own country, a place where he was likely to encounter persecution. Before leaving, he told her, "We will meet again, perhaps in heaven. I am going to die for my own people." She challenged the young people to do the same. "Each one of us must feel ready to die, yes, for all humanity — because for a Gen, this is the measure of a person's soul — but also to die for one's *own* people."[1]

Each of the Focolare's "mass movements" reflects this commitment to embrace the particular as well as the universal. They promote solidarity and extend social outreach on a local level, and they work with the Movement as a whole to address needs globally. As Chiara explained to a group of young people: "If we really want to be another Jesus, we have to have his mentality, which is both universal and particular; we cannot live to love only those who are far without doing something for those who are near. We need to root ourselves in our own land as well, and show our love with facts, right where we are."[2] They also organize public events that promote the idea of a united world. These have included large-scale international symposiums, with participants at a hub city linked by satellite or Internet to multiple sites throughout the world. In several respects, the Focolare has been a pioneer in using media technology to bring the world together.

The sections below outline the local and global dimensions of "New Families," "New Humanity," "Youth for a United World," and "Teens for Unity." Another field of action, parish life, will be discussed in Chapter Five, "The Focolare Movement and the Church."

NEW FAMILIES

The Focolare lifestyle has been a part of Karen and Luke O'Leary's married life almost as long as they have been a couple. Luke's parents, Patrick and Catherine, have been active in the Focolare community for years. In its spirituality, they found the resources to help their son and daughter-in-law grow during their engagement, and as a married couple. Karen gives a glimpse of what this support means to her. "You know what it's like, 'Your in-laws come, and then it's time for them to go?' With mine, it's like, you never want them to go."

Both generations of O'Learys have faced the challenge of keeping their families united during the disruptions of military service. Patrick, an Army officer, was deployed to Bosnia in 1998; Luke, an officer like his father, was deployed to Iraq in 2005 and to Afghanistan in 2010. Karen has drawn strength from Catherine's experience: "It helps to talk to her and know that she's done this and that I can do this."

Since becoming a father, Luke has discovered deeper ways to live the Focolare spirituality. "To lay down your life for another is the most precious gift anyone can give," he says. "In many ways to do that physically is easy. To choose to give your life for your children, daily, hourly, minute by minute — that is tough. I thought I was a patient person before I had children," he adds. "The truth is, you cannot just say at one time you are going to be a patient person or that you are going to love your children completely every day from now on. You have to make that decision daily to try with all of your heart and soul to love them completely."

Karen and Luke draw upon the Focolare spirituality in their family life. Karen reflects, "So many times Luke and I have had to start over because we see things differently or because one of us was unkind to the other. Also with our four small children — if we weren't able to love them that day or in a particular moment, we just start over and the past is gone." Luke adds, "I have to start over a lot. Certainly our anger and fear make us hold on to the things of the past, but once you let go of them, once you start over, you can love completely right away. For me the hard part is learning to start over before I get to the point where I don't want to start over, before the anger and resentment even have a chance to settle."

The New Families Movement serves couples like Karen and Luke as they live the day-to-day challenges and joys of marriage and parenting. The Movement sponsors courses of formation through which couples strengthen their relationships, and families learn to apply the gospel to their everyday lives.

Therese and Paulo have been married for twelve years; both have lived the Focolare spirituality since childhood. They live in New York City with their four children, aged ten, eight, six, and three. Amid the constant demands of work and school, it has helped them to maintain focus on nourishing their relationships. Therese notes, "We try our best to lessen 'screen time' in front of the TV or computer. It can be like a game to find moments to do simple things together that have to be done anyway. Debi, our five year-old, loves to fold clothes, for example. It takes longer to get the laundry done, but what fun we have together!"

Living on a limited budget, they rarely hire a babysitter, so they have "nights in" instead of "nights out." Paulo explains, "We feed the kids a little earlier than usual and we put them to bed. Then we cook a meal together and set the table and actually sit down. We take the time to talk. It amazes us how much time we can find, especially if the TV is turned off."

The New Families Movement also provides support to couples facing particular challenges within their marriage. Gerarda, who is Catholic, explains how the community helped her in a difficult moment with her husband, who is Jewish: "At a certain point cultural differences started to surface where we didn't think we would have a problem. I felt like everything was being destroyed, and we were growing in completely different directions. It was unity with my Focolare friends that gave me the courage to look at the suffering, and summon the strength to take the steps that I needed to take to change. From that point, the relationship between me and my husband grew stronger. At times he would say, 'I think you need to go spend more time with the Focolare!' because he saw that it was helping me and our relationship."

Particular care is extended to the divorced and widowed, as well as to single parents. Diane reflects, "My relationship with my ex-husband had been difficult. Now, the difficulty has become a springboard for me to take the initiative in loving. I no longer react to him, and he has become sensitive to the love of God he receives from me."

The experience of B.D., who lives in the Southwest, and his teenage son demonstrates how in family life, unconditional love transforms human failings, even things that might be considered irredeemable. B.D. and his girlfriend gave birth to a son, but they never married. He supported her and the boy, but could only participate in his life from a distance. She did not raise him in any particular faith; attending the summer Mariapolis was his only exposure to religion.

When the boy was thirteen, however, he asked a question that opened up their relationship and set in motion a chain of events that transformed both of their lives:

> He asked me about the circumstances surrounding my relationship with his mother and the pregnancy. I told him how we met; how our relationship was on and off for three years; and about the night she told me she was pregnant. I told him: "I was in shock for a split second, but then immediately realized that you would be the most important reality in my life. I got a glimpse of what my life would be with you in it and at that moment you became a part of me forever and the greatest gift God ever gave to me."
>
> He began asking if he could come live with me. At first I told him that his place was with his mom, but I began to see that as a thirteen-year-old, perhaps he really needed me more. When his mom understood that he had made the request, she agreed. In fact, just prior to this she had begun another relationship, and was content to move on. Both my son and I have maintained a positive relationship with her and her husband.

My son is a logical, problem-solving thinker. His favorite subject is math. He recently had been given an article, "The Mathematical Concept of Infinity," inspired by the writings of Chiara Lubich. He read it but didn't speak about it.

A few days later, with tears in his eyes, he shared how he was struck by Chiara's understanding of "the ultimate infinity" and how it relates to God. Many things began to pour out of him. "I know why Christ suffered. He showed us the way, he emptied himself and generated life in all of us. His death and resurrection makes our transformation possible." It was as if his unbelief never existed. I had always left him free and believed that faith is a gift that I couldn't give him. It was a moment when I felt the personal love that God has for both of us.

Couples and families see their own difficulties as a springboard to reach out to others with similar problems. Igino Giordani, Focolare co-founder, husband and father of four, captures this well: "The family is not closed within itself, but grows like a cell that lives as much for others as for itself. A new society is born ... from families that live the gospel."[3]

The New Families Movement also works to ensure that families throughout the world can live a dignified life and provide for their children. It currently supports 100 development projects involving 15,200 children in 45 different countries. Specific programs include literacy, work training and parenting skills, as well as projects to supply food, clean water, health care, and education. The New Families also sustain the "One Family, One Home" project in the poorest quarters of Manila. This model has also been replicated in the impoverished neighborhoods of Cochabamba, Bolivia as well as in Thailand and Sri Lanka following the 2004 tsunami.

The periodic "Familyfest" has gathered thousands to share their efforts in building a more united world. In 2005 the festival linked via satellite and Internet 200 cities in 78 countries.

New Humanity

Just as New Families support efforts to live a spirituality of unity in family life, the New Humanity Movement aims to bring this spirit into society — workplaces, neighborhoods, towns, and every area of civic commitment.

Adriana works as a clinical social worker at a medical center. She finds a sense of collaboration and collegiality among the staff, but strong differences concerning a woman's decision to abort a pregnancy. She describes her own view:

> Each life is a gift from God, and so I am troubled that any-one, particularly a medical professional, would encourage anyone to have an abortion. At the beginning of my work experience, I began to wonder whether I should stay at this job or not. At that moment we were three case managers in the clinic. I realized that if I remained, at least a third of the clients might have an opportunity to meet someone who would not only listen to their pain, but also inform them of other alternatives and help them to overcome the obstacles to a decision in favor of life. So, with the support of my supervisor, I decided to stay, even if it meant working in the midst of this tension with my colleagues.
>
> One day I was walking along the hallway when a young lady ran up behind me. "Do you remember me?" she asked, smiling. I did. "How are you?" She answered with tears in her eyes: "Four years ago, I came to see you and I felt am-bivalent about keeping my pregnancy. Your respect, your words and your conviction about the value of life helped me decide to keep my baby. I now have a beautiful four-year-old daughter who has filled my life with joy. I can't imagine what life would be without her. Thank you."

The New Humanity Movement often operates through "action cells" in workplaces where two or more people live the Focolare spiri-tuality. They maintain a commitment to mutual love, and identify how they might build a spirit of unity in their work environment.

Mary, a registered nurse, works at pre-school in Brooklyn for two-to five-year-olds with emotional disturbances and learning disabilities. The school's founders hoped to have a positive effect on the pupils and their families by optimizing the children's development through a holistic approach. She explains:

> I was especially excited by this goal, and convinced that it could be achieved not only by providing educational and therapeutic services to the children and families but, most of all, by fostering positive interactions among staff through dialogue, collaboration, and collegiality.
>
> "Every person is a candidate to unity," I would often remind myself. There was the school secretary to greet and

at times cheer up with a piece of chocolate. On days when she seemed overwhelmed, I would encourage her by sharing my own efforts to "live the present moment."

One of the social workers seemed especially sensitive to this approach. I invited her to a New Humanity conference, and she found its ideas appealing. Anne, the school's executive director, also wanted to learn more after hearing Chiara Lubich speak about unity at a United Nations conference.

Within the first two years of the school's founding, in addition to the administrative team, the action cell grew to include an educational director, a teacher, two occupational therapists, two physical therapists, a speech therapist, two bookkeepers, a secretary, and a clerk. They were Christian, Jewish and Muslim.

Three years later, they decided to propose their interdisciplinary model to the entire staff. The first step was to meet with each department, giving everyone a chance to speak freely to the Director about the strengths, weaknesses, and conflicts that they perceived. This helped to create a positive atmosphere that was receptive to new ideas. A month later, the core group organized a staff development day to present feedback on these conversations and to give everyone the chance to speak openly about both negative and positive dynamics in the school. After this meeting, the action cell elaborated a "unity" approach to resolve conflicts and offered "The Art of Living the Golden Rule" as a set of guidelines:

1. Be the first to serve your co-worker.
2. Be the first to reach out when you have a conflict with a co-worker. Be the first to let a co-worker reach out to you.
3. Be inclusive and reach out to everyone, not just to a few you consider friends or have a good rapport with already.
4. Be open to others' ideas and do not be attached to "your way." Remember, we all have different temperaments and different ways of getting things done. A better collective idea may emerge when you are open!
5. "Make yourself one." Try to put yourself in "the other person's shoes" so you can really understand and share what he or she is going through. This means losing your ideas or wishes to make room for the other person's ideas or wishes. This means forgetting yourself to serve the other.

6. Conflicts can be springboards to unity. Remember that a moment of anger, disagreement, or misunderstanding with a co-worker does not need to end a relationship. Instead, ask yourself, "If I were her or him, how would I want to be treated?" If we keep unity in mind, a difficult experience with a co-worker can be the beginning of an even better working relationship.

7. Hear the other person's point of view before passing judgment. Do not take any given negative incident, whether real or perceived, personally. Give your co-worker a chance to explain and listen to the end so you can have the whole picture in any given situation.

8. Allow yourself and others to start over again when there is a conflict. Think of the golden rule: "Do unto others what you would have them do unto you."

Mary sums up the change in their school: "At the first team meeting after the staff development day I saw clinicians, who normally clung to their own ideas, let go in order to defer to another. One psychologist commented that for the first time she felt the freedom to share her observations without worrying about being judged, or her ideas not being appreciated."

The New Humanity "action cell" approach has also been applied in neighborhood settings. Carole Spale lives in North Riverside, a suburb of about 6,000 near Chicago. She recounts how she became more involved in the life of her town.

> Our son, David, is severely disabled and needs constant attention. Part of his physical therapy program required the assistance of three people at a time. The natural goodness of our neighbors overwhelmed us. A core group of about 20 came seven days a week, twice a day, for six years. Even the firemen helped on weekends and holidays. I felt such gratitude that I asked God to show our family how to give something back to this town and its residents.[4]

Because Carole took the time to respond to a letter the mayor sent soliciting ideas for his newly-formed Neighborhood Services Committee, he asked her to coordinate the project. In order to show the seventy-two "block captains" how "to make each block like a family, where no one would feel alone," Carole adapted the Focolare's "art of loving" into what she termed the "Art of Caring":

- ❧ Be the first to reach out to others.
- ❧ Reach out to everyone.
- ❧ Care concretely.
- ❧ Be one with joys and sorrows.

She communicated these principles to the other block captains using her own experiences, or quotations from famous people like Mother Teresa. In response, some began to share their own stories. One recounted how he tried to love the owner of the barking dogs that were disturbing the rest of the block by baking cookies and helping him to retrieve the dogs when they escaped. Only then did he broach how the dogs were disturbing a newborn baby next door. "Care concretely" led to finding a working stove for an older couple. "We send cards, bring food, listen to people's troubles. We use e-mail to communicate special needs." Stories of the mayor and the town's trustees trying to put the principles into practice are also shared at the block captain meetings. During the holiday season, a town "giving tree" provides a way to allow needs and resources to circulate. During the year a "sharing board" lists furniture and other items that people have made available.

For one lady who was about to be evicted from her apartment, the villagers provided food and emergency money, dealt with the legal proceedings on the back rent she owed, located another apartment, and even found her a better job. In gratitude, the lady came by bus to the village center to help package cookies for the gift baskets to be shared with others in need.[5] For an elderly couple in poor health whose property was falling into disrepair, the team raked leaves, found a working refrigerator, and located grant money for repairs through the Council on Aging.[6]

Other towns have asked how to replicate the Art of Caring program. "I believe that the art of loving can transform a town from top to bottom," Carole reflects. "What touches my heart most is something one resident said a few months ago: 'I am so lucky to live in a village with a caring heart.'"[7]

YOUTH FOR A UNITED WORLD AND TEENS FOR UNITY

"Bienvenidos al mundo del amor" (Welcome to the world of love), whispered one little girl. With hugs, she and her schoolmates greeted their visitors from Houston. These ten members of Teens4Unity from a Catholic high school had come to spend a week at Café con Leche, an elementary school in the Dominican Republic.

The teens rolled up their sleeves and embarked on returning the children's love. Despite the absence of things that the Houston students considered necessities — air conditioning, continuous electrical power, cool water — the children never complained. "They were always happy," said Larissa, 18. "They were always giving. It was quite amazing." Teens4Unity Club sponsor Christina recalls, "I was cutting out some paper shapes for the children. After we finished, I was going to throw away the left over pieces. One child took a marker, wrote on one of those pieces and gave it to me. He was thanking me for being there with them. After him, every single boy and girl at the table did the same, giving me a personal note."

"The little things we taught them made the kids so happy," said Lisette, 16. "But really — really — they taught us so much more." "I learned to love more deeply," Marina, 17, said. "I learned there is more to saying, 'I love you.' I learned to prove my love to people, to act it out, to sacrifice — to give my whole heart. When I looked in the eyes of those children so poor, so in need, and yet so happy, I knew God was there in them."

Like other Teens4Unity around the world, the Houston group has raised funds for disadvantaged children, including earthquake victims in Peru and survivors of the tsunami in Indonesia. They also work close to home, visiting nursing homes and homeless shelters, helping repaint houses in the aftermath of Hurricane Ike, stocking shelves in the city's food bank, and playing with children at the Catholic Worker's Casa Juan Diego, which provides hospitality to new immigrants.

Local and international projects such as the working trip to Café con Leche are sponsored by Youth for a United World (for college age young adults) and Teens4Unity (for high schoolers). They encourage young people to live for others and spread peace, unity, and solidarity in their local environment.

International Gatherings for Young People

Since Woodstock, the younger generation has used mega-festivals to make their collective mark on public opinion. The Gen, too, hold international festivals that feature their own "united world culture" of music, theatre, and dance demonstrating how they build bridges of unity in their daily lives.

The 1990 "Genfest" drew 20,000 young people to the Palaeur Stadium in Rome. There, Chiara challenged them to put the radical love of Jesus' new commandment at the core of their lives. Friendship, kindness, philanthropy, solidarity and non-violence are not enough. She urged them:

> [Radical love] asks that we live no longer for ourselves, but for the others. It requires sacrifice and effort. It asks everyone to change from being spineless and egotistical individuals, concerned only with their own interests, only with their own things, into small everyday heroes who, day after day, are at the service of their neighbors, ready to give even their lives for them. Dearest young people, your vocation calls you to this if you do not want your ideas to vanish into utopian dreams.[8]

The 2002 "Supercongress" drew 9,000 boys and girls from 93 different countries. As part of this event, which took place shortly after the tragedy of 9/11, young people rallied at the Coliseum to demonstrate how their vision of a united world embraced differences in culture and religion.

These international youth festivals generate much more than a one-time "high." They make a permanent mark on these young lives. Helena, from Los Angeles, is now in her mid-twenties. She describes the lasting impact of the Supercongress: "I witnessed a connection that I had never experienced before — other young people from different countries, speaking different languages yet living for the same ideal: a united world. This shaped my outlook. I began to see the world around me in a different way. It made me aware that there is something greater to live for — not just my grades, material things, or status — but a better world. I continue to see how, in everything I do, in the choices I make I can contribute to making it so."

Initiatives for Global Unity on a Local Level

The Focolare young people have found creative strategies for generating public interest in the possibility of a united world. "World Unity Week" includes local events and a global conference call to showcase what they are doing on every continent to build unity.[9]

In "Run4Unity," an around-the-world relay race first conducted in 2005, teens choose as their guide one common text such as the Golden Rule: "Do to others as you would have them do to you" (Lk 6:31). Over the course of twenty-four hours, 330 local sites stay connected through the Internet, passing a virtual "baton" through each time-zone. They share in real time how they have been putting the text into practice in their daily interactions. At each local site, the Teens4Unity organize sports, games, and service projects to promote and reinforce their message.[10]

In projects such as "Color the City with Love," teens seek out the "gray" areas of their communities where people might be lonely or marginalized and find ways to reach out. As part of this project, teens in Chicago, New York, Washington DC, Los Angeles and El Paso have worked with local residents to restore public parks in inner-city neighborhoods, and have visited nursing homes. The group from Chicago took this approach:

> First we read together this meditation by Chiara Lubich: "Lord, give me everyone who is lonely…. Who will console their weeping? Let me be in this world, my God, the tangible sacrament of your Love, let me be your arms that embrace and transform into love all the loneliness of the world."
>
> We went to a local nursing home to bring the presence of Jesus in our midst to the residents there. At first we were rather shy, and a little scared. Whenever we entered a new room, we would ask how they were, how their family was, how long they had been living there, and so on. They were delighted and surprised to see us, because they had very few visitors. This made us even more determined to bring them joy. We took pictures with them and promised to come back soon.
>
> Two months later, we invited as many of our friends as possible to join us. The fifteen of us split into groups so we could visit even more residents. We had a wonderful time there again. One lady loved to sing gospel songs, and so we all sang and danced with her, which made her (and us) happy!
>
> We continue to visit every couple of months, and each time we read the Word of Life before going. It sets us on the right track. It is really touching to see how the residents light up when they see us!

The Cube of Love

The "Cube of Love" is a game-like activity in which different statements from the "art of loving" are featured on the six sides of a die.[11] Children roll it at the beginning of the day to set a particular behavioral goal for themselves. Teachers and students have found it helpful in establishing respect, love and positive interaction. At Holy Trinity elementary school, Poughkeepsie, New York, the teachers also see how the Cube of Love has changed behavior. One comments:

You see children sharing toys, offering to accompany a student to the nurse and reminding one another about the day's phrase. A boy in the second grade saw one of his classmates off by herself, so he invited her to play with him and his group. But she said no and that she really wanted to play with another group. Rather than just walk away, he approached the other group and convinced them to let his classmate join them. He later commented, "This is how I lived our point of love today which was to 'share the other's joy or hurt.'" The girls in the other group added that they all had fun playing together with their new friend.[12]

St. Ambrose School in Old Bridge, New Jersey, has integrated the Cube of Love into its religion curriculum. The principal, Joseph Norris, writes how the Cube has helped teachers to frame religious instruction around "deep spiritual concepts" that are "approachable and applicable."[13]

Norris also notes that the Cube has helped students and staff alike address the problem of bullying. "Practical elements, such as how to deal with bullies, are used in the classroom to help illustrate the gospel values of loving your enemies."[14] Sr. Betty Ann Martinez, F.M.A., former Coordinator for Religious Education at St. John the Evangelist School in Pensacola, Florida, saw that the Cube improved relations among students at her school, too. One student reported, "I try not to bully anymore and when I see someone being bullied, I help them." "I used to be an enemy with someone; now I love him." "It's really hard to love my enemy, but I do it."[15] A student from another school describes how the Cube helped to shift his reasoning: "Before I was a bully 'cause I thought it was cool. Then I saw the words on the Cube one day and thought about them. I knew I wouldn't like people to bully me. 'Why do I do it?' I asked myself, so then I stopped. Now I help in my family, too."[16]

Social Service Projects

Throughout the world, members of the Focolare have reached out to their closest neighbors, generating over a thousand projects for social and economic development. Some of these have expanded to include large numbers of people working together to improve health, education, and living conditions. These include, to note just a few, a camp for

Burmese refugees at Mae-La, Thailand; housing for homeless families at Mont Organisé, in the northeast of Haiti; and a center for homeless children, "Nuevo Sol," near Buenos Aires.[17] One of the largest and most developed projects is in Fontem, Cameroon.

Mary Help of Africa Hospital specializes in tropical diseases and AIDS treatment. As noted earlier, Focolare doctors arrived in Fontem in the mid-1960s in response to a request from the Bangwa people for help in addressing their dramatic infant mortality rate due to sleeping sickness (see p. 33). Fontem is now the site of a large village where the Bangwa and Focolare members live together in a spirit of mutual love. In addition to the hospital, Fontem includes 600 homes, a school, a hydroelectric plant, a church, and several small industries.

Young people from the United States have volunteered at Mary Help of Africa. They acquire valuable professional experience, and learn the Focolare's approach to health care and development. Chiarelle, from Los Angeles, devoted six months to volunteering her skills as a nurse there. She describes their approach quoting Chiara's hopes for the hospital: "When people come to this hospital, they should not say, 'what a great hospital!' but 'what a great community!'" This spirit of community was evident in how teachers and doctors worked together to help a student recover from his illness while not slipping too far behind in his studies. When a patient needed a special type of splint for a complex fracture, the Fontem carpentry shop made it for him. Even though it does not have a blood bank the patients always can get transfusions because hospital employees or townspeople spontaneously donate whenever blood is needed.

The greatest gift that she received from her experience in Fontem, Chiarelle says, was spiritual orientation for her work as a nurse.

> After a few months, the job was becoming difficult. It was painful and emotionally draining to be constantly surrounded by so much suffering. I was also faced with tropical diseases like malaria and sleeping sickness, which I knew nothing about, and with traditional beliefs and practices that sometimes interfered with our treatment plans. I had to put aside everything that I learned at school to make room for a new way of doing things.
>
> One morning when I arrived at work, the nurse from the night shift told us that one patient was in end-stage kidney failure and might die soon. My mind and heart were racing

as we called the doctor to go over his care plan. We altered the medicine as needed, continued to watch him closely, and did everything we could to make him feel better. At a certain point, though, there was nothing more we could do.

I had been helping other patients, but this news left me frozen and close to tears. Then, I remembered that month's Word of Life. It was the passage in which Isaiah feels unworthy to take on the task God is asking of him. Nonetheless, when God asked him "Whom shall I send?" Isaiah responded with faith, "Here am I, send me!" (Is 6:8). I, too, sent up my silent prayer to God: "Here I am, what do you want me to do next?"

A relative came to me saying that the dying man wanted me to call a priest. I called the parish, but before the priest could arrive, I found out that the man wasn't breathing anymore. With another nurse and the doctor, we were able to revive him long enough for him to receive the sacrament of the sick. He passed away peacefully an hour later.

After this experience, it dawned on me that God wasn't asking me to perform miracles, to preserve lives or do the impossible. He was simply asking me to love and do his will moment by moment.

In school I learned a holistic approach to nursing but before this experience, I hadn't heard much about the spiritual aspect. My time in Fontem completed my training as a nurse, and helped me to see what in the end grants true comfort to the sick.

Americans have also volunteered at the Focolare's *Bukas Palad* ("With Open Hands") social service centers in the Philippines — a network of twenty-three programs assisting more than 6,000 families with education, walk-in medical services, food distribution, TB prevention, housing assistance, and infrastructure development. In addition, a micro-loan program funds entrepreneurs and business development around the country.

During natural disasters or other emergencies, the Focolare's global networks facilitate the communication of victims' immediate needs and channel resources directly to the recipients. Because of the strong bonds of mutual love that permeate this global network, disaster relief can reinforce the personal relationships that already have been built, transcending the anonymous distribution of goods.

The Focolare takes a more systematic approach to development funding through "Action for a United World," an NGO known internationally by its Italian name, *Azione per un mondo unito* (AMU).[18] AMU raises funds and awards grants for international development work conducted from the perspective of a spirituality of unity, promoting participation and shared responsibility, reciprocity, and respect for the dignity of local cultures and social structures. Another entity, the Focolare's nongovernmental organization, *"New Humanity,"* is now recognized by the United Nations Economic and Social Council (ECOSOC) as one of the 122 NGOs worldwide that enjoy General Consultative Status.[19]

Cultural Renewal

THE *ABBA* SCHOOL AND THE "INUNDATIONS"

Since the early days of the Movement, Chiara intuited how its spirituality would contribute to cultural renewal. She explains: "On the one hand, it is the offspring of the Christian tradition, but at the same time, it is new, because it is enlightened by this charism."[20] In 1949 she wrote, "We need to allow God to be reborn within us and keep him alive … among us by loving one another…. So everything is renewed: politics and art, school and religion, private life and entertainment. Everything."[21] As the Movement grew and its ideas spread beyond its own structures, the "specific characteristics" of this culture came into relief, prompting the study of its doctrine.[22]

Since January 1991, the Focolare's interdisciplinary study center (known familiarly as the *"Abba* School") has held regular sessions in which they assess the spiritual legacy of the Movement in light of Christian doctrine and tradition, and explore what it can contribute to different fields of research. The group includes professors and researchers who work in twenty-five areas including theology, philosophy, psychology, mathematics, literature, history, law, economics, education, medicine, art, music, and the natural sciences.

Sessions begin with a "pact" in which each declares his or her readiness to give their lives, spiritually and intellectually, out of love. It requires the readiness to suspend or "let go" of one's own way of thinking in order to enter into the thought of the other. For example, an expert in Thomism "lets go" of this expertise in order to "enter into" the thought of an expert in Bonaventure. From this communion new intuitions emerge. The same method is used to explore not only differing perspectives on theology, but also the various disciplines represented, the beliefs of Christian churches outside the Roman Catholic tradition, and the traditions of other religions.[23]

In his introduction to a collection of essays by members of the study center, theologian David Schindler summarizes the *Abba* School methodology. He notes that it "testifies to how we must resist assuming that the response needed to the problems of our time can be realized easily or quickly — for example, through management techniques or political strategies or 'expert' analyses." Schindler surmises that the center embodies a more promising method: "namely, a reflection sustained by and centered in a life of community and entailing a transformation of one's being and consciousness through prayer, the suffering of difference, and the like, all of which presuppose the duration of time."[24]

The *Abba* School provides leadership and service for the Focolare's developing dialogue with culture. It sponsors periodic conferences where Focolare members who work in academic environments throughout the world enter into and learn from the work of others in their own field and profit from the interdisciplinary exchange.

Chiara explains, "the encounter between the people of unity and its doctrine has given rise to what we call 'inundations,' or 'torrents of living water,' using an expression taken from St. John Chrysostom."[25] Through the inundations, the Movement applies intuitions that emerge from its spirituality to the various professional fields — politics, economics, mass media, art, science, sociology, education, medicine, and so on.[26] Sociologist Vera Araújo, a member of the *Abba* School, describes the inundations as bringing "to light the action of the Holy Spirit in human realities."[27]

In the field of education, since the earliest days of the Focolare in North America the local communities have included professors, teachers, school administrators, counselors, students, and parents who want to bring a spirituality of unity to their work. These steady, patient efforts crystallized in 2000, when the Catholic University of America conferred an honorary doctorate in education upon Chiara Lubich; the title of her address there named the clear connection between "The Charism of Unity and Education."[28]

Education's Highest Aim: Teaching and Learning through a Spirituality of Communion,[29] published by New City Press in 2010, constitutes an ini-

tial effort to reflect systematically on application of the spirituality of
unity in the theory and practice of education in various North American contexts. Upon its release, communities across the United States
and Canada held conferences where educational professionals studied
the book and compared their own experiences to those that it presents.
An elementary school teacher from Prince Georges County, Maryland,
attended the session in Baltimore. She comments, "I was impressed
and inspired by the courage and boldness of the Focolare group to
apply a spirituality of communion directly in the public schools, which
generally do not acknowledge spirituality. You have launched what is
necessary to touch the hearts of the younger generation by inculcating
values and formation. If students learn goodness and love in school,
they will live by those values."

In his scholarship, Donald W. Mitchell, professor of Eastern
Religions at Purdue University, has drawn on his formation in the
Focolare spirituality and his involvement in Buddhist-Christian
dialogue. *Spirituality and Emptiness: The Dynamics of Spiritual Life in
Buddhism and Christianity*,[30] presents his analysis of kenosis, or self-
emptying, in Buddhist and Christian spiritual traditions. He explores
the notions of creation as the pouring forth of God, the negative
kenosis of the Fall, Redemption through the kenosis of Christ, the
pouring forth of the Holy Spirit in the process of sanctification, the
place of kenosis in spiritual life, and Mary as a model of kenosis.[31]

Other examples of North American scholarship include Judith
Povilus' *United in His Name*, which draws out some of the ecclesiological
and sociological aspects of living out the sentence, "Where two or three
are gathered in my name, there I am in the midst of them (Mt 18:20)."[32]
Paul O'Hara's "Interpretations of Reality" appeared in Piero Coda and
Roberto Priscilla's *Interpretations of Reality: Theology, Philosophy and Science
in Dialogue*.[33] In *Faith and the Media: Reflections by Christian Communicators*,[34]
published by Paulist Press in 2010, seven experts present their notions
of how faith perspectives, including a spirituality of unity, might inform
communications theory and practice. Implications of a spirituality of
unity for various areas of legal theory and legal education have been
explored in a series of law review articles.[35]

SOPHIA UNIVERSITY INSTITUTE

Beginning in 2001, the *Abba* School conducted four-week Summer Institutes in which young people could try its methodology for themselves and learn from its insights. Rainer, who holds a bachelor's in international relations from Boston College, describes his experience: "The summer school gave me a taste of how God might see unity in diversity. Being with 200 students from all around the world who were able to come together to become a family and mutually enrich each other's lives and thinking, I saw and touched the reality of one human family. The program both engaged my intellect and deepened my faith. It helped me to see how faith and reason are mutual gifts for each other and for all of humanity."[36]

On the basis of this successful pilot project, in October 2008, the Focolare inaugurated its international interdisciplinary graduate program, the Sophia University Institute. Located in the Focolare's little city of Loppiano, near Florence, it offers master's and doctoral degrees in "Foundations and Perspectives on a Culture of Unity." Unique features of the program include time for reflection together on a sentence of scripture that professors and students alike put into practice. The master's program begins with courses grouped into four areas: theology, philosophy, logic and scientific reasoning, and social sciences. The social sciences include economics, political science, and social ethics. In the second year, students choose between tracks in philosophy-theology or politics-economics.

The program aims to foster in each student a quest for truth and to form mature leaders who can respond to the challenges of their times. The program also helps students develop the interpersonal skills that will help them to build relationships of unity in any academic or professional environment.

The Vatican Congregation for Education has approved Sophia as a Pontifical Institute, which allows it to participate in a pan-European agreement that facilitates recognition of its credits and degrees across Europe. Vatican Secretary of State, Cardinal Tarcisio Bertone described Sophia as "a gift for the Church and for the society of our time."[37]

NEW LIGHT ON ART AND MEDIA

Beauty has always had a "home" in the Focolare. Even from the very beginning, reactions to the ideas and spirituality that Chiara presented were not "How true!" or "How good!" but "How beautiful!"[38] She notes, "Beauty had found a place in our Movement because the word our charism began to speak to the world was one alone: unity. And unity means the highest harmony. And it was this vocation to harmony that characterized even the smallest, most concrete details of the culture that was beginning to flourish as an effect of the charism."[39]

The Focolare spirituality offers artists inspiration for their work, for their relationships with fellow artists, audiences, and patrons, and for their vision of art in society. Since 1966, two international performing arts groups, Gen Verde and Gen Rosso, have been demonstrating how musical theatre, performance, and dance can be informed by a spirituality of unity. Like Sophia, both are based in Loppiano.

Nancy Uelmen encountered the Focolare Movement in her native Los Angeles when she was in elementary school. She has worked with Gen Verde as a composer and performer since 1992.

> When I began working with Gen Verde, "unity as the utmost harmony" became tangible. Before every show, before the daily work in our studio, we renew the "pact" to love one another to the point of being ready to give our lives for each other. Our composition team includes artists from three different continents. Working together calls for a new creative process in which each of us welcomes the others' idea as our own, listening not only with our ears, but with something deeper, so that the others can clarify the concept that might be emerging. When we freely share our ideas in this way, what emerges is often even more beautiful than the initial idea, no longer "mine" or "hers" but "ours."

Gen Verde applies the same method while mounting a multimedia show that involves singers, instrumentalists, dancers, actors, and the technicians who operate the sound, light and media. Nancy describes what it meant for the group to choreograph a hip-hop number in "unity."

> I had put my whole self, all of my creativity, into writing the music for the number. Full of enthusiasm, I brought it to the dance studio, sure that they would love it. They didn't. My first thought was, "Okay, just do it yourselves!" Then I remembered our "pact" and realized it meant being ready to start from scratch. I asked them to show me the steps, and noted the places where they hoped the music could

give a particular effect or energy to their dance. This kind of collaboration produced much stronger results.

The Focolare spirituality has led Maria Hartmann Kastan, a New York painter and sculptor, to an "open studio mentality." She notes, "Along with scheduled biannual open studios, I would always leave my door open for an artist on a break to peek in to chat, and I was open to anyone who wanted to give me a ring and drop by. It has taken years of practice to feel that I am not abandoning focus, but to recognize in each visit a moment of visual rest. More often than not the interaction would give me insight into their personality and a 'new eye' to re-engage the piece I had been working on. This relationship is what supports my own spiritual and artistic goal — to initiate dialogue!"[40]

The Focolare perspective can also inform an artist's choice of topic and point of view. In his short film "Hidden in Time," Ed Roy examines the common humanity of two men from contrasting social, cultural and religious backgrounds.

> I wrote the script for the film after reading an article in the *New York Times* about a Muslim man in Iraq who lost his wife and children to an errant U.S. missile that hit a residential building in Baghdad where they lived. It saddened me that his personal story of grief and loss is hidden in our times. The film is a journey through our stereotypes, a recognition of the sacrifices we all make for those we love and the consequences that our choices can have on those to whom we are indifferent.[41]

The Focolare spirituality also helps Ed to place his work in an ever-broader perspective.

> I have discovered that I contribute to a better world not so much through my films but through this embrace of a lifestyle of love. The stories I work on may or may not have an impact on the viewer, but the way I treat my neighbors each day with love and respect, sometimes even sacrificing my own opinions or creative impulses as a gift of love for them, is what makes a difference to them. At times I can see how it filters into my work and somehow makes it more complete.[42]

Ron Austin is a veteran writer and producer with over a hundred credits in film and television. A member of the Academy of Motion Picture Arts and Sciences, the Director's Guild, and a founding member of Catholics in Media, he has won two life-time achievement awards from the Writer's Guild of America for his service to writers and to the Hollywood community. Austin sees a growing receptivity to a sense of the transcendent among his Hollywood peers. "What this spiritual inquiry needs to connect with now is a way of living it, not only proposing questions."[43] According to Austin:

> Chiara's charism of unity has a special application in Hollywood. First, we need to be united as people. We put such stress on success, on celebrity and on money that sometimes we don't see each other as people. We need to see each other as human beings and be united as a family. This will lead us to a new vision of our relationship with the audience. We should not see them as the "mass audience" but as individual persons. This unity is important for our own lives and how we relate to our audience.[44]

A spirituality of unity also sheds light on actors' work. Austin notes:

> Paradoxically, what might seem the most ego-driven art, acting, depends upon a profound loss of self and a radical opening to others, at least during the creative process. The origins of art and culture are sacred, and art loses its power and significance if and when it is no longer in touch with the divine. We needn't invent or try to will this connection. It exists, and we simply must be open to it. Opening ourselves is the challenge. God will do the rest."[45]

"Mariapolis": Model of a Society Renewed by Love

As mentioned in Chapter One, the "Mariapolis" summer gatherings held in the Dolomite Mountains throughout the 1950s brought together people from a wide variety of ages and walks of life — small children, youth and young couples, men and women of religious orders, priests, and bishops too. They also came from a cross-section of professions — it was a place where students and doctors, blue-collar workers and politicians could experience their common dignity and equality. The last large gathering there, in 1959, brought together people from twenty-six countries, who spoke nine languages, perhaps a sign of the Movement's vocation to work toward a "united world."

The Mariapolis continues throughout the world as Focolare members and friends gather in local regions for a three- to five-day meeting, generally during the summer. During the Mariapolis, the spirituality is presented, explained, and most of all, lived. Depending on the country, numbers range from a few hundred to several thousand.

In 1961, Chiara had a preliminary intuition of how the Mariapolis experience might become a "permanent" reality. Gazing down at the abbey of Einseideln, Switzerland, she was impressed by how the complex, which included not only a church, but also workshops for carpentry and other trades and a farm, embodied the Benedictine vocation — *ora et labora*, pray and work. Chiara understood that God might be asking something similar of the Focolare Movement: "a real little city, but suited to these times, with houses, exhibit halls, industries, sports fields, schools and businesses."[46]

Three years later, the Movement was bequeathed a sizable piece of land near the town of Incisa Val d'Arno, about twenty kilometers southeast of Florence. Loppiano, the largest of the Movement's "little cities," has about 800 inhabitants from seventy different countries. They demonstrate with their lives the effectiveness of mutual love. Loppiano welcomes the spiritual and cultural riches of its diverse inhabitants, and facilitates an exchange of their gifts. It is a "school" where Focolare members come from all over the world for periods of "formation" — shorter periods for couples and entire families, Volunteers, Gen, religious and priests; and three years for those preparing to live in a Focolare house.

Loppiano is a city in every sense of the word. It is self-sustaining, its inhabitants supporting themselves by working in one of its businesses, such as those that manufacture furniture, clothing or ceramics, or through the wine and olive oil cooperative. In 2005 a shrine to "Mary the Mother of God, *Theotokos*," designed by Loppiano's studio for art and architecture, was dedicated. Its purpose, and that of each of the thirty-five permanent Mariapolises spread throughout the world, is to be a "city built on a hill" (Mt 5:14). These "little cities" are not isolated from the world; rather, they aim to be like "laboratories," places to experience what happens when God is allowed to permeate every aspect of life.[47]

In North America, the permanent Mariapolis is located in the Hudson Valley, about eighty miles north of New York City. On September 14, 1986, twenty-five years to the day after the first Focolare houses in

North America were opened, Mariapolis Luminosa was inaugurated. Chiara could not be present due to illness, but she sent one of her first companions, Natalia Dellapiccola, to deliver the inaugural message. It called for Luminosa to be a center for ecumenical and interreligious dialogue because "it must be an expression of this nation, a nation made up of people who have come here from every part of the world." In 1990, Chiara visited Luminosa for the first time. After visiting the little city, she proposed guidelines for its continued development. Over the years, Luminosa has served as a focal point for North American schools of formation for the various Focolare vocations. Its work for intercultural and interreligious dialogue is reflected in the "Luminosa Award," given to recognize persons or groups whose lives and works contribute to unity and universal brotherhood.[48] These awards, as well the dozens of conferences and cultural events held there testify to the possibility of genuine unity in an American context.

5

The Focolare Movement
and the Church

People who hear about the Focolare often have questions about connections between the Movement and the Church. As David recounts, "in the Focolare I saw none of the devotions that I associated with trustworthy Catholic groups." Those with a more "traditional" experience, like David, might find a "contrast between the style of Catholicism that [they] had always known and the *modus operandi* of the Movement" (p. 17).

Others have more structural questions about how ecclesial movements such as the Focolare operate within a diocese or parish. Further, given its ecumenical and interreligious work, some wonder where it fits within hierarchical structures. This chapter addresses these questions, and then highlights how the Focolare spirituality and its structures serve to strengthen the life of the Catholic Church in the United States, as well as the Church's commitments to ecumenical dialogue.

A Brief History of the Approval by the Roman Catholic Church

The Focolare Movement has always acknowledged the necessity of unity with the Church. As Chiara explains, the initial group was "touched in a special way" by the sentence, "Whoever listens to you listens to me (Lk 10:16)"[1] She saw unity with the hierarchy as essential to the new Movement being fully incorporated within the Church. From the first stirrings of the community in Trent, she sought the approval of its bishop, Carlo De Ferrari; he concluded, "*Digitus Dei hic est*" — the finger of God is here. After further study, in 1947 he granted the first official diocesan approval.

In the 1950s, when the Church was studying whether the Movement should be approved, questions and concerns emerged. Unlike the spiritualities and ecclesial structures of that time, the Focolare posed some striking, and for some, alarming, characteristics. First, in an era when reading the Bible was almost always mediated by the clergy or by catechetical instruction, it was unusual for a Catholic group to be promoting the direct reading of scripture. As the French Catholic convert and writer Paul Claudel quipped, "Catholics show tremendous respect for the Bible — they stay as far away from it as possible."[2] Because they read the gospel for their daily spiritual nourishment, *focolarini* were actually accused of being Protestants masquerading as Catholics.[3] A second concern was that their practice of sharing material goods and dedication to "unity" brought them dangerously close to communism, a grave concern in post-war Italian society.[4] Prior to Vatican II, it was not common for lay groups — much less a group of young women — to stress ideas such as "God is love." In that regard, some in the Italian Bishops' Conference at the time were troubled by the Movement because it was led by a woman.[5]

Chiara declined to speak openly about the Focolare's lengthy period of testing and trial, but she did include an account in *The Cry*, a book that she describes as "a love letter to Jesus Forsaken." Within the broader question of the Movement's relationship with the institutional church, several aspects of her account are striking.

First, it conveys an attitude of humility and openness to correction. For example, she writes that there was no truth to the accusation of communist tendencies, but states, "It was undeniable that there were attitudes among us, young and inexperienced as we were, that could be naïve and hence in need of greater purification and greater maturity, and so requiring to be set right."[6]

Her account also reflects a capacity to give the benefit of the doubt to all involved, both accusers and investigators, and in this spirit to welcome the direction of Church authorities: "We know how these things can happen. Someone criticizes, perhaps in good faith, attitudes of others which appear suspect. Zealously, authorities are informed, who have no choice but to intervene. The Church intervenes because of its duty of discernment. So began a long and thorough study of our case."[7]

Further, Chiara could also trace, as the investigation unfolded, its constructive nature. Bishop Montini, the future Pope Paul VI, assured her that the investigation was "a protection and a guarantee" for the Movement. Taking comfort from those words, she appreciated that "it was something positive."[8] "[S]uffering does not exhaust itself only in the pain that it brings, but God has some purpose for it in mind. And since God is love, its purpose is love."[9]

Finally, her account demonstrates an extraordinary capacity to interpret all circumstances, including extremely painful events, through the lens of an ongoing and ever-deepening relationship with God, particularly with Jesus crucified and forsaken, whom she had chosen as the love of her life. She appreciated the process deeply, yet was frank about what the investigation meant for her. "For the Church it was something simple and dutiful, but for us it meant suspension and uncertainty."[10] "We felt alone. It was again Jesus forsaken, the lonely one *par excellence*, who supported us in this trial, this death, this solemn pruning of the already flourishing tree of our Movement."[11]

In a letter to a priest going through a difficult moment, Chiara described her own feelings during this process: "The waiting, the suspension, is Jesus forsaken. To feel out of place is Jesus forsaken; he, God of the universe, the One who was expelled from heaven and earth.... All souls who don't feel that they are in the right place can mirror themselves in Jesus forsaken."[12] She sums up the entire experience in these words: "During that period of trial, our love for Jesus forsaken was increasing: seeking him, preferring him, loving him without analyzing the pain, never taking our gaze off of him, joyfully welcoming him, not putting up with him but loving him, living together with him, loving him exclusively."[13]

On March 23, 1962, Pope John XXIII issued an official approval of the Movement. Although Chiara welcomed it with joy and relief, she realized that the "birth pangs" were not over.[14] Because the Code of Canon Law at that time could not accommodate the uniqueness of this new structure in the life of the Church, the terms of the Movement's approval caused her considerable concern. The Church faced the difficult task of approving a structure that included men and women, both clerical and lay. The approval as issued divided the Movement into two parts, one for men and one for women. Chiara explains: "The Focolare ended up formed of two separate trunks, one for men, the other for women: an impossible new face of Jesus forsaken, the divided one, to embrace."[15] Chiara wondered, "Could God who lives in the Church and God who had done this work contradict himself?"[16] Over the years, the Movement's extensive and substantial contacts with other Christian churches and with other religions further complicated its status with the Church. Canon lawyers faced the challenge of approving under Roman Catholic rubrics the statutes of an association with non-Catholic and non-Christian participants, some of whom felt a vocation to live in Focolare houses, and who were in fact, already imbedded in these communities.

Over an extraordinary period of history, including the Second Vatican Council and the open, receptive, and creative pontificates of Paul VI and John Paul II, these challenges were overcome. In 1964, before all of these problems had been addressed, Paul VI told Chiara, "Things which seem rather unusual, later become possible."[17]

In 1990, the President of the Pontifical Council for the Laity issued the Holy See's approval of the General Statutes of the Work of Mary, a "private, universal association of the faithful, of pontifical right ... containing the norms of life and of government for all the persons who are part of the Work of Mary" (Part One, Ch. I, Art. 1). The same article explicitly acknowledges participants of other Christian churches, other religions, and those with no religious affiliation:

> Christians of other Churches and ecclesial communities live the spirituality inasmuch as the differences in Christian faith and the praxis of their single Churches and ecclesial communities will allow. On the basis of a shared religious foundation, believers of other religions are also part of the Work of Mary, living its spirit in varying degrees. Persons with no particular religious faith are also a part of the Movement and wish to share its goals, insofar as their conscience allows, by practicing unconditional love and respect toward every neighbor and basing their actions on a spirit of fraternity. (Art. 1)

All of the aspects that provoked questions and concerns during the investigations of the 1950s are included in the 1990 General Statutes as essential characteristics of the Movement's mission and identity. Article 8, "The Spirit of the Work of Mary," reads: "Those who are part of the Focolare Movement walk along the way of Christian love in accordance with the Gospel-based spirituality of the Movement." Section 3 of that article reads: "In order to carry out God's will, they strive to live the Gospel, nourishing themselves daily with the Word of God so as to acquire his way of thinking, of willing, of loving. To do this, they put into practice a passage from the Holy Scripture, sharing with one another the resulting experiences for the edification of all."

In Part III of the General Statutes, "The Concrete Aspects of the Life of the Work of Mary," Chapter One presents "Communion of Goods, Economy and Work." Article 24 reads:

> The New Commandment (see Jn 15:12) is at the basis of the life of all those persons who are part of the Work of

Mary. Consequently, the communion of goods is practiced by all, in ways that differ according to the various vocations. The early Christian communities are seen as a model: "The community of believers was of one heart and mind, and no one claimed that any of his possessions was his own, but they had everything in common" (Acts 4:32).

Finally, Article 98 of Chapter IV, "The Central Governing Body of the Work of Mary," specifies that the President of the Work of Mary must be a laywoman, selected from among the *focolarine* with perpetual vows. In a September 1985 conversation, when Chiara asked John Paul II what he thought of this idea, he affirmed, "Indeed! Why not?" The co-president is selected from among the *focolarini* with perpetual vows who have also been ordained. The General Statutes build gender equality into all aspects of the Movement's day-to-day governance and decision-making. For example, its Central Governing Body and General Council are both made up of an even number of men and women. Similarly, in the various geographical regions, called "zones," two "zone directors," a *focolarino* and a *focolarina*, are entrusted "together" with overseeing and promoting the goals and activities of the Movement (Art. 117–118). These provisions solve the problem of the separation between men and women in the first approval.

Focolare and the Local Church

Like David's account in the introduction, many Roman Catholics who first hear about the Focolare attempt to situate the Movement within familiar local structures. Their first question is often, "Where do you go to Mass?" The short answer is that Catholic Focolare members go to Sunday Mass in their neighborhood parish. Many also attend daily Mass in a location convenient for their work schedules. Focolare members are active in their parishes, serving as liturgical ministers, leaders for adult formation and marriage preparation, and as members of committees and councils.

The inquiry "Where do you go to Mass?" however, often points to a deeper set of questions and concerns. Why doesn't the Focolare pour its energy into established parish structures? Don't separate programs and courses of formation drain or ultimately threaten the basic organizational structure of Church life — the parish — which in the United States seems to be working so well?

Such questions need to be examined from broader perspectives. The first is historical. Drawing spiritual nourishment and formation from a "movement" is a deep and ancient pattern within Church life. In a 1998 address on the theological place of ecclesial movements like the Focolare, then-Cardinal Joseph Ratzinger outlined how from seventh-century missionary monasticism, to the thirteenth-century Franciscan and Dominican movements, to Ignatius of Loyola's sixteenth-century movement for evangelization, to the founding of various missionary congregations in the nineteenth century, the faithful have sought to deepen their spiritual lives through groups and movements that are independent of diocesan structures.[18]

Cardinal Ratzinger explains: "Waves of movements are always sweeping through [the Church] that reinstate and reapply the universalist aspect of the apostolic mission and the radical dimension of the gospel and thus serve to promote the spiritual life and truth of the local Churches."[19] In light of this history, Cardinal Ratzinger affirmed: "There must always be in the Church ministries and missions that do not belong purely to the local Church but serve the task given the whole Church, the task of spreading the gospel."[20]

Some Catholics tend to place almost exclusive emphasis on the Church's hierarchical and clerical dimensions: the pope, bishops, and priests, who administer the sacraments, preside over its governance, and guard the magisterial tradition. This perspective risks failing to appreciate all of the ways in which the Holy Spirit intends to work in the world. Quoting *Lumen Gentium*, the Second Vatican Council's Dogmatic Constitution on the Church, Pope John Paul II affirmed that "it is not only through the sacraments and the ministrations of the Church that the Holy Spirit makes holy the people … Allotting his gifts according as he wills, he also distributes special graces among the faithful of every rank … He makes them fit and ready to undertake various tasks and offices for the renewal and building up of the Church."[21]

Chiara's experience with the Church's investigation of the Focolare Movement in the 1950s suggests that trust and unity between movements and parishes can be nurtured through humility, openness to the direction of Church authorities, and transparent honesty. In this fashion, movements can find ways to express and share the particular gifts that the Holy Spirit might be sending for the good of the entire Church.

The path to learning this kind of humility and openness includes mistakes. Neophyte zeal, lack of judgment, and lack of spiritual maturity can cause misunderstandings. Divine treasure is always carried in the "clay jars" (2 Cor 4:7) of human weakness, at times manifested in pride, impatience, or other shortcomings that create or intensify tension in Church communities. In his 1998 analysis, then-Cardinal Ratzinger noted how the development of the ecclesial movements has included "various infancy sicknesses": "There were tendencies toward being exclusive, toward having one-sided emphases and thus, of being incapable of fitting into the life of the local Church."[22]

When Tom, from Brooklyn, first met the Focolare, he felt a new excitement and passion for the faith. Thinking that he was applying the lessons he was learning from the Movement, he began to challenge his pastor to improve certain aspects of parish life. The tension between them led to noticeable division among the parishioners. As Tom began to understand the Focolare's principles more deeply, he realized that he had gotten it all wrong. He explains: "One weekday morning there was no altar boy, so I served. During Mass, I realized I had to change. I had to stop competing with my pastor and try to love him. I knew I couldn't receive the Eucharist unless I promised God I would love this man." Tom's apology opened a heart-to-heart discussion, which transformed their relationship. "We became close friends. In the months to come, without me pushing him, he instituted some of the changes I had proposed."[23]

Reflecting on the recent experience of the ecclesial movements in the United States, theologian Richard Gaillardetz warned against elitist "Super Catholic" tendencies. "It's easy to applaud these groups in wanting to associate with other Christians who take their faith seriously, those who understand that to be a Christian means being marked for a dramatically different way of life ... But the shadow side is that it can encourage a kind of elitism, a sense that the only way one can grow in Christ is to associate exclusively with other likeminded, committed Christians."[24]

Focolare members have discovered that a spirituality of unity offers resources for learning how to appreciate the manifold gifts of the Spirit and attend to the diverse needs of the Church. In a meditation from 1950, Chiara imagines herself in a "great garden full of flowers." She acknowledges the tendency to gaze with love on one single flower without noticing the others. "God — because of the collective spirituality he has given us — asks us to look at all the flowers, because he is in them all, and by observing them all we love him more than the individual flowers. God who is in me, who has shaped my soul, who lives there as Trinity, is also in the heart of my brothers and sisters."[25] Living a spirituality of unity entails contemplating the beauty of all that God is working in the garden of the Church.

When he was a parish priest, Bishop Michael Mulvey began a new assignment in the Diocese of Austin, Texas, with such a spirit of openness. Upon his arrival, he met with the Spiritual Life Committee, which was researching how they could contribute to parishioners' lives. As he listened to their ideas and plans, he saw a parallel with the efforts to build unity among ecclesial movements and new communities following the first World Congress of Ecclesial Movements in 1998. Seven spiritualities were present in the parish: two secular orders (Franciscans and Carmelites) and five ecclesial movements — Charismatic Renewal, Schoenstatt, Focolare, Marriage Encounter and the Oblates of the Congregation of St. John. Drawing on that international experience, he invited the leaders of these groups to a meeting with just two agenda items: to have them get to know one another and the spirituality each was living; and to discuss how to make the wider parish aware of these spiritualities.

The leaders then agreed to assist the Spiritual Life Committee in putting together a "Day of Spirituality" for the parish. To prepare, they met monthly to deepen their understanding of each spirituality and their appreciation of the contribution that such movements bring to the Church.

On the Day of Spirituality, representatives took turns summarizing the origin of their particular spirituality and its unique gifts. Following these introductions participants could attend two of the workshops, offered by the seven groups. Parishioners appreciated the opportunity to learn about these spiritualities and their presence in the parish. Some expressed interest in knowing more.

Bishop Mulvey reflects, "Beyond the increase in awareness, I believed it was equally important that a real communion among the groups would grow. We began meeting together monthly and each movement took a turn hosting us in one of their homes. As the knowledge of one another's spirituality grew, it became obvious that their various expressions were not in competition, but were different reflections of the one Spirit. They found that communion can and must exist among all of them in order to express fully the presence of the Spirit in the Church."

The gatherings continued, and membership in the various groups grew. The two secular Carmelites came to have twenty-six people in their Carmelite study group. The Secular Franciscans grew from one member to ten. The Schoenstatt family began to sponsor regular pilgrimages from the parish to their shrine in Corpus Christi, Texas, and during the Year of the Rosary (2002) were supported in promoting the family rosary. The Charismatic prayer group was revitalized, and the number of participants in the Focolare "Word of Life" meetings also grew. Each of the groups remained at the service of the entire parish, participating in renewal weekends twice a year. At the end of the weekend they offered their service to parishioners who wanted to continue deepening their spiritual life.

The initial step to look beyond one's own group or approach is demanding. For Chiara, Mary "desolate" at the foot of the cross is the model *par excellence* of the essential attitude for any kind of work within the Church:

> Mary Desolate! We may have lost everything, we may not be attached to anything, but still there can remain something that we believe we can possess, that we must show and take pleasure in: the gifts of God! If the Desolate sacrificed God for God, we have to know how to lose the gifts of God for God. Therefore, we should not stop to consider them, or fill our soul with spiritual pride as we admire them, but empty ourselves so as to be filled with the Spirit of God. If you have gifts, these talents ought to be put to use with the same charity that should always envelop everything we do…. But it is best then to forget, to let go, in order to be only love in front of souls and the works of the Church. Love thinks of the beloved, not itself.[26]

At the conclusion of the 1998 Pentecost gathering of ecclesial movements and new communities in St. Peter's Square, Chiara put the "gifts" of the Movement at the disposition of the Church when she made a promise to Pope John Paul II: "We know that the Church desires full communion, unity among the Movements, and this has already begun. We want to assure you that, since our specific charism is unity, we will make every effort to contribute, with all our strength, toward fully accomplishing it."[27]

Serving and Enriching Parish Life

For Focolare members drawn to liturgical ministry or catechesis, formation in its spirituality provides a solid foundation for service to the local Church. For example, for their more than thirty years in Houston, Dan and Mary have participated actively in their parish. They have served as members of family life committees, as sponsors for marriage preparation, lectors, and extraordinary Eucharistic ministers. Now in their eighties, they can no longer continue with these commitments, but they say:

> We are not yet too old or too infirm to love and serve Jesus in others, especially by bringing the Eucharist to the homebound. When we visit these friends, their suffering becomes our suffering, and over time a close relationship develops.
>
> Sometimes they have adult children and grandchildren that live in distant parts of the country, which is a hardship for them. They welcome the fact that someone listens to them as they work through different issues. We occasionally can assist with other errands or drive them to medical appointments. And when they are hospitalized, we go to visit them.

They explain how this sense of family often extends to parishioners' relatives as well. "Often, when their family members are living nearby, we develop friendships with them, too. In one instance, we brought the Eucharist to a lady for nearly eight years. When she died at age 106 the family asked only us to speak at her funeral Mass. We were honored and deeply moved with this one last visit with our dear friend."

When Carla was in her early 50s, she realized that in her large Bronx parish quite a few women were going through divorce and raising their children alone. Several years earlier, during a difficult divorce, Carla herself found that the Focolare spirituality of unity gave her the strength to raise her five children. "I knew that I could love these women in my parish and help them by sharing what had happened to me," she says. With the pastor's blessing, she began to meet with them regularly to share the "Word of Life" and other key points of the Focolare spirituality of unity that relate to their circumstances. In turn they shared their efforts to put it into practice in their daily lives. "We helped each other by putting the art of loving into practice first among ourselves and then with those around us. We received strength from each other, from Jesus in our midst and from the Eucharist. Some of these women began to participate in local Focolare activities as well."

Even when it might have been more comfortable to switch parishes, Focolare members often stay in order to help heal painful situations. For example, one family found it difficult to build a relationship with their pastor because of his dry and negative approach. In addition, the liturgy was held in a gym, where the noise distracted their children. The husband comments, "We realized that we shouldn't run from this, but try to bring love, right there." They decided to reach out to the pastor when their two sons received first communion by offering him a book as a small gift. He was deeply touched. From the pulpit the next day he said that it was the first time in years that anyone had ever given him a present at first communion time. Reading a quote from the book by St. Thérèse of Lisieux, "Charity is love for the ones that we find unbearable," he explained how he realized that he could do a better job, for example, by loving the parishioners who complain. He encouraged the congregation to do the same.

Fr. Dan began his service as an administrator for a predominantly Spanish-speaking parish in St. Louis at a particularly difficult time. For the previous ten years, the parish had had a succession of pastors who did not speak Spanish. In addition, since the church building required over two million dollars in repairs, it seemed likely that the parish would be closed. In the midst of these challenges, Fr. Dan discovered that the colon cancer that had been in remission for two years had metastasized to his liver. Chemotherapy would prevent him from doing half of his administrative duties and allow him to celebrate only one of the four Sunday Masses. "It seemed I was a constant bearer of bad news for the parishioners. The stability that they were seeking continued to elude them no matter how hard we tried. I encouraged them to look to the future with hope, but inside I felt that everything was falling apart. Increasing fatigue from the chemotherapy further reduced my energy and the time that I could spend with them."

The Focolare spirituality of unity, and support from his brother priests who lived it with him, helped Fr. Dan to see how the circumstances were an occasion to deepen his own love for Jesus crucified and forsaken. "I realized that I could pray and embrace this suffering throughout Lent as we prepared for the celebration of Jesus' resurrection on Easter Sunday. I encouraged our parishioners, who were going through their own personal trials, sufferings and struggles, to pray also."

What seemed the bleakest moment for the parish became an opportunity to build a true sense of community. At a prayer vigil before the Blessed Sacrament that a group of parishioners organized every Friday evening, they prayed for Fr. Dan's health. They conveyed their concern in a variety of ways, always inquiring about how he was feeling. Fr. Dan recounts:

> Our suffering together turned into a deep experience
> of reciprocal love and unity that culminated on Easter
> morning. Our typical separation of English-speaking and

Spanish-speaking Masses was set aside and we joined together in one celebration, a communion of people with distinct gifts yet all one family. I discovered that my personal efforts to be first in loving, to embrace Jesus in this suffering and to speak a message of hope, and all of our communal efforts to love had been used by God to create unity among us. His presence gave us the assurance that it was really he who was guiding our future. We experienced new joy and hope. In all my thirty-five years as a priest I have never been through a more transforming experience. When I was my weakest, Jesus was the strongest and used my nothingness to be present among us.

"We don't do anything big or dramatic — nothing to put in a book. It is just trying to be totally empty, listening a lot, and loving where God puts us." This, in a nutshell, sums up the presence of Focolare members Lyle and Sue Anne in their local parish. With each pastor, they have worked to build a personal relationship through which he can feel their support. "I love your concepts of listening and your idea of unity" — one pastor told them — "we need more of that on our staff." Sue Anne empathizes with the difficulties a pastor cannot avoid. "Sometimes it seems that they can do no right; it's like a mother with teenagers. When I hear criticism, I try to slip into the conversation somewhere a positive experience that I have had with that priest."

Because they had a gift for building a sense of family at the daily Mass, Lyle and Sue Anne were asked to organize a monthly breakfast club, a social setting to welcome those who otherwise might keep their distance from the community. They were also asked to coordinate their parish's involvement in local ecumenical and interfaith events. Serving on a committee to explore the parish's response to the bishop's evangelization program, Lyle helped everyone to see the value of what their active ministries were already doing.

Miriam is the Director of Religious Education of her St. Louis, Missouri parish. She reflects on how the Focolare spirituality has informed her own approach and their work as a community.

> One of the most difficult tasks I face is trying to achieve faith development in such a way that the head can stay connected to the heart. Often parishioners approach adult and youth education with the idea that it is a matter of learning the knowledge of their faith. Incorporating the Focolare spirituality into our approach helps us to go beyond just

intellectual knowledge. We see more clearly how to integrate our faith into a way of living and loving each other, and those outside the parish community. This creates an environment of hospitality and family, making my ministry as a director of religious education a more joyful experience.

The Cube of Love (see pp. 96–97) is a daily challenge to practice this love, and it enriches our curriculum, too. For example, when we teach the Corporal Works of Mercy in the upper grades, our students do not learn them as information for a test. Rather, they learn them because they are additional ways that we can practice the Cube of Love — "Feed the hungry" takes on a different meaning when it is seen as a way to "be the first to love."

Already in 1966, Paul VI had encouraged members of the Focolare to "do all you can" to help make the parish a place in which "love is truly lived."[28] The "Parish Movement" brings together the clergy, religious and laity who live a spirituality of unity in the context of their work in a parish so that it might become, in the words of John Paul II, "the home and the school of communion."[29] At occasional international and local meetings, they exchange ideas and encourage one another in this vital service to the Church.

Ecumenical Commitment: "A Passion for Unity"

A Movement dedicated to working toward the fulfillment of "that they may all be one" cannot help but work for the full unity of all Christians. As noted by Sr. Joan McGuire, O.P., Director of the Archdiocese of Chicago's Office of Ecumenical Affairs, "Whatever we do as an office, you can count on the Focolare to be present and supportive, and you can be confident that they understand what the Church teaches. It makes a big difference to have a whole group of people who work with a passion for unity."

The Focolare's ecumenical work has often begun with personal relationships. For example, in 1961, a group of German Lutherans who met Chiara were especially touched by the Movement's approach to putting scripture into practice, and a deep relationship began to develop. That same year, the Focolare opened an international office for ecumenism, "Centro Uno," with Igino Giordani as its first director. In 1965, a handful of Anglican ministers came from England to attend an ecumenical meeting at the Movement's center in Rocca di Papa, near Rome. This experience so impressed them that the following year they chartered a plane to bring 100 Anglicans and Catholics to the subsequent conference. Out of Chiara's personal relationship with Patriarch Athenagoras, which through the 1960s helped to open and sustain the dialogue between the Patriarch and Pope Paul VI, emerged deep relationships with Orthodox Churches in a number of countries.

By living the gospel together, experiencing the presence of Christ in the community, Christians discover the richness of their common heritage: baptism, scripture, the early councils, the creed, the Fathers of the Church, the martyrs. These discoveries reinforce the reality that they are brothers and sisters, distinct yet united in the gifts that each one shares.[30] Reverend Dr. Sherman Hicks, former bishop of the Evangelical Lutheran Church in America's Metropolitan Chicago Synod, describes what the Focolare contributes to the ecumenical dynamic:

> In a time when a consumer approach informs how one decides where to go to church, the Focolare helps people to understand what it means to have a sense of identity, not in order to separate oneself, but to understand what the unique parts bring to the whole. How the Focolare lives unity in diversity brings a very important contribution to the ecumenical movement. We have the parts, but that should not keep us from the spirit of unity. It should contribute to it.

Members of Focolare communities who come from different Christian churches emphasize the importance of participating fully in the life of the church in which he or she was baptized. Celine, an Orthodox married *focolarina* from Brooklyn describes her experience:

> The Focolare spirituality helped me to go more in depth, to go back to my Antiochian Orthodox Church to learn more about its riches and be faithful to its teachings. I also became more active in my parish by helping in the church school. There I met my husband, Joseph, and we now have four children. The spirituality of unity has been a great gift to our family. Joseph and I read the Word of Life together and share how we live it. It helps us focus our day and put God first in our decisions and actions.

Gerald met the Focolare while studying cultural anthropology at Temple University in Philadelphia. He was struggling to reconcile his Christian missionary upbringing with his North American Mennonite roots.

I met the Focolare Movement at a time in my life when the materialism and denominationalism as practiced by many Protestant and Evangelical Christians were leading me to cynicism about religious life in North America. I was asking, why bother being different? Was Christian faith and practice really worth the trouble? I really wanted to know if any Christian group tried to make their "walk and talk" match and if any group was actually succeeding at this.

Focolare life surprised and challenged me to become a consistent active adult Christian. That challenge remains central to my current adult participation in Focolare activities and witness. Focolare leadership insisted that I own my own Christian story and embrace my own church background. I come from a strong Christian home and a distinctive Mennonite Christian heritage. Living the "Word of Life" each month challenged me to re-examine my relationships and my attitudes toward those from my own church, community, and family, and to take personal responsibility for my life.

As Celine and Gerald explain, the Focolare spirituality speaks to people from different churches, calling them to go into depth in their own traditions. Bishop Demetrios of Mokissos describes how the Focolare spirituality has provided him a way to appreciate his own heritage more deeply:

Speaking in general terms, in Orthodox thought, there tends to be less of an emphasis on the cross and more of a focus on the resurrection. The Focolare spirituality has helped me to come to a heightened sense of my own spirituality. It makes me look at the resurrection in more hopeful and real terms. Without the cross there is no resurrection; we need both. We can't negate one or highlight one over the other. Putting them together, you have this amazing sense of redemption, wholeness, and healing for the world. Because of what I have understood from the Focolare spirituality about Jesus crucified and forsaken, I have been better able to understand painful moments within my communion and metropolis, and the painful situations of our clergy. This sheds a whole new light.

Similarly, Dr. Paul Crow, president emeritus of the Council on Christian Unity of the Christian Church (Disciples of Christ), affirms:

> I really had to keep reminding myself that Chiara was a Roman Catholic, because as I read her, I felt that my faith was being articulated. If she had written about the nature of the church and how the church should be structured, then I would have recognized that she was a Roman Catholic, which would have been fine. But that was not her witness. Her witness was to the faith. I think that is why she has been so universally accepted. That is why people of all cultures and traditions have found that she has penetrated our own religious experience.

When touched by the fullness of the charism of unity, Orthodox, Christians of many traditions, as well as Roman Catholics share an experience of unity in diversity. As Dr. Hicks explains:

> In so many ways the manner in which Focolare members live reminds me of what I read of the first century Christians — how they acted, how they cared for one another, how they carried one another's burdens. I think that too many experiences across faith traditions have been a matter of trying to indoctrinate people and show how we're right and you're wrong. With the Focolare this was not the case. It was an example of unity that did not negate the parts, [rather it was] unity that learned from the parts, unity that shared with the parts, unity that respected the parts. This leads to a truly meaningful relationship with Christ as the center or the head, and it is so refreshing.

Chiara has used the image of rays emanating from the sun to describe the effects of the charism of unity. "Each one of the sun's rays is still the sun itself, but its light grows in intensity the closer it gets to the sun. It is similar for those who live unity. They live by allowing themselves to penetrate always more into God. They grow always closer to God, who lives in their hearts, and the closer they get to him, the closer they get to the hearts of their brothers and sisters."[31]

This is the Focolare's gift to every church and to the unity of all Christians.

Part III
The Focolare Spirituality and Contemporary Culture in the United States

Part II has presented people in the United States who have found that a spirituality of unity is accessible, relevant, and helpful for their personal lives and for the life of their communities. This suggests that the Focolare has to a significant degree adapted itself to the North American context. Part III approaches inculturation from a slightly different angle. It aims to show how Focolare members in the United States have engaged contemporary cultural questions and values.

Before considering specific themes, a few guideposts might help orient readers to a Focolare methodology for cultural engagement. Americans tend to be problem-solvers. Whatever the challenge, they like to get a handle on the situation, consider the resources at hand, and then innovate. They may look for a list of things to do each day, and expect that "doing" them will advance their lives toward fulfillment and happiness. *New York Times* columnist David Brooks describes a recent article in the *Harvard Business Review* that exhorts students to reflect on the purpose of their lives, and then allocate their time, energy and talents accordingly. When this process is complete, Brooks states, "[L]ife comes to appear as a well-designed project, carefully conceived in the beginning, reviewed and adjusted along the way and brought toward a well-rounded fruition."[1] "In America," Brooks observes, "we have been taught to admire the lone free agent who creates new worlds."[2]

The Focolare approach runs counter to this model in several ways. First, in contrast to Brooks's "Well-Planned Life," the Focolare spirituality begins from a stance of receptivity — openness to the experience of God and the discovery that the principal force in one's own life and in the life of the community is God, who is love. While the Focolare certainly encourages reflecting on ultimate purpose and meaning, such reflection is grounded in the readiness to let go of control over "well-designed projects" in order to receive God's plans. Second, although members of Focolare communities reflect deeply on how to respond to people's questions and needs, they begin with the spiritual dimension. While they are working through a particular challenge, their conversations tend to begin from questions such as: how can we help each other to love, to live the gospel in these circumstances? How can we recognize and love the face of Jesus abandoned on the cross in this particular tension or conflict, and work together to build the kind of unity that might help to heal it? They do focus on addressing and solving problems, but they begin this process by letting a life of love transform personal and community perspectives.

Third, for those who live the Focolare spirituality of unity, the one who "creates new worlds" is not the "lone free agent" but the presence of the living God in the life of the community. They hope that relationships founded in mutual love generate the capacity to receive the gift of unity, which Christians experience as the presence of Christ: "where two or three are gathered in my name, I am there among them" (Mt 18:20). The presence of Christ helps them to see meaning in their lives, and how "all things hold together," as Paul wrote to the Colossians (Col 1:17).

These characteristics of the Focolare spirituality's engagement with culture — a receptive stance that leads to personal spiritual transformation with a strong accent on communal expression — are not unique to the Movement. Other spiritual currents within the Catholic tradition, other Christian spiritualities, as well as many other religious traditions also share such an approach. Considering how the Focolare spirituality interacts with broader cultural questions might also shed light on the more general question of how spiritual currents challenge the paradigm of the "lone free agent who creates new worlds."

Each of the next four chapters opens with what we have identified as a "quest" to realize values in American culture: the search for happiness, for freedom, for community, for the common good. Each begins with a description of the cultural tensions implicit in each quest, then turns to the lived experience of individuals and communities in the Focolare Movement throughout the United States.

Focolare members live shoulder to shoulder with family, friends and neighbors in urban, suburban and rural communities, immersed in the challenges of daily life that complicate the search for these four values.

They nourish themselves with a spirituality of unity, usually through frequent contact with the Focolare structures that sustain their commitments to build relationships of love and community in their daily lives. It might be evident by now that they are storytellers. If asked for their thoughts on a particular cultural or social problem, many begin by relating "an experience." The simplicity of these narratives belies the complex social and cultural renewal that they describe.

Chapters Six reflects on the value Americans give to "the pursuit of happiness" — the quest to find a sense of the self, of personal identity. The American spirit embodies creative energy and optimistic drive, as well as tendencies toward individual isolation, conformity, and consumerism. The daily experience of Focolare members shows how a stance that is receptive and open to God's love clarifies questions of professional identity and decisions about material goods. Chapter Seven considers how such receptivity also generates an alternative definition of freedom which shapes moral perspectives on building relationships and on facing illness and death.

Chapter Eight reflects on the enduring quest for community in a pluralistic society: *e pluribus unum*. Careful observers of American culture, alarmed by a perceived loss of social cohesion, lament the shrinking social space where people can transcend their differences. Focolare communities provide a living laboratory to test tools for building social cohesion across a range of ethnic, racial, social and religious differences. They also help people to develop the perspectives, attitudes and habits they need to build social cohesion where they live.

Chapter Nine explores the quest for the common good in an increasingly polarized and fragmented culture. Focolare members work to sustain political and civic commitments for the common good and to bridge partisan differences. The chapter presents the diversity of political opinion within Focolare communities in the United States, the worldwide experience of the Movement for Unity in Politics, and recent efforts to develop the tools and skills for entering into dialogue about such differences within the framework of a spirituality of unity.

6
The Focolare Spirituality and "The Pursuit of Happiness"

Between Lonely Independence and Comfortable Conformity

The American nation and its culture were born from revolution. "In the course of human events," the Declaration of Independence states, the time had come for its citizens to claim "certain unalienable rights" of "life, liberty and the pursuit of happiness" and to begin forging a new way of life.[1] An early immigrant, J. Hector St. John de Crèvecoeur, captured the tone of this new nation's people: "The American is a new man, who acts upon new principles; he must therefore entertain new ideas, and form new opinions."[2] That same spirit still courses through Americans' cultural veins — urging them to throw off old ways to embrace the new, to push beyond settled boundaries and patterns.

One aspect of this new way of life is how Americans connect work and its rewards. Crèvecoeur explains, "From involuntary idleness, servile dependence, penury, and useless labour, he [the American farmer] has passed to toils of a very different nature, rewarded by ample subsistence." As a result, "We are all animated with the spirit of an industry which is unfettered and unrestrained because each person works for himself."[3]

This revolutionary spirit of independence, individual initiative, and eager embrace of the new generates boundless energy, optimism and creativity. Yet it also drives Americans toward isolation. American literature is replete with rugged, solitary and self-reliant heroes whose self-sufficiency allows them to challenge the natural and social world. In the 1830s, Alexis de Tocqueville observed that the people he met during his travels in the United States "owe nothing to anyone, they expect . . . nothing from anyone . . . they are in the habit of always considering themselves in isolation, and they willingly fancy that their whole destiny is in their hands."[4]

Such tendency carries a risk: "it constantly leads him back toward himself alone, and threatens finally to confine him wholly in the solitude of his own heart."[5] Tocqueville coined the term "individualism" to describe what he saw: "a reflective and peaceable sentiment that disposes each citizen to isolate himself from the mass of those like

129

him and to withdraw to one side with his family and friends, so that after having thus created a little society for his own use, he willingly abandons society at large to itself."[6]

Of course, Americans also have a deep sense of selflessness and community. As the Massachusetts Bay colonists disembarked from the Arabella, John Winthrop urged them to "delight in each other, make others' conditions our own, rejoice together, mourn together, labour and suffer together, always having before our eyes ... our community as members of the same body."[7] American history and literature contains example after example of a spirit of community and generosity that propagated towns, regions, and the entire nation. That spirit extends into the twentieth century, as seen in Dr. Martin Luther King's description of the "beloved community," which spurred the national imagination toward positive social change.

Nevertheless, Americans tend to see themselves as individuals. They continue to suffer the malady that Robert Bellah calls "ontological individualism" — "the idea that the individual is the only firm reality."[8] On this foundation, many define freedom as the rejection of other people's values, ideas or lifestyles, so as to be free of "arbitrary authority" in work, family and political life.[9]

Bellah's *Habits of the Heart* concludes that for Americans "to be free is not simply to be left alone by others; it is also somehow to be your own person in the sense that you have defined who you are, decided for yourself what you want out of life, free as much as possible from the demands of conformity to family, friends or community."[10] Ironically, this understanding of "freedom" can lead to its opposite — conformity. Bellah summarizes Tocqueville's observations: "When one can no longer rely on tradition or authority, one inevitably looks to others for confirmation of one's judgments. Refusal to accept established opinion and anxious conformity to the opinions of one's peers turn out to be two sides of the same coin."[11]

The absence of "fixed standards" to define status can generate consumerism, whereby a person's worth is measured by "gross standards of income, consumption, and conformity to rational procedures for attaining ends"[12] — keeping up with the Joneses. Bellah notes the result: "a classic case of ambivalence.... We strongly assert the value of our self-reliance and autonomy. We deeply feel the emptiness of a life without sustaining social commitments. Yet we are hesitant to articulate our sense that we need one another as much as we need to stand alone, for fear that if we did we would lose our independence altogether."[13]

Is this tension between lonely independence and comfortable conformity inevitable? Tocqueville points out one way that Americans deal with this problem. Religion not only reinforces self-control and maintains moral standards, but also captures a positive and even contemplative vision that inspires benevolence and self-sacrifice. Christianity, he writes, teaches "that one ought to do good to those like oneself out of love for God. [Man] sees that the goal of God is order; he freely associates himself with that great design; and all the while sacrificing his particular interests to the admirable order of all things, he expects no other recompense than the pleasure of contemplating it."[14]

Bellah also suggests that traditions of "civic republicanism" and biblical religion offer ways of seeing "the individual in relation to the larger whole, a community and a tradition ... capable of sustaining genuine individuality and nurturing both public and private life."[15] Canadian philosopher Charles Taylor suggests that our modern world, plagued by a loss of meaning and a sense of interior fragmentation, needs something more. Resources for commitment to the greater whole must be grounded not only in exterior traditions, but also make sense within the interior search for meaning. People need to grasp, in Taylor's phrase, "an order inseparably indexed to a personal vision."[16] The experience of people living the Focolare spirituality in the United States responds to the concerns of both Bellah and Taylor.

In the United States, an individual's identity is often formed and judged by his or her occupation, and happiness is thought to come from success at work or in a profession. How does this dynamic play out in the lives of American members of the Focolare? The subsequent sections of this chapter focus on personal identity and fulfillment and how they have engaged questions regarding work, professional identity, money, and material goods.

Personal Identity and Fulfillment in the Discovery of God's Love

"When a person discovers that God loves him, when you discover this for yourself and you believe it, then everything is different. The more you live it, the more God allows you to understand, and everything changes." Nassor and his wife Eshe, Focolare members in pursuit of the "American dream," emigrated from Egypt to the Baltimore area in the early 1990s. "It's not an easy task," Nassor muses, "to move from a different culture to establish your life again in the U.S. Whatever English we spoke was with a British accent that made people laugh, so we said, 'It is better not to speak until we learn.'" While raising their two children, they did not always see eye to eye about what to retain from their own culture, and what "good things" from U.S. culture to adopt. "But God was patient with us," he said, "and seemed to be saying, 'Just love,' because it is under his control, not ours."

Both hold degrees in engineering, but when they arrived in the U.S. they worked in fast-food jobs to sustain their family. As Nassor assumed increasing responsibility within the hotel industry, he asked himself:

> So what kind of manager are you going to be? My co-workers don't have much education, and I don't really have the skills to give them all that they are lacking. But I do know that we have to consider the human being in every decision we make. If they need me to be the father or older brother, I'll be that. I took the opportunity a lot of times to attend funerals and weddings to really show them I care. I don't want to be a manager that just gets the job done, or some brilliant guy. I want to be what God wants me to be. I fail more than I succeed, but I would never change anything or go back, because from every single incident I have learned something to help me today to do what is right.

Nassor turned down a promotion that would have removed him from daily contact with the staff, "because this is where I feel fulfilled.... Why go elsewhere to boss everyone around? It's not about the money. That's not me."

• • •

"I had come so close to finishing my first year as a fourth-grade teacher. This was the fun part of the school year filled with award ceremonies and field trips, but God had other plans." Beth-Anne's limbs had started to fall asleep easily, followed by episodes of dizziness and vertigo. Then one morning she felt pressure in the back of her head, followed by a tingling sensation in her legs. By evening, when she could barely lift them, she headed to the emergency room. "On the way to the ER," Beth-Anne says, "I sent out a text message to all the Focolare young people in Boston asking for their prayers. Immediately, my cell phone was buzzing with supportive responses. I felt at peace; I was not alone. I was living this with them and for them." She reflects:

While in the hospital I was amazed at the love and support
of friends from the Focolare. Clare, who was in the middle
of studying for finals and preparing to go to Florida for a
presentation, came just to be with me in the hospital while
my mom went home to be with my little brother and sister.
When she had to leave, Paul who was also in the middle of
studying for finals, came and waited for two hours while I
was getting MRIs done. During this experience, these friends
gave me a big gift. They taught me the beauty of being able
to share my needs. I learned that by allowing myself to receive help and love, I can also love the one who is helping.

At twenty-five, Beth-Anne found herself borrowing her grandmother's cane. "As she handed it to me, she said, 'Here. This is your
new best friend.'" With a Focolare friend in his seventies she had a very
"unifying" conversation about the merits of a cane versus a walker.
"We both decided that a walker gives you more balance; I felt my hips
start to get out of place as I kept leaning to one side with the cane.
Strange how God gives you situations that allow you to have insight
into others' lives that you otherwise could not imagine." She continues:

The more I worked, the worse my symptoms became.
Upon my doctor's recommendation, I had to take medical
leave. I began to understand more that the only thing that
matters is to love. This I could do, love.

And I could use these moments to gain an appreciation
of those who also suffer. I reflected a lot on my younger
brother who had been ill and out of school for an
incredibly long time. Until my own experience of illness,
I did not know how to show him the compassion he
deserved because I did not grasp his suffering. As I began
to understand his situation more, I felt closer to him. This
insight alone was worth the whole experience.

Her doctors still do not understand the cause of her illness.

Not knowing what was wrong was a huge suffering. I prayed,
"God, the doctors don't understand what is happening
with my body, but you do and you are the ultimate healer.
You are the one to whom I need to entrust everything."
In the past I had asked for the ability to live in the present

moment and to be able to live with a faith so strong that I could entrust everything to God and feel at peace even in the most troubling times.

Well, God answered my prayers. As I had no idea of how my health would be in the future, I could only live in the present moment. This also helped me to gain insight on how to spend my time. I used to be always rushing from one thing to the next, not taking time to reflect on my blessings, or always focusing on what was next on my "to do list" rather than taking a few moments to have a conversation with my family, friends and coworkers.

As I began to focus more on the present moment, I began to feel a deep joy in my heart that had not been there in a long time. Things that before caused me anxiety, now seemed trivial. I had a renewed feeling of peace and found joy in the most daily activities; even brushing my teeth became a treat!

I realize that I might never discover what has caused this sickness, or be healed of it. But I have seen how it is bringing me closer to God. I have been able to let go of some of my old thoughts and habits that kept me away from God. This all is happening out of God's love for me. When I think of how much I've gained from this experience, I feel like I haven't lost anything.

• • •

How do Nassor and Beth-Anne perceive and live "the pursuit of happiness"? They both have the interpretive key that opens the door to the entire Focolare spirituality: receptivity to an experience of God's personal love, which transforms their perspective. This, in turn, shapes their sense of identity and reveals the meaning of their lives and their activity in the world.

Often, the story of Chiara Lubich's own discovery and experience of God's love provides an introduction for people who are learning about the Focolare. Many draw analogies between the uncertainty or suffering in their own lives and the context of the Movement's origins, a heavily bombed city where "everything was crumbling" — youthful plans to pursue a career, dreams of a beautiful and secure house, desire for a perfect family. In Taylor's framework, the source of identity and meaning they are poised to receive from *outside* the self at the same time resonates *within* — a sense of meaning "inseparably indexed to a personal vision."[17]

In 1943, Chiara was teaching in an orphanage when a young priest asked her to offer a part of her day for his intentions. She answered generously, "Why not the entire day?" Touched by her response, he responded, "Remember that God loves you immensely."[18] Chiara recalled, "It was like a lightning bolt — God loves me, God loves me!" She repeated it to her friends: "God loves you, God loves us immensely.... Since that moment we perceived God present everywhere with his love, in our enthusiasm, in our resolutions, in joyful and comforting events, in situations that were sad, awkward and difficult."[19]

From that moment, they felt God take the initiative in their lives, "present everywhere with his love ... not a God who is distant, immovable and inaccessible to people. God-Love who comes to meet every person in thousands of ways ... love in himself, love for all of his creation."[20] Chiara expresses her experience in a language of personal resonance. God "explained to us" in personal terms that "everything is love: all that we are and all that concerned us; that we were his children and he was our Father; that nothing escaped his love, not even our mistakes, because he permitted them; that his love enveloped Christians such as us, the church, the world, and the entire universe."[21]

For the group that first gathered around Chiara, God-Love became the frame of reference and the strength that bound them together. Chiara writes, "It is he, my God and your God, who has established a bond between us that is stronger than death."[22] This experience of believing in God's love became their name, the heart of their identity. "We believe in love. This is our new life. For this reason we have expressed our desire — should we die in the war — to be buried in a single tomb with the words that express our being, written as our name: 'And we have believed in love' (see 1 Jn 4:16)."[23]

This experience of God as love called forth a response — loving in return — which also shaped their identity. As she wrote to one of her young friends in 1944: "It is Love that has called us to love! ... You hope, you believe — in order to Love. This is your future, your present, your past. All is summed up in this word: Love! ... This is the destiny of every human being — Love! Let's leave to our hearts a single desire: to Love! Let's leave to our minds the measuring of every thought without exception against the infinite and immense love of God."[24] Later she reflects, "We would not have had any meaning in the world if we were not a little flame of this infinite fire: love that responds to Love."[25]

What did it mean for the initial group, and what does it mean for those, like Nassor and Beth-Anne, who live the Focolare spirituality now, to take as their framework the experience of believing in God's love and responding with love in return? A few defining features might help to interpret these experiences.

First, they are all *receptive*. In contrast to an insistence on individual self-definition, Chiara's experience was grounded in receiving the reality of God's love, "listening" to what God was saying to her about her life and their life together. Doing this did not suppress or impinge on her sense of freedom or personal fulfillment. On the contrary, the experience of God's personal love enveloping "all that we are and all that concerned us" filled their lives with meaning and purpose. As Nassor puts it, "when you discover this for yourself and you believe it, then everything is different." Their experience of an *external* source of meaning and purpose — God — opened them to an *internal* source of meaning — Love.

Second, the experience was and continues to be *relational*, in two ways. Right away, Chiara shared her insight with her friends and invited them to make the same discovery. "God loves me" extended from her individual experience to "God loves you, God loves us." In the Focolare spirituality, the dynamic relationship between self, neighbor, and God is "all one kingdom" (see p. 39). The path to God is found precisely in recognizing both how much God loves me and how much God loves my neighbor. Beth-Anne's experience of God's love in her illness helped her to build deeper relationships with others who had suffered — her grandmother, her older friend, and her brother — and with the young people she knew in Boston. Nassor saw that in his work as a manager he could be "a father or an older brother" if that is what the employees needed.

Because "all is summed up" in love, for Chiara and her initial group of friends love itself became their deepest sense of reality — their "name"; their "single desire"; the lens through which they could interpret their future, present, and past; their way of "measuring" reality; and a vision of "the destiny of every human being." Because love is "the destiny of every human being," finding one's identity in love resolves the seemingly irreconcilable tension between the interests of the self and those of others.

Third, the framework acknowledges the unmistakable value of *suffering*. Chiara and her friends made their discovery amid the chaos and darkness of World War II, in a city reduced to rubble, when destruction and hatred still threatened to have the last word. Like Chiara, Focolare members still see God-love present everywhere, not just in "joyful and comforting events," but also "in situations that were sad, awkward and difficult," even "in our mistakes." Jesus who cried out from the cross, "My God, my God, why have you forsaken me" (Mt 27:46), continues to be the model for people in the Focolare to recognize the loving hand of God amid difficult choices; in personal, familial and communal suffering; in encounters with failure and limitations; in receptivity to what God accomplishes in an individual's life through illness and ultimately through death. Beth-Anne puts it well: "This suffering was bringing me closer to God. This all happened out of God's love for me. When I think of how much I've gained from this experience, I feel like I haven't lost anything." Or as Nassor explains: "I can take any sadness, any discouragement, any disappointment, and see what God has done in our lives, and I find hope." In this way, suffering takes on a new meaning. It becomes a place to find the consoling presence of God and deeper union with him. It also becomes a springboard beyond suffering into a place of love for others.

This interpretive scheme includes not just the few people mentioned in these experiences, but everyone. "His love enveloped Christians such as us, the Church, the world, and the entire universe." The discovery of God's universal love for humankind establishes bonds that transcend social, economic, racial, ethnic, and generational divides. Within this vision people can experience being connected within the one human family, and so be inspired to work toward the social and economic well-being of their brothers and sisters.

Work and Professional Identity Grounded in Love

How does believing in God's love, and loving God and others in return affect a person's work and professional identity? Because the Focolare emerged from an essentially "lay" (not clerical) experience, and since most Focolare members support themselves by holding jobs, the spirituality projects a deep respect and regard for work. Chiara notes that Jesus, Mary, and Joseph were all workers.[26] Within the Movement, work is important not only as a means of economic support, but also as a spiritual path for cooperating with God as "co-creators," putting gifts and talents at the service of the larger community, and sharing with those in need.[27]

There is social pressure to derive a sense of identity and self-worth from what is done for a living. "So what do you do? Where do you work?" is often the first question when meeting someone, sometimes even before asking the person's name. The Focolare spirituality shifts this focus. A person's identity is grounded in the fact that they are immensely and personally loved by God, and in loving God in return.

Dennis, an engineering professor from Houston, describes how he has shifted his focus:

> Prior to meeting the Focolare, I had been living for the future, which for me meant getting tenure and a permanent faculty position. After meeting the Focolare, my focus changed, and I tried to love the person in front of me in the present moment. At day's end, I would ask myself how often I had loved or failed to love, rather than how much closer I was to getting tenure. After six years I was promoted and tenured, and although I worked hard at teaching and research, I saw in this the hundredfold promised to those who seek first the kingdom of God (see Mt 6:33).

Specifically, the Focolare spirituality shifts the perspective on work in at least two ways: first, in relation to those who because they are less "productive" might otherwise be marginalized from society; second, in relation to other time commitments and aspects of one's life.

Because those who live the spirituality are receptive to God's loving hand in suffering, "active" contribution and service to the community takes on a new meaning. Chiara explains the "hierarchy of love":

> At times we are tempted to see people who are suffering as marginal cases to be looked after, to be visited … to be helped if we can so that they may soon resume their activity, as if such activity were our primary duty, the center of our life. But this is not so. Those among us who are suffering, who are lying ill, who are dying, are the chosen ones. They are at the center of the hierarchy of love in the Movement. They are the ones who do the most, who achieve the most.[28]

Jerry and Sharon are married *focolarini* who moved from Chicago to Mariapolis Luminosa so they could put their skills at the disposition of the Movement. Jerry, a carpenter, dedicated a large part of his career to contracting and construction work for the Focolare community. Sharon was active in sustaining the Focolare families and other outreach activities. Twenty years into their marriage, Sharon was diagnosed with multiple sclerosis. Their journey as a couple living with the disease illustrates what it means in the Focolare to place those who are ill "at the center of the hierarchy of love."

Jerry describes his first reaction to the news: "When I first heard the word MS, I thought of all the people I had known with it and the crippling effects it had on them. I felt sick at the thought that this could happen to Sharon, but I knew I could not let her feel my fear. While together in the hospital, we talked about these changes in our life. We held firmly to the conviction that God loves us as a father, and this was in some way a gift for our family."

Due to the side effects of her medication, Sharon found herself struggling with unexpected anxiety and bouts of depression. "I was beginning to feel alone and forsaken. I did not want to give in to these feelings, but at times they were so strong that I felt I could not control them, and this too frightened me. I realized that in my own small measure I was going through something like what Jesus must have experienced when he felt abandoned on the cross." But then, an important turning point:

> One day in the hospital, as I struggled to conquer one of those moments, I read a spiritual thought by Chiara Lubich entitled, "Love of neighbor and our way to sanctity." I glanced to the person in the bed next to mine. I had been so wrapped up in my own concerns that I had totally lost sight of who was next to me. I introduced myself and we began to converse. I listened while she described all her problems and I felt peace come into my soul, and my own suffering slowly disappeared. Looking back, I realize that this was the turning point in my life.

Acknowledging that those who are ill "do the most" is not just a turn of a phrase. Jerry reflects:

> I could see Sharon was greeting people at the hospital with love, not looking for sympathy. This gave me the courage to do the same. Her illness was forcing us to change both our lives, but the changes she had to make were so much

greater than mine. She had been an outgoing person, involved in the activities of our five sons and capable of handling a lot of responsibility. Now she had to give up many of these commitments.

Her ability to do the will of God defined by this illness amazed me. She was still the same person but simply organized herself to deal with her illness, following all the directives from her doctor. He had told her she should rest two hours then she could work two hours. If I came home early for lunch, I'd say, "Let's eat," and she would answer, "Ten minutes more." Then she would get up and, because she was so organized, would accomplish a great deal, cooking meals, doing the laundry and being a comfort with her listening ear to me and all those who called or visited our home. When I came home from work exhausted or preoccupied, I would open the door to find her there welcoming me with her beautiful smile, as if she had no other concern but to be there totally for me. This melted my heart and made me forget all my burdens.

Our sons matured in a very balanced and wholesome way. The experience of watching how their mother has handled her sickness has given them the ability to be more sensitive and compassionate to others. What initially seemed like a tragedy turned out to be a gift from God, enriching our whole family and changing our lives. The difficulties and sufferings were turned into love.

The Focolare spirituality works a change in the way members perceive what lies at the center of life. Chiara perceived early on that God's love embraces "all that we are and all that concerned us" — not just work. Crèvecoeur's American farmer was animated with an "unfettered and unrestrained" spirit of industry, "because each person works for himself." In contrast, those who live the Focolare spirituality aim to "fetter" and "restrain" their work lest it consume the time they need for other aspects of life and for maintaining their relationships.

John directs a network of charter schools in inner-city Newark. At the beginning of his career he and his wife Daniela had made the choice to preserve time for each other, and for their three young children. At the beginning of his job, John got a clear message from his boss that if he wanted to grow in his job and to become a leader he would have to work very late hours. He and Daniela prayed about this, and decided that their family came first. They set aside six to nine in the evening as "sacred time together." With only a few exceptions, they have been able to maintain this commitment, and John was still able to grow in his career. "God continued to show us the way," he notes. "Seven years later, my boss actually offered me his job when he moved on, and we grew from one school to six."

The Focolare spirituality proposes that daily life be ordered according to seven expressions of love. Those who live in this way discover a sense of integrity in giving equal value to each of these aspects. They judge the time devoted to labor in light of their entire lives. Work is only one of seven aspects, alongside outreach, prayer and spiritual growth, care for personal health and the health of the community, care for clothing and the beauty of one's home, study, and attention to the means of social communication (see pp. 43–45).

Through this lens, time is not merely money, but a gift and an opportunity to love. Attention to aspects other than work becomes not just a mechanism for survival or stress relief, but an expression of love, each with its own place and value. "Non-work" chores such as cooking, cleaning, and laundry become opportunities to love one's family or community. Certainly moments arrive when deadlines or other work rhythms require extraordinary hours. But living the spirituality helps one to distinguish between genuine emergencies and the temptation to idolize work or professional advancement.

How does a spirituality of unity inform an approach to work? First, it allows an individual to cross boundaries set by professional hierarchies and levels of experience. Rosemarie, a physician, recounts one such example:

> One day as I was doing my rounds I asked one of the nurses a question regarding a patient. She answered me rudely, saying that she would feel much better if instead of asking the question I would bring her a cup of coffee. Feeling insulted, my first impulse was to answer back, but something inside of me suggested: "Don't miss your chance to understand and love this nurse. She is probably very tired." As soon as I had finished with the patients on that floor, I went to the cafeteria, bought a cup of coffee and a muffin, and brought them to her. She was surprised yet

happy with this simple gesture of love. A new relationship of trust and collaboration was established.

Leonard is the CEO of a medium-sized manufacturing business. One Monday morning an employee, Anton, came into his office with great excitement. He showed Leonard a real estate flyer and said, "My wife and I have found our own house to buy, and we can afford it! We are making an offer this afternoon." Anton had recently emigrated from Bosnia, and knew little about how financial matters worked in the United States. Leonard congratulated him, and asked if he had a mortgage commitment from a bank. Anton had no idea that he needed one. Leonard saw in this employee's predicament an opportunity to love. Setting aside his own agenda for that day, he used his business contacts to help Anton secure a mortgage. That evening the seller accepted their offer.

On another occasion an employee asked for a $1000 loan to help pay for a relative's funeral. At that moment the company did not have much money to spare. Nevertheless, Leonard gave this employee a $1000 check not as a loan, but as a bonus. Back in his office, he began to open the morning mail. The first envelope contained the largest check the company had ever received — an unexpected early payment from a dealer.

The Focolare spirituality also suggests how love can transform certain professional norms. John, a fourth year Houston medical student, had been assigned to a rotation in the Intensive Care Unit. On one occasion, he needed to discuss with a patient and her husband a care plan for the final stages of her illness. "Because of the pressures in the ICU, the time I could spend with the couple was limited but I managed to convey the reality that the patient was near death and any medical intervention would be fruitless. In the days that followed, recognizing how much the husband was suffering, I felt drawn to the bedside to offer whatever help I could."

At a certain point the husband asked John, "Would you pray with me?" "I was taken aback and felt a little embarrassed as I wondered what the other medical staff might think if they saw me praying with a patient. But then within an instant I overcame myself, realizing that it was more important to love than to save face. We prayed together every day until his wife died." After the funeral, the husband came back to thank the medical staff and John in particular. "He told me that if I act in the same way with all of my other patients, I will be an extraordinary physician. This confirmed for me why I had chosen to be a doctor and renewed my commitment to love."

Finding one's identity in love provides the strength to work through the conflicts that can arise in professional settings. Monica, the Director of Social Services in a shelter for homeless families in the South Bronx, recounts:

> One client greeted me with a barrage of foul language and accusations every time I had an encounter with her. At first I was taken aback. How could this woman stand there and accuse me of not doing my job! I became frustrated and entertained the thought of returning some of the aggression. Eventually, though, I chose a different kind of revenge: every time her venomous words attacked me, I countered with words and actions of love. I listened to her concerns and made them my own. Making it a priority to support her, I doubled my efforts and found housing for her and her family, without expecting anything in return. On her last day at the facility, she came to my office and graciously thanked me. The woman who had been visibly aggressive was now smiling.

Javier works in the customer service department of a Florida cell phone company. At the end of a long day he received a call from an irate customer who told him straight off that he did not know how to do his job.

> My first reaction was to tell her that what was happening in her account was her responsibility because she had not followed up in a timely manner. In that moment, however, a phrase of the gospel came to my mind: "Just as you did it to one of the least … you did it to me" (Mt 25:40). I tried to love her, first by listening attentively as she went on for a while explaining herself. By the time I finally got the chance to say something, I had already made up my mind that I wanted to speak to her as I would to Jesus. I could sense her surprise; she told me that when she calls the company, whoever answers always argues with her. She went on to apologize, recognizing that her case was not my fault, nor the company's.
>
> As we continued our conversation, I discovered in her a beautiful person. She shared that she had cancer and

was receiving chemotherapy. She was feeling terrible and scared. What started out as an aggressive phone call became a moment of God. A week later I had a chance to talk to her again, and she told me that she had kept our chat deep in her heart, and it had given her a new vision of each moment. I realized that Jesus had given me the chance to announce the gospel mostly through my listening.

Brianna, a doctoral student in immunology, does research in a New York City laboratory. Her project had been going well, producing original and possibly important results that needed to be written up. At the same time she had to focus on her qualifying comprehensive exams. Although the others in her lab seemed helpful on the surface, she could sense that they were positioning themselves to take credit for her work by putting their names in as authors of the paper. As she put it, "Friendly sharks are always sharks." She struggled: "How can I defend myself and my work, and still be a person who loves? Do I have the right personality to be working in such an ambitious and competitive environment?" She shared these concerns with other Focolare young people:

> Talking this through with the Gen helped me to name the frustration that I felt — Jesus forsaken was also surrounded, taken advantage of, not given credit. I realized that the cross that I had to pick up was to study for the comprehensive exam, and really accept that I might not be able to write the paper. For me, this discussion was like the "enzymatic catalyzer" that gave me positive energy to approach the situation from a better angle. In order to focus fully on the exam, I went to the lab, froze down my cells, and was able to let go completely.

She found that a sense of peace in doing "what God wanted from me right now" also helped her to love her colleagues in the lab. In this context, a short time later, the laboratory director recognized her hard work and made sure that she would appear as first author on the paper.

Frank is one of six members of the corporate leadership team for the worldwide operations of a large trading company. He explains how he lives a spirituality of unity in this context:

> During a global conference for 250 of our senior leaders, our team answered their questions live, on stage. There was no way to anticipate what I would be asked, nor how my

colleagues and I might help one another. As my colleagues were answering, I tried to empty myself of my own thoughts, worries, and ideas, listening with an open mind to everything they said. Despite the pressure and the responsibility I had to bear at that time, I felt no reason to fear anything.

The questions were not easy, but as the session continued, a sense of peace and collaboration spread through the team. If someone had something to add or to clarify, he offered his ideas respectfully. Even in cases where we differed in our opinions or in the information that we could offer, we did so with respect, charity, collaboration, even humor. I could see that the way we related to each was making a strong impression on the senior leaders.

After the session one of them commented, "The things that each of you actually said didn't matter so much, because the image we saw, one united team, cohesive, respectful, and supportive of each other, sent a far more powerful message than anything else."

Charles is the CEO of a software company in Northern Virginia. He recounts how the rest of the staff responded when one of their consultants was diagnosed with leukemia.

As the treatments went ahead, weeks became months, and we were moving toward long-term disability. Because of the atmosphere of mutual support that we have tried to sustain in the company for several years, at this point the employees all rallied together for their colleague. We sat down with the accountants and tax consultants, who explained that we could donate vacation days into a community pool. On the first shot, we managed to gather enough days so that our colleague could have full salary and benefits extended to eleven months. This totally changed his outlook.

In times of economic difficulty Focolare members, like many others, have had to participate in painful decisions about downsizing and layoffs. At the end of 2008, Charles asked himself, "How can I manage to love my workers and keep the company alive at the same time?" After pursuing all other cost-saving options, he had no option other than to downsize by thirty percent, affecting the lives of twenty-five workers. He knew that each of these people would have to seek employment in a very tight job market. Charles recounts: "I proposed to the board that we use our precious cash in order to give each employee the highest possible severance package. They looked at me as if I were crazy, but decided to approve it because we had been responsible in the past." Charles then spent a great deal of time helping each person find another position. "I got on the phone, working every possible contact, and serving as a reference for each employee." Before they had used up their severance packages, all twenty-five were able to find new positions. Two years later, when the firm began hiring again, Charles asked interviewees why they wanted to work for the company. Through Facebook, they were in contact with those who had been laid off, and they were following the glowing recommendations they had heard.

Daniel, a human resources manager for a California-based semiconductor company was dismayed to see his name on the list for a third round of layoffs. Knowing well how difficult the market was, he was filled with anxiety. What would he say to his son, who had his heart set on attending college the following fall? Then Daniel's boss asked if he was willing to manage the layoffs in his group before he would be laid off himself. If he said no, he would not have to make hard decisions as to who might be cut, nor would he have to face close to fifty employees, many of whom would be hard hit. But he decided to say yes. He explains: "I wanted to stay in the loop because I knew the people better than anyone else, and I might be able to help relocate some of them within the company. I decided to let go of my own hurt in order to do the right thing for the people in my group." Although he was not able to find another position for himself, he worked tirelessly to find openings within the company for others. He was able to place more than half of those who would have been laid off.

Perspectives on Money and Material Goods

What happens when believing in God's love and wanting to love God and others in return becomes the basis for relating to money and material goods? The Focolare spirituality does not render people immune to materialism and consumerism, but it does offer an ethical framework and sense of perspective. If people measure their economic and material needs against, to use Chiara's phrase, "the infinite and immense love of God," they are less likely to become caught up in comparing their income and consumption levels with those of their neighbors.[29] Nassor illustrates such a measure in his reasons for turning down a promotion: "It's not about the money. That's not me."

Similarly, Keith, who grew up in a family that "did not have a lot," reflects on how the Focolare spirituality changed his perspective on material goods:

> Growing up, when I saw people who had everything, I would come to the general conclusion that they must be happy. But then I realized that this was not the case, and it was confusing. Getting to understand more about the Focolare life, I started to find an answer to this question, and the pieces came together. I saw that being with people who loved one another, who did not go after material possessions, but who tried to be there for one another, in all their struggles and in life's difficulties, brought me the happiness I was seeking.

In the Focolare spirituality, sharing material goods has positive consequences. In addition to satisfying actual material needs, it also offers those who share an opportunity to grow in love for their neighbors, and opens individuals and the community to the providential love of God who meets his children's needs in unexpected ways.[30] Reflecting on choices about spending money, even small amounts, presents the opportunity to consider the needs of one's neighbors and to experience the ways that God meets daily needs and desires. For example, a person might put into common for others' needs the $5 saved from her lunch budget because she received a salami as a gift, or $2.25 when a beautiful day allowed her to walk instead of riding the bus. The amounts might seem insignificant, but these daily gestures reinforce an alternative approach to spending.

At first glance these choices to "deprive" oneself of goods might seem, to use Chiara's own words, "difficult, arduous, heroic." But, she insists, "It is not, because the human person, made in the image of God who is Love, finds fulfillment precisely in loving, in giving. This need to love lies in the deepest core of our being, whether we are believers or not."[31] For Focolare members, the virtue of poverty lies not in warding off the negative effects of excess goods, but in the positive expression of living as a family that cares for one another's material needs. Since its origins in war-torn Trent, the Focolare has emulated the first Christian community by practicing a "communion of goods" (see Acts 2:44–45).

Chiara suggested the regular practice of making a "bundle" of things that could be shared with those who need them, or sold. Her underlying rationale was to keep love "real." As she explained, "We know how easy it is, living in the world, to gradually accumulate objects which are useful more or less, or superfluous, and keep them in our homes. . . . If we collect our surplus and give it away, our charity toward our neighbor shall be real."[32] To explain the communion of goods, Chiara often used images from nature, advising young people to be like beautiful flowers that take from the ground only what they need.[33] Who does not want to be beautiful?

Children who grow up in an environment where the communion of goods is a fact of life become sensitive to this alternative perspective. For her seventh birthday, Mara asked not to receive any gifts, but instead that people make a donation to a school for low-income students in rural Mexico. Her friends' parents were so touched by Mara's gesture that they donated over $400, which the school used for sports equipment. At almost every birthday party, Mara and her younger sister Elisabeta make things to sell in order to raise money for various causes. Mara describes this practice to other children as "our own little way to holiness." After hearing about this, another little girl whose birthday was coming up wanted to do the same.

Frances, a fourth grader, came to her Gen meeting upset because a classmate had ripped her winter jacket, and her family could not afford to replace it. Perceiving this need as their own, the other children spread the word and within a day they found a new jacket for her.

Focolare communities also put their goods in common in response to specific needs. Caitlin, from New Jersey, recalls how the community responded when a family on a tight budget could not afford to repair their broken vacuum cleaner.

> That month's Word of Life was, "Sell your possessions, and give alms" (Lk 12:33). I lent them my vacuum cleaner for a week, confident that we would find one through God's providence. I sent an e-mail to our group, sharing the need. The following morning two friends called to say they each had an extra vacuum cleaner and another offered to check out what the local thrift shop might have. Not only did God take care of this need, he even offered the family a choice.

Business Life and Economic Development:
The Economy of Communion

In a recent interview, John Allen pressed Archbishop John Onaiyekan of Abuja, Nigeria, "to get concrete about what the West ought to do for Africa" — for example, lowering trade barriers or restructuring debt owed to the International Monetary Fund. When the bishop demurred, Allen asked directly, "What's the problem?" "The problem," the bishop answered, "is the way you phrased the question. You asked how the West can 'help' Africa. We're not interested in 'help' in the sense [that] we are exclusively the receivers of your generosity. We're interested in a new kind of relationship, in which all of us, as equals, work out the right way forward." What is needed, he challenged is a "change of mentality" — including within the Church. Economic development must be addressed, the archbishop added, "as brothers and sisters in one church, not as patrons in the West confronting objects of charity."[34]

What might such a "change of mentality" look like? The Focolare's project for an "Economy of Communion in Freedom" (EOC) illustrates the potential of a system of economic development based upon relationships of reciprocal giving and receiving. The EOC is grounded in the same practices concerning money and material goods discussed in the previous section. It embodies the conviction that human persons, as Chiara describes them, "find fulfillment precisely in loving, in giving."[35]

As the Movement spread throughout the world, people in the Focolare strived to meet the material needs of everyone in the community. Such needs, however, often outstripped resources. During a visit to Brazil in 1991, Chiara was moved by the circumstances of the people, including Focolare members, living in the *favelas* that surround Sao Paolo. Reflecting with the community on how to respond to these needs, the idea emerged to launch a new economic model. EOC businesses would generate jobs and commit to a three-part division of their profits: 1) direct aid to people in need; 2) educational projects to help foster a "culture of giving"; and 3) the continued growth and development of the business. There are now more than 700 businesses, most small and medium-sized; a few have more than 100 employees.

In his 2009 social encyclical, *Caritas in veritate*, Pope Benedict XVI notes one recent sign of economic hope — the development of a "broad intermediate area" of "traditional companies which nonetheless subscribe to social aid agreements in support of underdeveloped countries . . . and the diversified world of the so-called 'civil economy' and the 'economy of communion.'"[36] Many have connected the pope's description of businesses that consider profit as "a means for achieving human and social ends" and the Focolare's global EOC network.[37] George Weigel acknowledges the influence that the Focolare's "economy of communion" academics had in drafting the document, noting that this school of thought merits further discussion.[38] In the United States, EOC businesses include an environmental engineering firm, a violin atelier, a language school, a tutoring service, a law office, an organic farm, and various consulting businesses. North American EOC firms sustain their vision through contact with local Focolare communities and their "business to business" network with other EOC firms throughout the continent and the world. Quarterly conference calls, an annual national convention, and occasional international meetings provide opportunities to sustain their commitment to the project and refine their ideas.

Clare Marie DuMontier's Visitation Law Office in Appleton, Wisconsin, provides guardianship services for the elderly. An interview in *Our Sunday Visitor* describes a simple yet essential benefit of her connection with the EOC: "What I love about working in an Economy of Communion business," DuMontier notes, "is that my entire life in Christ is united — my work, as well as my family life and community life."[39] She had considered leaving the profession because of the conflict that suffused the legal environments in which she had worked. A spirituality of unity has given her the tools "to stay calm and persevere, and to love in the most stressful circumstances."[40]

The businesses commit themselves to infusing all their relation-ships — with employees, customers, suppliers, regulatory agencies, the general public, and the environment around them — with values of love and respect. For example, John Welch is CEO of Consort International, which produces high-quality stringed instruments. He needed to check on the status of a large outstanding balance from a dealer who he knew was having serious financial trouble. From time to time, Welch would call to see how he was doing. During one of these calls, the dealer got choked up and said, "John, everyone else calls to threaten me. You call to give me encouragement."

How do EOC businesses function in a competitive environment? A former student asked Miriam Turri, who operates "La Parola," an

Italian language school in Denver, to help his wife set up what in effect would be a competitor. Turri recounts how the Golden Rule spurred her to love. "I invited the wife to participate as an observer at a beginners' class. I gave her copies of all my materials and ideas for games that I use with my students. She has since become a dear friend of mine, and her children too. Her business is coming along and I continue to offer my help."

John Mundell is the founder and CEO of Mundell & Associates, an environmental reclamation consulting firm in Indianapolis.

> It's a twist on the American way, but in an EOC business, we try to see competitors not as the ones to beat, but as people with whom we can build relationships. Since we started, we have tried to follow the principle of never speaking ill of a competitor. It's tempting when someone calls seeking negative information about them, but we refrain. We compete only by the quality of our product and our service. We have even helped people in our area to start similar companies, sharing with them how we started, how to avoid the mistakes that we made, and sending along resumes of good people when they don't serve our own employment needs.
>
> Also, when asked to testify in court, it is tempting to go on about a competitor's mistakes. But I try to make it a point to also say what they did right. We saw one result of building these kinds of relationships when we were involved in a fairly large bid for a sophisticated project in another state. When the attorney for the city stood up to say how our references checked out, he confessed that he had spoken not only with our client referrals, but also with our competitors. "I tried to get the dirt on this company, to find out what they do not do well, and I have never heard such glowing remarks from competitors. I have no reservations about hiring these people."

EOC businesses also consider how to foster reciprocal relationships in their local environments. For example, Mundell decided to relocate their offices, to encourage economic development in a distressed part of the city.

> We decided to hire local people to fix the roof and do the landscaping. We have developed close relationships with the smaller coffee shops and restaurants in the neighborhood, and have offered our employees gift certificates to

be used at these businesses. The local Catholic school was not able to support much curricular enrichment, so we sponsored a workshop for them on protecting wildlife and hired another business that was also going through a hard time to develop it. Our employees also volunteer at the food pantry in the nearby Disciples of Christ church. As a service to the community, some of our employees and their spouses helped to fix up a run-down house in a poorer part of our neighborhood. It just so happened that a television crew came by that day, and seeing what we were doing they featured us on the evening news. Because of that coverage, three years later we obtained a $50,000 contract.

Some of the more developed EOC businesses have been able to offer internship programs so undergraduate and graduate students can experience from the inside how these firms operate. Elizabeth, who had done research on the EOC model in college, interned with Mundell & Associates. The experience helped her, as she puts it, to "see the challenges in a clearer way, especially in understanding relationships with employees. I came away convinced that you can build a sense of family in a workplace. This experience has had a big influence on my career choices, and my current work with small business and microfinance."

Those helped by EOC businesses are active participants in the project, part of the same community, committed to living the culture of giving.[41] This culture assumes that everyone, of any economic status, has something to give — understanding, attention, forgiveness, a smile, time, talents, ideas and help. In fact, those in need participated in founding the initial EOC businesses. Hundreds pooled their resources, often selling chickens or other livestock to purchase "shares" to raise initial capital. Sharing one's needs, with dignity and sincerity, is an essential contribution to the life of communion.

Direct aid from the EOC has been used primarily to provide temporary assistance for the unemployed, for students who cannot afford schooling, and for those facing unexpected illness or personal calamity. Many of those who receive help relinquish it as soon as they establish minimal economic independence. A young man from Nigeria who used EOC aid to finish high school and find a better job wrote, "Now it is time for me to help someone else whom I do not know but who needs my small contribution, as I was helped. I ask God that he may always give me a heart as big as his, in order to see others' needs."[42]

The EOC has also established credit and micro-credit programs. For example, a Serbian mushroom farm used an EOC loan to install a heating, ventilation and irrigation system and to purchase a delivery van. A small Indonesian supermarket received seed funds to subsidize prices so that those without means could buy necessities at a discount; the store in turn was able to employ fourteen additional people. A Brazilian bakery purchased start-up equipment and now employs four full time and two part-time workers. A loan helped a Bulgarian family farm survive a drought; within the year they repaid a large part of the loan. EOC funds helped a Croatian stocking factory purchase a fabric machine, creating new jobs.

Surveying the U.S. experience, EOC businesses are neither the first nor will they be the last experiment with "hybrids" that integrate aspects of non-profit, profit-based, and socially responsible business models. The tendency to link "self-interest" with concern for the common good runs deep in the American mentality. Tocqueville observed that Americans "are pleased to explain almost all the actions of their life with the aid of self-interest well understood; they complacently show how the enlightened love of themselves constantly brings them to aid each other and disposes them willingly to sacrifice a part of their time and their wealth to the good of the state."[43] Ever practical, Tocqueville notes, "American moralists do not claim that one must sacrifice oneself to those like oneself because it is great to do it; but they say boldly that such sacrifices are as necessary to the one who imposes them on himself as to the one who profits from them."[44]

To what extent does the Focolare's economic experience resemble Tocqueville's principle of "self-interest well understood"? Is the "culture of giving" an example of that quintessentially American tendency to explain "how the enlightened love of themselves" leads Americans "to aid each other" and to sacrifice their time and their wealth? Can the EOC be considered an example of how "such sacrifices are as necessary" to the one who makes them as to the one who benefits? Is this the vein that Chiara was tapping when she explained that the "culture of giving" might seem to be difficult, arduous and heroic, but it is not?

Some who study the intersection of religious and corporate social responsibility ask how religion might be "used" to encourage a broader and deeper commitment to the common good. They hope to harness for good the tendency to pursue material interests rather than let such pursuit run wild. But Tocqueville worried that "self-interest well understood" might not be strong enough to ground a culture over time. Political theorist Brian Danoff explains Tocqueville's fears that "utilitarian and economistic arguments for civil commitment may, over time, fail to rein in or 'master' the destructive passions of the human soul."[45]

The Economy of Communion offers more staying power than "self-interest well understood." It is founded on the belief that human beings, made in the image of God who is Love, find their true "self-interest" in loving, in giving. In *Caritas in veritate* Pope Benedict XVI explains that the "more authentically" one lives in the dynamic of interpersonal relationships, the more one's own "personal identity" matures.[46] Chiara affirms, "I am myself ... when I give myself."[47]

For those who participate in the Economy of Communion, sharing their profits with those in need is simply a logical expression of their identity as members of the universal human family, and a sign of their connection to this family. Similarly, the protagonist in the work of the Focolare community to improve economic and social structures is not the generous individual or the ingenious problem-solver. Rather it is the presence of Christ in the community that emerges through relationships of mutual love by which all discover how they have been created as "gift" for each other.

7
The Focolare Spirituality, the Moral Life, and the Quest for Freedom

Let Freedom Ring

"Proclaim liberty throughout all the land unto all the inhabitants thereof," reads the inscription on the Liberty Bell, which on July 8, 1776 rang out from Independence Hall, summoning the citizens of Philadelphia to the first public reading of the Declaration of Independence. According to Robert Bellah, "Freedom is perhaps the most resonant, deeply held American value.... In some ways, it defines the good in both personal and political life." The quest for freedom, understood as the power to "be your own person," to define who you are and decide for yourself what you want, "free as much as possible from the demands of conformity to family, friends or community,"[1] pervades American culture and daily life.

In *Planned Parenthood v. Casey,* a ruling on an abortion regulation case, a plurality of the United States Supreme Court articulates this notion of freedom: "At the heart of liberty is the right to define one's own concept of existence, of meaning, of the universe, and of the mystery of human life."[2]

What happens when such a definition of freedom alone informs a person's core sense of self? Bellah explains: "If the self is defined by its ability to choose its own values ... there is simply no objectifiable criterion for choosing one value or course of action over another.... The right act is simply the one that yields ... the most exciting challenge or the most good feeling."[3]

A framework of freedom in this sense provides little guidance in approaching fundamental questions in life. "Ideas of the self's inner expansion reveal nothing of the shape moral character should take, the limits it should respect, and the community it should serve.... Why should we do one thing rather than another, especially when we don't happen to feel like it or don't find it profitable?"[4]

Ironically, a system of social interactions in which each self "constitutes its own moral universe" and "feelings become our only moral guide"[5] leads to its own kind of slavish conformity.[6] One of the

155

interviewees in *Habits of the Heart* describes such a life as "a big pinball game and you have to be able to move and adjust yourself to situations if you are going to enjoy it."[7] "A self free of absolute values or rigid moral obligations can alter its behavior to adapt to others and to various social roles," Bellah notes. "It can play all of them as a game, keeping particular social identities at an arm's length, yet never changing its own 'basic' identity, because that identity depends only on discovering and pursuing its own personal wants and inner impulses."[8]

Where do those who reject the "pinball" version of life find clear standards to evaluate fundamental questions and guide their social interactions without sacrificing their freedom? Charles Taylor's caution bears repeating. Moral guidelines need to be expressed in a language suited for their times. Turning to *outside* sources of moral guidance does not eliminate the need for a language that allows these standards to resonate *within*.[9] While absolute values never change, how a moral guideline is expressed in one era may not be clear in another.

The remaining sections of this chapter explore how the Focolare spirituality defines and illuminates freedom, and how individuals reconcile their personal identity with external sources of moral authority. It also considers how they face and find meaning in circumstances beyond their control, such as illness and death.

Discovering Freedom through Living a Spirituality of Unity

"My mother and father taught us the value of honesty and integrity in school," Laura, a middle-school student from Texas, reflects.

> But I have sometimes found myself in conflict, especially for the simplest things, like not letting other students copy my homework. My classmates would come to me sometimes because they had forgotten to do their homework or because they couldn't understand a problem. I would think: "They are my friends. How could I not help them?" Sometimes I would give in and slip them a few answers, but each time I would dread the feeling I had inside because — even if it was so insignificant, or I did it just once in a while — dishonesty was dishonesty. I hated cheating and letting others cheat off of me. One day, risking mockery from my friends, I finally told them how I felt and talked to them about this issue in light of the ideal of mutual love that I try to live. To my surprise, my friends actually seemed

to understand my reasoning. Now, they come up to me not to cheat, but to ask how to do something or even to tell me that they finished their homework on their own! Doing their own homework, they are doing better in our classes.

The experience of Keri, a ten-year-old from Indiana, demonstrates how she has constructed a "personal vision" in the exercise of freedom.

A boy in my class in school was making fun of me. My friends said he was mean, and they began to say bad things about him. I decided to be the one to love and to forgive him for saying things about me. I complimented him on the things he was good at, and he stopped making fun of me and everyone else, too! When he changed, my friends thought better of him. I think this is the way Jesus wants me to love!

Elizabeth, twenty-five, lives and works in Boston.

When people see the choices I am making in my life, I get both positive and negative reactions. I think that depends on whether they feel threatened, because it can be frightening to be challenged to work through your own values. For a while I focused more on living and giving an example. But lately I feel that I need to become more verbal. For example, when a conversation is taking a turn that I disagree with, sometimes on topics regarding sexuality, I have started to interject something about what I think. Sometimes it makes someone uncomfortable, and I get labeled as a goody-goody. Other times I encounter respect. Recently I was walking to the train with a colleague and just out of the blue she looked at me and said, "You are a Christian, aren't you?" I felt like she was trying to put together the pieces of what she saw in various interactions. So this started a long conversation where I mostly just listened, trying to give space for her to share what was in her soul, because she is really searching.

• • •

Children, young people, and adults find in the Focolare spirituality a template for constructing a coherent sense of self and moral orientation. *External* authority (God) becomes *internal*, a source of meaning that comes from within (Love). Keri's joyful simplicity captures this well: "I think this is the way Jesus wants me to love!"

Equally important for those who live the Focolare spirituality is their commitment to travel this path of love *together*, whether as a family, as a small group, or as a larger community. This bond of love, the presence of Christ in the community (see Mt 18:20), helps each person tap into the insight needed for understanding in particular situations what it means to love. Monica describes this commitment:

> Alone I could arrive to an intellectual understanding that the unity of humanity through love is essential, but it was from those who live the Focolare spirituality that I learned how to put this love into practice freely. It is really my choice to do it. This caused significant changes in my way of life — to put others first and to value suffering. I learned that as long as my love for God is my compass and love for others is my map, I will not get lost. I will find my way. When I become discouraged and overwhelmed with negative emotions, living the spirituality of unity provides me with strength in my day-to-day life.

For Chiara and her friends, the desire to live a life of "love that responds to Love" directed them to another external source of authority through which they could orient themselves: the gospel, which they read and put into practice, phrase by phrase. "Whenever the sirens sounded we rushed into the shelters, unable to bring anything along other than a small book of the gospels. In it we could find what Jesus wanted of us — his will. So we opened it. It was wonderful. Those words which we had heard many times were illuminated as though lit from within."[10] The guidelines for daily life that emerged from scripture were not cold or "rigid" obligations standing in the way of free "adjustments" in the pinball game of life. Instead, they were something "wonderful" — a lighted path that led to the freedom to live a life of love in response to God's love.

This same sense of freedom and gratitude permeates how Focolare members perceive and accept external norms of behavior. Many find in its spirituality an entry point for understanding, engaging with and eventually adhering to the moral guidance that their own church or religious community offers.

In the light of the presence of Christ in the community, by whom "all things hold together" (Col 1:17), moral teaching comes to be seen as God's own gift of love. Chiara explains:

When reciprocal love is lived, isn't it Jesus, alive in our midst, whom we experience? Isn't He the one whom others meet when they come into contact with us, and in their turn, make this same experience? But it is precisely because they either directly or indirectly make this experience of God that persons who are far from Him accept as logical, almost without rationalizing, everything that lies behind this experience…. They accept all things whose purpose is to draw people to God, to allow them to make the experience of God and His Kingdom.[11]

Ed's story reflects deep gratitude for a path that helped him to adhere to the moral principles of his faith. He grew up in the middle of farm country in rural Washington State. Following graduation from high school, he enlisted in the Air Force and found himself confronted with moral and ethical challenges.

When I entered the military I had a fairly clear understanding of my own convictions and values, but soon discovered that I had much to learn about how to hold on to them and express them openly. Like most newly enlisted, I wanted to be part of the group, but certain lifestyle choices contradicted my beliefs and how I understood I should live a Christian life. I was in turmoil. I found I didn't have the courage to be different. I simply didn't want to be left out.

One Sunday during church services I felt particularly troubled. I had been out with my "new buddies" the night before and had nearly compromised my core values. During Mass all I could do was weigh my options — let go of my convictions and just have "fun," or make a definitive choice to follow God. It wasn't easy. As I prayed I told God that if he wanted me to succeed he'd have to help me find friends who shared the same values and convictions. I received a response almost immediately.

During my final two years of service, at a base in New Mexico, I met a member of the Focolare, who in turn invited me to meet his friends. I was impressed with their sincerity and genuine efforts and struggles to put the gospel message of love into daily action. Their experiences of the gospel "lived" challenged me in ways I hadn't considered, and I found myself doing small yet courageous acts of unconditional love that I would have never done before. The way my fellow airmen expressed their approval of how I responded to difficult choices led me to the conviction that the world is thirsting to see love in action.

Resources for Personal Growth and Decision-Making

Bellah notes that many Americans define the heart of "psychological freedom" as "separating oneself from the values imposed by one's past or by conformity to one's social milieu, so that one can discover what one really wants."[12] Robert Wuthnow, a sociologist of religion, points out an unintended consequence of defining freedom in this way. In his study of self-help and support groups, Wuthnow observes that some might seem to be caring for and helping one another, but actually are perpetuating the problem by "being alone together."

> Some small groups merely provide occasions for individuals to focus on themselves in the presence of others. The social contract binding members together asserts only the weakest of obligations. Come if you have time. Talk if you feel like it. Respect everyone's opinion. Never criticize. Leave quietly if you become dissatisfied.... We can imagine that [these small groups] really substitute for families, neighborhoods, and broader community attachments that may demand lifelong commitments, when, in fact, they do not.[13]

As described in Chapter Three, Focolare members generally participate in small communities that share the same vocational path. They offer each other practical help in the course of their spiritual journey through the "instruments" of the spirituality of unity. Several features of these small group dynamics keep them from devolving into "being alone together."

For example, those sharing an experience of living the Word of Life do not speak merely because "[they] feel like it." Instead, they recognize that they have a responsibility to communicate the gift of the work of God within them. "Communion of soul" might include details about personal struggles and efforts, but here, the protagonist is God at work in each person's life.

Those who listen, receive, and respond do so not with the superficial distance of "respect everyone's opinion," but with the intention to love as Jesus loved — he gave his life. Empty of all preconceptions and judgments, they generate a dynamic in which the presence of Christ himself can illuminate what the other has to say and the work of God in each person in the group (see Mt 18:20). Advice to "never criticize" or "leave quietly if you become dissatisfied" demonstrates a reluctance to address differences or faults. In contrast, the "pact" of mutual love calls forth the responsibility to provide for one's neighbor an "eye in the back of their head" that helps them see how to grow and improve.

Scott, a professional in his mid-twenties, lives and works in Indianapolis. As he prepares to make life decisions concerning career and family, he describes how he has shaped his "personal vision" through interaction with other young men from diverse backgrounds.

> Communitarian life is not unique to the Gen, but it is an important part of who we are. Part of what Gen do is put their experiences in common. I remember when I was in high school, during a trip to Rome, talking with a Gen who was much older than I. It was the first time I had an open conversation about boy-girl relationships with someone older than me who was not married. It was great to have advice from someone older, to bat around experiences and ideas about what is wrong and right. Gen are diverse, and that's the point. There are city Gen, rural Gen, older, younger, and we are all trying to do the same thing.

As a recently divorced mother with two small children, trying to sort out her relationship with their father, Jorie found herself full of questions: Didn't I need to protect myself? Didn't I need to listen to my attorney? Her Focolare friends helped her to work this through. "They encouraged me to put unity first, not only with the boys, but also in my interactions with their father. This helped me to begin to try to make decisions that would lead to unity rather than disunity."

The experience of "Jesus in the midst," the fulfillment of his promise to be there "wherever two or more are gathered in my name" (Mt 18:20), helps to burn away tendencies to "focus on oneself in the presence of others." The presence of Christ in the small group is experienced as a bond of unity between the interior and the exterior — the interior life of the presence of Christ in each person with the exterior life of the others and with the group as a whole. In fact, Chiara has described this presence as a "loudspeaker" that amplifies the voice of God within each person, allowing them to hear what they need to make a decision, or to confirm their resolve to maintain a certain course of action.

Elizabeth describes this dynamic among the Gen:

> When I had to make important decisions about my studies, such as figuring out what to do for my senior research project, I was in constant communication with the other Gen and with my Gen assistant.* I grew up with a tendency, like many young people in the U.S., to be strongly independent and self-reliant. Sometimes it takes a concerted effort to share with others what I am thinking. The image of "Jesus in the midst" as an "amplifier" for the voice of God within has been helpful for me, leading to beautiful moments of communion with the others. When there is this presence of Jesus in the midst, you feel that something in you changes, it gives you more clarity. It was not that these moments gave me a direct answer. That came later.

After a night of freshman college drinking, Tamar remembers attending a meeting at the Focolare house with other young people. Although the effects of her hangover were probably visible, none of the women in the house gave the least hint of noticing, other than, perhaps, to give her a glass of water. But the "loudspeaker" of the presence of Christ in the community was more than effective. She recalls word for word the question that Jesus himself planted in her heart: "So when are you going to stop living a double life?"

Freedom in Dating, Engagement, and Marriage

The Focolare spirituality provides a framework for young people as they enter into deeper intimacy through dating, engagement, and marriage. The community often provides the support and encouragement they need to swim against the tide of prevailing social mores, and also to generate new trends in the environments where they live and work. Elizabeth explains:

> When I think about what living the Focolare spirituality brings to a dating experience, I see how it is enhanced by

---

* While the Gen assume leadership for the youth branches, the small groups are also accompanied by an adult, usually a *focolarino* or *focolarina*, who assists in their formation and helps them to live the Focolare spirituality in their daily lives and activities.

being part of a larger community. Introducing other people into our experience as a couple opens us up to the possibility of discovering a new kind of love that doesn't turn in on itself but reflects the divine commandment — "love one another as I have loved you." This has helped us to understand how we, as a couple who are dating and discerning our vocations, can be a gift for those around us as much as others are a gift for us.

Elizabeth's boyfriend, Paul, also lives the Focolare spirituality. He adds:

I agree that being open to the presence of others helps us to grow as a couple. In social situations, witnessing Elizabeth's love for others enriches my love for her. I have also understood that it is important to love someone enough to leave them free, even if that separates us as a couple. This goes against the possessiveness rampant in modern relationships. It brings you to the point where letting the other discern what God may want for them becomes as important to you as discerning what God wants from you.

Bridget, who grew up in Kentucky, has been a Gen since childhood. Liam, from rural Illinois, knew nothing of the Focolare until they met in college. Their journey through dating and engagement to marriage illustrates how a young couple can find guidance and support from peers and adults as they embark on a life together.

Liam explains how their relationship began.

We took the time to form a friendship slowly and to approach it as naturally as possible, without forcing the development. This was key in cultivating a healthy foundation. We discovered that many of the decisions we had made before we met each other had really prepared us for the relationship we would have. We both were uncomfortable with how our friends would jump into serious relationships one after another. We liked the idea of having many friends, and never forcing ourselves into something that did not seem right. In this way, when we met, we both felt comfortable around each other and never had any pressure to pretend we were something we were not. This freedom allowed us to express how we felt about many things in life, our faith, and what we wanted to do in the future, including what was right for a relationship before marriage.

Bridget explains how the decision she and Liam had made affected them:

> The absence of sex allowed space for our faith to grow, together, rather than allowing sex to take over the relationship. Now that we are married, with all the graces of the sacrament, we can see how developing our faith together was also important for the future physical aspect of our marriage, and for learning to appreciate and love each other in many different ways. Waiting until marriage allowed each of us to remain truly free and open to God's will, always asking if our relationship was what he wanted for us. We both had the freedom to end it, without regretting anything, knowing that even the time invested was worthwhile because we had learned how to love.

Therese and Paulo both grew up living the Focolare spirituality, and have made it an integral part of how they relate to each other, particularly when they disagree.

> Therese: There are moments when our relationship is not going well. Sometimes it seems like there is no way out, and I understand why people separate.

> Paulo: Once, we had been arguing about the same question for days, to the point of exhaustion. She would not budge, and I would certainly not move.

> Therese: Then I really put my foot in my mouth and our relationship was shattered. I felt like I hit a wall, and thought there is no way I can make our relationship open again. That's it. But at that moment, I remembered Jesus forsaken. I can look at this disunity and see Jesus. This is you. I love you, even if this disunity will not go away for eons. Then the next step is to go out of myself to love in that moment. Change the diaper. Make the dinner. In making the effort to love Jesus forsaken, I understood that I was the one who was not listening. I was the one who was not ready to let go of my idea.

Paulo: I don't recall how it happened. We started to listen to each other, we tried to accept one another and accept our different ideas. This helped us to begin opening up.

Therese: When we finally did talk about this problem, I put my foot in my mouth again. Recognizing Jesus forsaken in our moments of suffering is not magic. But at a certain point our talking went from arguing to sharing.

Paulo: I don't think that the argument itself was resolved. But her view was now also mine, and mine became hers. In that moment we felt united. The problems and difficulties did not go away. But we felt a load off our shoulders, we saw things more clearly and we were at peace. We could go ahead.

Illness and Death in the Light of a Spirituality of Unity

A youth-oriented and health-focused culture tends to marginalize experiences of illness and preparations for death. These inescapable facts of life trump the freedom individuals think they have to define their own existence and to control external circumstances. The Focolare spirituality offers a way to evaluate these fundamental questions, while drawing on the support of the community. In its "hierarchy of love," suffering, illness and preparing for death become central to the life of unity. Openness to the living presence of Christ, who sustains not only the ill or the dying but all those around them, has brought to Focolare communities particular light and strength.

Anthony, a married *focolarino,* lives in New Jersey. His kidney problems had worsened for several years, requiring at one point that he receive dialysis three times a week.

With each visit I would entrust everything to God, and ask for the gift of being able to love the people beside me, and to share in their suffering. We are usually assigned the same seats for dialysis, so we get to know our seatmates. A few months into my treatment, I noticed that the lady on my right spoke Italian. I said a few words in Italian, and all of a sudden her eyes glowed with joy. I became her official translator because she had a hard time communicating with the nurses and the medical staff. One day her son, who usually picked her up after the treatment, approached me while I was still hooked up to the dialysis machine. He told me, "Anthony, you cannot imagine how happy my mother is to have you around."

I also tried to befriend the lady on my left. On one occasion, as I was leaving I greeted her, saying "have a nice weekend." She was so upset that she shouted back, "I'm not going to have a good weekend!" After that reaction, during our subsequent treatments I tried to be more sensitive, just giving her a smile or attending to what she needed, such as fixing her TV screen, buying her popcorn (which she loved), or just listening when she wanted to talk. Then one day, all of a sudden she became very friendly. She started to show me her paintings, and always brought me something — fruit, a cookie, or even chips. We were not allowed to eat during the four hour treatment and so she would tell me, "That's for later."

Anthony kept hoping for a donor match. In the meantime one of the *focolarini*, Peter, had moved from Chicago to Manhattan. Peter notes, "I considered Anthony as my brother, and it passed through my mind that maybe I could donate a kidney for him." Nothing came of that initial thought, but later, at a Holy Thursday liturgy, the idea unexpectedly returned. Peter recalls, "Out of the blue a question came up in my mind: 'Are you still willing to donate a kidney?' I was quite surprised, because I had not thought about it for some weeks. It felt like an inspiration, as if Jesus were asking me to do it. So I considered it very carefully and felt totally at peace with the idea."

Shortly afterwards, having learned by chance that he and Anthony shared the same blood type, Peter thought that this might be a confirmation. After talking this through with other *focolarini*, Peter and Anthony decided to go ahead with the transplant. After the procedure, Anthony no longer needed dialysis. Still, he chose to stay in touch with his fellow patients, with whom he had developed such close relationships. He explains:

> I wanted to go back to visit my friends, but was worried that they might feel bad seeing that I no longer needed dialysis while they still did. But the social worker suggested that I go ahead, as it might give them hope that one day they

could also live a normal life. When I entered the dialysis center, they were all happy to see me and to see how well I was doing. It was wonderful to reconnect, and this too was an experience of God's personal love.

The Focolare's "hierarchy of love" also transforms the preparation for death into an experience of the living presence of Christ. Sheri Schiltz lived in the outer suburbs of Chicago. When she was nine years old, she met the Focolare spirituality and it became an integral part of her life. When she was eighteen, the first symptoms of leukemia presented themselves. The disease advanced rapidly, and she and her mother went to Seattle for a bone marrow transplant procedure. She describes her experience there:

> In the room with me there was an older lady who had had the same kind of transplant two weeks before mine. I noticed that the same ailments from the therapy would eventually reach me too. Then one day I learned that she had died. This scared me, thinking the same thing will happen to me, too. But then I said "yes" to the will of God, and decided not to worry, sure of his love. With Mom we helped each other to live moment by moment. Many times we had to renew our faith in the love of God, certain that he would take care of us.[14]

One day during a particularly rough moment, almost unable to speak because of the sores in her mouth, she heard the other Gen, who had come to her home to sing for her. In their act of love, she found new courage to overcome the pain. After that episode, the disease went into remission. Reflecting on her experience, Sheri said, "Sometimes I feel overcome by the fear of a relapse, but each time I try to renew my 'yes' to God. I understand that none of us knows how long we will live. This experience has helped me to decide to live the gospel better than before."[15]

When the symptoms reappeared, she realized it was unlikely that she would get better. She explained the impact this had on her relationship with God: "Before I would pray to be healed. But now I understood that God wants to bring me closer to him, exactly with this illness. So now instead of praying only for physical health, I started to ask him, above all, for the grace to become closer to him."[16]

As the illness progressed, she continued to share what God was working in her. Unable to attend a summer school of formation at

Mariapolis Luminosa with the other Gen, she called them every morning to share together the resolutions they hoped to put into practice. Every evening they would call her to recount what had happened during the day. During these conversations, Sheri would not speak of her illness or of death, but of how she had lived. Her experiences were often as simple as picking something up off the floor for her mother, or how a medical visit had gone. For example: "There was a tense atmosphere in the waiting room. Next to me a lady was crocheting, so I asked her to show me how she does it. After we talked a while, I realized that she was much more peaceful."[17]

After Sheri had passed away, many of her Catholic friends and family who had distanced themselves from practicing their faith returned to the sacraments. Before the onset of the illness, she had worked in a hospital office. After her death, her supervisor wrote, "This year we lost Sheri Schiltz, due to leukemia, at the age of twenty-five. She worked in the administrative office, and was an example for all of us. She never complained, even though the pain was great. She was a saint."[18]

Maria Pereira had immigrated to the United States from Cuba when she was fourteen. Life in America offered her everything that she had dreamed about — a good job, education, even a new Mustang. But at a certain point she became disillusioned and asked herself, "Is it possible that one day I will die and there will be nothing left? I had found that a new car could make me happy for a few days, a party for a few hours. I wanted much more out of life."[19]

At a Mariapolis she discovered a larger purpose for her life. "It struck me like lightning what all these people were trying to do, to work so that 'all may be one' (see Jn 17:21). For a moment I understood the greatness of this undertaking, a revolution of love that could change the whole world, and I wanted to be part of it." For thirty years, she lived in Focolare community houses throughout the U.S., Canada, and the Dominican Republic, often in positions of leadership.

While serving as co-director for the West Coast region, she was diagnosed with stomach cancer. She took this news as an occasion to share with the community the depth of her love for God and her readiness to do his will. She told a *focolarina* who lived in the Northern California Focolare house, "We are in God's hands. He has a plan for me and for all of you." Realizing that her friend was crying, Maria said, "Even in this suffering we have to be strong for the others."

"She was saying this with so much peace," says the other *focolarina*, "it gave me the strength to say yes." Then, so that her friend would not lose hope, Maria added that they could still pray for a miracle. Doctors tried every possible therapy, but the tumor continued to grow. Eventually, Maria was brought home from the hospital to die. Although she could no longer speak or open her eyes, the *focolarine* prepared her room at her Focolare house with flowers and pictures. They left the door open onto the living and dining rooms so that the familiar sounds of life could reach her. They took turns being her eyes, describing everything that happened: who had come in after the doorbell rang, who had brought flowers, what meal was being prepared. They read her mail aloud to her, and let her know who had telephoned. She shared their life, and they shared her preparation for departure. They said morning and evening prayers with her, and Mass was celebrated daily in her room. One of her friends reflected on Maria's last days:

> We learned to recognize from the slightest movement of her eyebrows or facial expression whether she was saying "yes" or "no" to something. A few days passed that were so beautiful it seemed like living in eternity, and then she stopped breathing. We could hardly believe it. It was an exceptional experience of unity, of being community, in which, because of Jesus present among those who love one another, one can see how extraordinarily normal it is to live and die together.

Redefining "Holiness"

Maria and Sheri are but two of the Focolare members who have concluded their "holy journey" completely reconciled to God's loving plan. These stories demonstrate vividly how loving and living a life of unity bring peaceful normality to circumstances generally considered dramatic or tragic. Such "peaceful normality" is one of the most striking characteristics of the life of an Italian teenager, Chiara Luce Badano, who was beatified on September 25, 2010.

Chiara Luce, together with her parents, met the Focolare when she was in elementary school. She lived the Gen life with enthusiasm and commitment. When she was seventeen, the diagnosis of a particularly aggressive form of bone cancer introduced her to Jesus forsaken, a relationship that would grow deeper and deeper.

At first she hoped for a cure. Learning the actual prognosis, starting with the fact that she would lose her hair, placed her before the physical and spiritual reality she would have to face. Her mother describes the moment when Chiara Luce returned from the hospital:

> She had a fixed, almost absent look on her face as she came into the house. I asked her how it had gone, and she replied, "Not now, let's not talk now." She threw herself down on the bed, her eyes closed. I was dying inside, but the only thing to do was to stay beside her, in silence, suffering with her. It was a battle. After twenty-five minutes she turned towards me, smiling. "Now we can talk," she said. It was done. She had said her "yes," and she never turned back.[20]

How she lived the illness generated a profound experience of reciprocal love and unity with her family and with the young people of her community. On her part, Chiara Luce relied on her relationship with other young people, whose support and love were an integral part of her journey. As she wrote to her Focolare friends who lived nearby, "I feel your unity very strongly, your offerings, your prayers which allow me to renew my 'yes' moment by moment."[21]

That love flowed both ways — the other young men and women received from Chiara Luce a precious gift, that of sharing deeply in her "splendid adventure of love with God." One of them, Fernando Garetto, describes what passed between them:

> At the beginning we all thought that we were going there to support her. But we soon realized that we could not do it without her. It was as if we were drawn by a magnet. Every time we went into her room, we felt that we had to "adjust" our souls; and then in those brief moments spent with her, we were filled with joy. It felt as if we were being projected, without any merit on our part, into her splendid adventure of love with God. And yet Chiara did not pronounce any extraordinary words, did not write pages and pages in her diary. She just loved.[22]

Chiara Luce's family experienced a similar exchange. As he watched his only child weaken, Ruggero, her father, reflected on how his daughter's relationship with Jesus was intertwined with the whole family's spiritual journey:

> We saw the hand of God in the illness. I discovered a family that I didn't realize I had. And Chiara's relationship with

> Jesus helped us take the necessary spiritual steps ahead.
> Chiara was seriously ill, and yet we never fell into despair,
> because in her there was always Jesus. I remember one oc-
> casion when we had done a meditation together. Chiara
> said, "When we have Jesus present in our midst, we are the
> happiest family in the world."[23]

Letters written shortly before her death reveal her growing intimacy with Jesus forsaken. To Chiara Lubich, she confided:

> [W]ill I manage to be faithful to Jesus forsaken and live to
> meet him ...? I feel so small and the road ahead is so hard.
> Often I feel overwhelmed by suffering. But it's my spouse
> who is coming to visit me, right? Yes, I will repeat, with
> you, "If you want it, Jesus, I want it too."[24]

Lubich wrote back, encouraging her: "Chiara, don't be afraid to say
your 'yes' to him moment by moment. He will give you the strength, be
sure of it! I too am praying for this and am always there with you. God
loves you immensely. He wants to penetrate the most intimate part of
your soul to give you a little taste of heaven."[25]

The Church has confirmed that Chiara Luce indeed had a "little
taste of heaven" here on earth. In comments delivered the day after
her beatification, Pope Benedict XVI noted:

> Only Love with a capital "L" can give us true happiness!
> This has been demonstrated by Chiara Badano.... [Today
> is] a feast for all young people who can find an example of
> Christian integrity in her. Her last words of full adherence to
> God's will were: "Bye, Mom. Be happy because I am." ... We
> give praise to God, because his love is stronger than evil and
> death; and we thank the Virgin Mary who guides the young,
> even through difficulty and sufferings, to fall in love with
> Jesus and to rediscover the beauty of life.[26]

8

E Pluribus Unum — The Focolare Spirituality and the Quest for Community in a Pluralistic Society

The Ties that Bind — and Divide

In his analysis of the tendency among Americans to be independent, Tocqueville observed a counterbalancing force: the habit of forming associations. "Americans of all ages, all conditions, all minds constantly unite. Not only do they have commercial and industrial associations in which all take part, but they also have a thousand other kinds: religious, moral, grave, futile, very general and very particular, immense and very small."[1] Associations, he surmised, counteract the tendencies of individuals to close themselves off from others because in such associations "Sentiments and ideas renew themselves, the heart is enlarged, and the human mind is developed only by the reciprocal action of men upon one another."[2] He concludes, "There is nothing, according to me, that deserves more to attract our regard than the intellectual and moral associations of America."[3]

In his 2000 study, *Bowling Alone*, Robert Putnam agrees with Tocqueville's assessment of how associations build social cohesion, or "social capital."[4] According to Putnam, associations serve two functions: *bonding* and *bridging*. "Bonding" is primarily "inward looking," reinforcing relationships among people who are similar. Putnam's examples include ethnic organizations and private country clubs. "Bridging," by contrast, is "outward looking," encompassing "people across diverse social cleavages." Putnam's examples include the civil rights movement, youth service groups, and ecumenical religious organizations.[5] In Putnam's analysis, bonding and bridging are not necessarily exclusive. Groups generally serve both functions, and may emphasize one dimension more than the other.[6] Putnam sums up his analysis with these images: "Bonding social capital constitutes a kind of sociological superglue, whereas bridging social capital provides a sociological WD–40."[7]

Toward the end of his study, Putnam acknowledges the tensions generated by the American tendency to form associations. "Strong in-group loyalty" may create "strong out-group antagonism."[8] At the

172

founding of the republic, James Madison expressed concern that some associations did more harm to the body politic than good: they were "mischiefs of faction," to be tolerated only in the name of liberty but kept in close check because of their readiness to sacrifice the good of the whole for the pet projects of the few.[9] Putnam also acknowledges how groups and associations can feed class antagonism, advancing the political power of those with education, money, status and connections.[10] Further, it is a sad truth that "American clubs and churches are even more racially segregated than our neighborhoods and schools."[11]

The forces necessary to build community pull in opposite directions. On the one hand, as political philosopher Amy Gutmann has observed, "Other things being equal, the more economically, ethnically, and religiously heterogeneous the membership of an association is, the greater its capacity to cultivate the kind of public discourse and deliberation that is conducive to democratic citizenship."[12] On the other hand, Putnam admits, "Social capital is often most easily created in opposition to something or someone else. Fraternity is most natural within socially homogenous groups."[13] Groups with diverse membership do the most good for society, but they are hard to form because people prefer to associate with others like themselves.

In *The Big Sort*, his 2008 analysis, Bill Bishop recounts how this tendency to cluster into like-minded communities feeds division and polarization. Americans, given "unprecedented choice about where and how they wanted to live," have gravitated toward the groups that make them most comfortable.[14] "Technology, migration, and material abundance all allow people to 'wrap themselves into cocoons entirely of their own making.'"[15] Observing the recent social trajectory in the United States, he explains:

> [It] wasn't a simple increase in political partisanship, but a more fundamental kind of self-perpetuating, self-reinforcing social division. The like-minded neighborhood supported the like-minded church, and both confirmed the image and beliefs of the tribe that lived and worshipped there. Americans were busy creating social resonators, and the hum that filled the air was the reverberated sound of their own voices and beliefs.[16]

As scholar of American religion Martin Marty explains, churches used to contribute to society by serving as a "town meeting place where people with very different commitments can meet and interact." Now this kind of "fertilization" across differences "simply doesn't happen."[17]

The Quest for Unity in Diversity

Tocqueville had been drawn to the American experience of voluntary associations because, in Robert Wuthnow's words, they could "forge connections across large segments of the population, spanning communities and religions, and drawing together people from different ethnic backgrounds and occupations."[18] Is this kind of "bonding" becoming extinct? Such a dynamic does seem to be alive and well within local Focolare communities. In the Focolare's experience, religious life does not draw participants into an exclusive enclave, but opens them to the widest social embrace. Consider these vignettes:

Joy, an African-American from Texas, was born in 1957.

> I grew up in a time when racism was certainly more apparent than it is today. My vision of this country was shaped by events such as my father's early experience, when he was forced to leave home and family for having only glanced at a person of a different race — she was white — and he was almost hanged.
>
> My mother, originally a Southern Baptist, and my father, a Catholic, met, married and had us four children. My mother's death when I was six years old turned my world upside down. Despite the love showered upon us by the relatives with whom we later lived, at times while growing up, I felt orphaned because my mother was not there.
>
> My aunts were especially careful to see that we grew up aware of our heritage as African-Americans and of the contribution that our race has made to this country. They managed to transmit a positive sense of pride rather than hate, and a trust in our own capabilities rather than distrust of what others might do to us. But this pride did not remove the sting of always being outside the mainstream of life.
>
> I was aware of racism, and had experienced it in my life — like when you are waiting in line and they skip over you to serve someone else. Generally I didn't let it bother me. I don't feel that I grew up with an edge. But I did have some strong experiences. Once when a group of students traveled with our science teacher to a white town for a science fair, we stopped for lunch at a jam-packed fast-food restaurant. By the time we got our food and sat down the place was completely empty. Our teacher turned red, he was so shocked and embarrassed.

Also the fact that my mother's family was Baptist and that they allowed us to remain Catholic forced me, at times in painful ways, to constantly face the differences even among Christians. I felt I was given a realistic vision of the world in which I lived, a world that offered all kinds of opportunities, but not to everyone, a world where even believers of the same faith did not necessarily understand one another, and where death seemed to bring about the ultimate division.

I encountered the Focolare when I was in college. Through a friend I experienced Christian love as never before (and certainly not from someone who was white), and this gradually led to my discovery of a life of the gospel and the spirituality of unity. Meeting the Focolare marked a decisive and radical transformation for me. I came to discover God's love, his personal love for me, and I began to see everything, everything that had ever happened to me as a fruit of that love. It is a love that finally made sense of all the sufferings, barriers, and divisions that I had experienced in my own life, giving me the possibility to heal the wounds and become, through this life of unity, a bridge for others. I see that, like Chiara, I only have to respond to love with love.

When I attended Chiara Lubich's funeral in March 2008, I looked around at all the people who were present, people who represented all of humanity. I had the impression that we were already one. Race no longer mattered, faith was not an issue, and the divisions between us no longer existed. We were truly all one family united in universal brotherhood. This gave me great hope and conviction that its full realization won't be a long time in coming.

• • •

John always dreamed of an America where people of different races and religions could live together in unity. This dream has become real for him and for the others who meet once a week at a local delicatessen.

Stop by any Wednesday for lunch at the deli and you might end up seated among our happily blended group, Christian and Muslim, black and white, in animated conversation. We share much more than lunch. Conversation usually revolves around our personal experiences, our successes and difficulties living in real life situations according to the teachings of our faith traditions.

In 1997, Chiara addressed the Muslim community of Imam W. Deen Mohammed at the Malcolm Shabazz Mosque in Harlem. Soon after, the local imam and I began having lunch together at the deli. We were soon joined by another imam and judge, and a local entrepreneur. Word spread. A Baptist minister whose son is a Muslim has become a regular, as well as a young pilot. Eventually people of a number of faiths — even some with no religious tradition — began joining us for lunch: priests, college professors, people who had simply read in the local newspapers about what we are doing.

We have taken part in one another's celebrations, such as wedding anniversaries and award ceremonies, and shouldered each other's burdens. We have helped each other as our parents have grown old and passed on. When a fire destroyed a Muslim family's home, we all pitched in to help them put their life back together.

Except during the Ramadan fast, our Wednesday lunches continue to be an oasis of unity that rejuvenates us, sending us back to work ready to love everyone.

• • •

Natalie, an Italian married to an American, has raised her family in Baltimore.

Our family was invited to a birthday party for one of the children of a family who had met the Focolare in Nigeria and had recently emigrated here. We realized that we were working with a different understanding of time when we showed up at the scheduled hour only to find that we were the only guests who had arrived. Rather than being embarrassed or worried, we just tried to love, helping as we could, setting up the chairs and decorations, trying to enter into this family's spirit of celebration. When the other guests started to arrive, our hosts insisted that we help them to welcome the others into their home. At that moment I realized that they consider us to be "family" in a very strong way. As it turned out, we were the only ones at the party not from Africa. At first my husband and I felt the difference, but once we had finished greeting the other guests and the party got under way, that feeling disappeared. We felt completely at home.

• • •

Using Putnam's terminology, the Focolare spirituality, structure and lifestyle serves *both* to "bond" and to "bridge." Even more, however, it draws those two forces, that seem to pull in opposite directions, into one. Bridge work operates at the core of Focolare identity and lifestyle, and the tightest bonds are forged in that process. To bridge *is* to bond, and in turn, each experience of bonding generates reflection on how to engage in further bridging.

The sections that follow examine this dynamic from several angles and consider how people from different ethnic, racial, social, and religious backgrounds have come to consider themselves part of the same "bridging" project. The chapter concludes with a reflection on how the Focolare experience in the United States extends what Robert Putnam and David Campbell have identified as "America's Grace," the fact that in a culture with extensive religious diversity, people with deep religious devotion coexist harmoniously.[19]

E pluribus unum within the Focolare Movement

People bring to the Focolare Movement a spectrum of opinions and experiences concerning social class and diversity. Some come from positions of privilege and wealth and others from financially constrained circumstances. Some are part of mainstream culture, others are ethnic minorities, and still others are recent immigrants. Regardless of their background, each person in the Movement has been touched by God's invitation to live for unity, to build unity in everyday relationships, and to work for the unity of the human family.

The Focolare worldwide is divided into geographical regions that sometimes even include more than one country. In the United States there are four: the whole East Coast down to Florida and including parts of the Caribbean, the Midwest states, the Southwest states, and the West Coast which includes Hawaii and Alaska. Therefore the distances are great and members often live far from one another. People travel regularly within their region to gather with others who share the same youth or adult vocation. Each of the small group gatherings brings together a cross section of American society. It is normal for people from different ethnic groups, social backgrounds, and levels of education to find themselves bound together in the intimate experience of accompanying one another on a shared spiritual journey. Gerarda, a Mexican-American, describes the small group of women with whom she meets regularly, which includes immigrants from Egypt, Italy, and Brazil: "Sometimes it is a challenge to step back and ask ourselves what is not connecting? What am I doing that reflects the blinders of my own culture? But it is beautiful to see how our relationships have grown."

The "bonding" that the Focolare in the United States exemplifies is limited because its membership is predominantly Roman Catholic. In Chapter Five, the reflections of Celine, Gerald, Bishop Demetrios, Rev. Dr. Hicks, and Dr. Crow indicate how bonding across Christian denominations is possible. Nevertheless, within the Movement, such experiences are more frequent in countries where Lutherans, Anglicans or Orthodox Christians form a larger segment of the population. For example, in Germany, England, and several countries of Eastern Europe, Focolare membership includes a significant number of Christians of various churches.

One way to appreciate the power of the bonding-bridging dynamic in the Focolare is to examine the spiritual resources on which members draw. Truly loving other persons entails making a space in one's heart for their experience, for their way of seeing things. It means entering into their life in order to embrace them as they are. Chiara was never naïve about the pain that the encounter with difference may provoke. Speaking to a group of young people in the early 1970s, she acknowledged the post-colonial realization that "there is a whole other way of seeing the same thing,"[20] which could lead to a profound sense of disorientation — like looking at the world "through a piece of shattered glass," or feeling that the earth is "trembling under one's feet."[21]

Reflecting on her own process of working through ethnic tensions as an African American, Joy explains:

> I understood that we have to look at our history and our experiences and see both the love of God and our relationship with Jesus forsaken. Until we allow this to heal our past, we cannot go forward. We have to look at it. It is real. It hurts. But I cannot stay in the hurt, because all of this is assumed and redeemed by Jesus on the cross. Only then will we be able to go out to the other. Only then will we be able to step forward and say that the spirituality permeates every part of who we are.

As Joy indicates, Jesus forsaken is the model for building unity with our neighbor, particularly the most marginalized and excluded. The God-man who enters into human experience so fully that he seems to have lost his sense of himself, his sense of being God, is the model of one who knows how to make room within so as to take on fully the experience of others. Chiara describes how Jesus forsaken is a model for loving: "We have to be one with our brother, feel how he feels, be him, empty ourselves completely, removing the ideas from our head, affections from our heart, everything from our will, in order to fully immerse ourselves in the others."[22]

Healing Racism

"Building bridges" sometimes occurs in highly personal circumstances. Teresa and her two daughters live in suburban New Jersey. One Friday afternoon, eight-year-old Diana came off the school bus very upset. During the ride home, a seventh-grade boy had made insulting comments about African Americans, and other children had chimed in. Teresa describes how they worked through the incident, first as a family and then with the school:

> My older daughter and I were incredibly angered by this and tried to comfort Diana by reminding her how special she is, being bi-racial. It seemed evident to all of us that we had to embrace this suffering and live up to our commitment to the gospel. We had to love even this boy.
>
> On Monday morning, I sent an e-mail to the principal, detailing the things that were said to Diana on the bus. He immediately called me and shared his plan to speak with Diana and the boy. He reprimanded the boy, had him apologize to Diana, and suspended him from school for several days. The principal asked if I would like to speak to the boy and his parents before he was scheduled to return to school after his suspension. I saw this as an opportunity to build a relationship with this family.
>
> Diana and I prayed together and then decided to do three things at the meeting: One, show the boy love and forgiveness. Two, educate the boy as to who Diana really is and where she comes from, because addressing the truth is also love. Three, promise to become an example to the other children of how

two kids who are expected to dislike each other (he had said nasty things, and she got him into trouble) can still show each other kindness and prove they can go beyond the incident.

The day of the meeting arrived. As Diana and I walked down the hall holding hands, I felt a special love accompanying us, as if Jesus were present among us, even knowing things might not go the way we hoped. Her little hand gave me enormous strength.

The boy and his mother, along with Diana and I, waited together in the front office. I overheard his mother say under her breath that this would be trouble, and I really felt the challenge to live the plan Diana and I agreed to. Sensing the other mother's hostility, Diana declined to go in with me.

I sat directly across from the boy's mother, and as I shared every point we wanted to make, I watched her expression change from embarrassment and defensiveness to acceptance. She was obviously surprised to hear something positive from me. At the conclusion of the meeting, the boy shook my hand and promised to try to be an example.

When I went back to work, I received a beautiful e-mail from the principal: "Thank you again for your gracious response and understanding of this incident and for those kind and uplifting words to the other family. I was very touched. Please know that I am at your service and that I look forward to seeing you again under happier circumstances."

During the last week of school, the boy saw Diana's big birthday pin on her jumper, and greeted her with a "Happy Birthday." She then reached into her backpack and gave him the last birthday doughnut. They were really friends in the end.

Muslim-Christian Dialogue:
"Encounters in the Spirit of Universal Brotherhood"

Since the late 1970s, many African American Muslims who initially had followed Nation of Islam founder Elijah Muhammad had been receptive to the efforts of his son, Imam W. Deen Mohammed. As one of his followers states, "He broadened our vision and our minds" and challenged the community "to see God as the Creator of everyone and everything." In the mid-1990s, during his work for interfaith dialogue, he heard about the Focolare Movement and its founder, Chiara Lubich. He decided to invite her to speak to African American Muslims in the United States.

"That blessed day" is how the followers of Imam Mohammed and Chiara Lubich refer to May 18, 1997, when Chiara, wrapped in a chador, stood before 3000 at the Malcolm Shabazz Mosque in Harlem, New York. Chiara concluded her talk with the hope that, "today will really be a milestone, the beginning of a new era in which we all love one another." In response, Imam Mohammed invited his followers to walk in his footsteps: "The idea that is in the Focolare is something that our soul knows and wants. For this reason I have embraced them as my friends."[23]

Imam Izak-el Pasha, leader of the Malcolm Shabazz Mosque since 1993, was instrumental in making the event possible. He reflects on the enduring significance of the encounter: "This is a living story that will be told for many generations to come. The impact of that meeting will endure the test of time and history. We continue to build upon that relationship to break barriers seen and unseen."[24]

The newly established relationship between the two communities continued with interreligious meetings in Rome, and regular local gatherings. Yusuf describes an inner change that came during a 1998 meeting of Muslim Friends of the Focolare in Castelgandolfo, near Rome. At first, he kept his distance. After a few days, still unsure of Focolare motives, Yusuf took a moment to reflect:

> As I stood looking in the bathroom mirror, the answer came gently into my mind and heart. I was judging these people, the Focolare, by my past experiences and prejudices. It occurred to me that not only was this unkind, it was also wrong. God permitted me to see that we have to accept people in the manner that they present themselves. I began to understand that if they had so much genuine love to share with others, where did they get it from, if God is the originator of love? I went back to my seat renewed and began the most exciting years of my entire life.

He began to "seriously study" the Focolare Movement, as Imam Mohammed had advised. "It was not a spectator affair. You had to jump into the pool and get wet — real wet." Each day he began to look for some way "to share an act of love with someone, preferably someone I did not know. I am committed to letting that light of love shine through me as much as I can." This commitment led Yusuf to initiate, with others, a Christian-Muslim dialogue group in Brooklyn, which has been meeting every month for over ten years.

Her encounter with people who live the Focolare spirituality helped Saadiqa, a Muslim from Rockford, Illinois, recognize how she could deepen the way she is living her own tradition.

> We have much in common. In one of his conversations, the Prophet Muhammad said "That which you want for yourself, seek for mankind," and Jesus said, "Love your neighbor as yourself." But when you actually see somebody living it, it is like a mirror, it helps you want to express it. It reminds you that this is what I'm supposed to be doing too, as a human being. So when I saw how these people were actually living the teachings of Jesus, it made me go back to my book, the Qu'ran.
>
> The Focolare spirit of fraternity is something that anybody can live, no matter what faith they are. When you express this and live this, naturally you feel good no matter who you run into, whether they have faith or not. It makes you want to treat everybody like a human being, no matter who they are.

Imam Mikal Saahir, from Indianapolis, expresses a similar insight: "One idea is to love the one near to you in that moment. I have found this to be a little more difficult than it sounds. But it just makes you a better person overall."

In October 1999 Imam Mohammed was chosen to deliver a message on behalf of the Muslim world to an interreligious gathering at St. Peter's Square, Rome. On that occasion he asked Pope John Paul II to bless his work with the Focolare and received great encouragement from him.

In November 2000 Chiara returned to the U.S. at Imam Mohammed's invitation, to address "Faith Communities Together" in Washington, D.C. Six thousand people attended. "America needs to hear your message. They need to see our unity," he told her. As she highlighted the parallel teachings on love in the Qur'an and the gospels, she told the participants, "We can already appreciate that what is taking place among us ... is not a mere dialogue of words: what we are experiencing is communion in God." At the same gathering, Imam Mohammed's response to Chiara's address suggests the depths of this communion: "I read in the Bible that Jesus Christ, peace be upon him, invited his followers to wash each other's feet, and I think that's just what we are doing. We are washing each other's feet."[25]

Chiara encouraged everyone: "Let us go deep down in our hearts where God is present, and let us tell him that we are committed to do this: we want to be people who are on the front lines bringing forward this peaceful revolution, involving many, many other groups of all religions, of all types of thinking, of all cultures, provided that they are in good faith and that they want to work for universal brotherhood."[26]

Many asked these two leaders how to continue on this path. Before she left, Chiara and Imam Mohammed proposed "Encounters in the Spirit of Universal Brotherhood," a program to promote forming the universal human family. It consists of regular, family-style meetings of Muslim and Focolare communities that give witness to shared values and growing friendship in their common journey.

The first such "encounter" took place in San Antonio, Texas, in February 2001. "No one tried to hide the differences between our two religions, or the fact that here we were whites and African Americans coming together," says Sharry Silvi, who at the time was Focolare co-director at Mariapolis Luminosa. "But one could feel that the relationship that has been established has taken us beyond the indifference, the pain and the barriers of the past, and made us a family — small perhaps, but sincerely united in a spirit of love and in the desire to help the world become one family as well."[27]

Throughout the country, in New York, New Jersey, Washington, D.C., Florida, Texas, Illinois, Indiana, California, and in other states local imams work with Focolare communities to prepare these "encounters" once or twice a year, alternating between a Muslim location and a Focolare venue. They provide a lived experience and the opportunity to put shared truths into practice on a daily basis.[28]

Muhsinah, from Houston, reflects on what these ongoing gatherings have meant to her, and the hope that they bring to others:

> Walking with the Focolare, I see how to apply the expressions of love that are in the Qur'an. That is the greatest benefit I have received from my relationship with the Focolare: learning how to live scripture, not just internalize it or think about it.
>
> Imam Mohammad understood that in the lifetime that God granted him he could not say everything, or have physical contact with all of us so that we could learn how to apply the scripture, but he saw in the work of the Honorable Lady Chiara and the work of her followers a people who were living for the purpose of doing God's

word. He knew that we could learn much from participating with them and building events so that we could enjoy each other's companionship on this life's journey.

Fires have been lit and the world is ready, the world is hungry to see human beings who have this kind of conduct with each other. It is not just Imam Mohammad's passion, we all have to go out and bring to others this spirit of hope that we can live together and live more.

Jewish-Christian Dialogue:
Building Trust for a Reciprocal Exchange of Gifts

At a 2007 conference marking the publication of Chiara Lubich's *Essential Writings*, Rabbi Tsvi Blanchard of the National Jewish Center for Learning and Leadership shared a *midrash* that illustrates how someone from a different religious tradition might interpret and experience Chiara's writings, work and spirituality.

> You can't miss the fact that her roots are thoroughly in the Roman Catholic Church. She speaks from who she is. But what grows from those roots, that tree, is going to reach out to honor and love others. She invites us to see that there's no contradiction between a profound particular faith commitment, and an ability to touch the hearts, souls, and minds of people of very different backgrounds than one's own. She wants to share, she says, what her heart says in this moment. The inner experience, the voice, and the message in the moment, is what will speak. We have a Talmudic expression, "Things that come from the heart speak to the heart." And it works like this — you can feel that she's speaking to you out of her own heart. And it goes into your heart as a result.

Rabbi Blanchard describes how in such a dialogue, both parties are certain of a reciprocal exchange of gifts:

> Above all, she says, we desire to know you. We want to create sisterly and brotherly relationships, loving and concrete relationships, we want them to be reciprocal, we want to get something from you, not just give something to you. She demonstrates a fundamental true openness and respect. And if you are not of a Roman Catholic tradition, you feel this

openness and respect. You understand that she sees us as brothers and sisters, and she's inviting a serious conversation. Not simply one that is going to "make nice," or tell us how good we can be together, but one that will actually engage. She is not afraid of encounter, she has no fear of the other. That is an enormously satisfying and reassuring feeling for a Jew.

We're all on the same page. I still get to be Jewish, I still have all of Jewish history with me. I can also hear the voice of this Christian theologian [Chiara Lubich] speaking to me, saying, "You know what this experience of being abandoned but refusing to give up faith is about. You know it is at the heart of your experience. You know it is why you are here and why you are still one people." She told us, "That same secret is what I am trying to bring to everybody, so we will all be one people, even though it sometimes feels like we are living in a world abandoned by God." So she lays it out in front of you. You cannot escape her ability to draw a circle that keeps you inside. If you do not want her theology, she will find a way that you will hear what she has to say. This is a real gift.

So when she says, look at the world around you, a lot of contemporary world culture is infected in some way with materialism, with secularism, with hedonism, with things that portray a sign of emptiness, and I offer you instead, as an invitation, I offer you love instead of selfishness, I offer you unity instead of fragmentation and separation, I offer you the will of God and concrete human solidarity in the face of suffering, I offer you this, instead of war and hatred, and you think to yourself, that's a good idea, how do I get that? So I would say, I welcome this, because one thing saints are able to do, whatever their religious tradition is, they make the presence of God real in a way that you cannot resist, because you can see what it is like to live in a world of the living presence of God.

Russ Pearce, who is Jewish, also recounts how his lived experience of love of neighbor transformed his outlook. He grew up in small towns in Pennsylvania and New Jersey where Jews were a minority. He had many friends who were Christian, but they never discussed religion and he does not remember ever attending Christian religious services. His experiences of Christianity consisted in the diminishment of his own identity, whether through explicit anti-Semitism or more subtle social exclusion.

He explains: "Like many Jewish Americans, my sense of fear and exclusion originated in the experience of my family. My grandparents were either immigrants or children of recent immigrants. They had left their homes in Eastern Europe because of their experience of persecution by largely Christian communities. We strongly identified with those who had family who died in the Holocaust, and were very much aware of the world's failure to act."

He continued living within this tension even as he began to engage in multi-faith work. Inside the Jewish community, he began to participate in the national social justice leadership of Reform Judaism, which places a priority on inter-faith conversation and dialogue. That work helped him to get his intellectual wheels turning, but it brought about only marginal change for him. Working at a Catholic university with Christian colleagues willing to exchange reflections on what it means to be a religious person opened a wider perspective, but he still felt uncomfortable.

In 2005 he participated in a Jewish-Christian symposium at Castel-gandolfo. He describes the transformative power of this experience:

> At the papal audience that we attended, where we had these really wonderful seats, very close, at some point I realized that I should have felt as uncomfortable and as fearful as I possibly could. Here was the pope, one of the greatest figures of Christianity, surrounded by an enormous crowd of very enthusiastic Catholics. Yet I found myself feeling very much at home and comfortable. What had happened was that the Focolare practice of love of neighbor that I had experienced at the symposium had transformed me, without my being fully conscious of it. It had made me very comfortable with Catholicism and Christianity. I am deeply indebted to the Focolare for this transformation in my view of Christianity, from fear to understanding and hopefully to love. But even more than that: it has helped and continues to help me to observe better the commandments of love of God and love of neighbor as a Jew.

Emily Soloff is national Associate Director of Interreligious and Intergroup Relations for the American Jewish Committee. She describes her first encounters with the Focolare:

> A lot of my work has to do with explaining Israel, and I got to know the Focolare at a time when international political circumstances were making relationships with some other

groups fraught with tension. Focolare meets you where you are — it is not a political debate and it is not a challenge. The approach illustrated for me the desire to live out that aspect of the charism that talks about loving people, and being loving, with no judgments. So going to lunch at the Focolare house was a chance to take a deep breath, relax, and not have to constantly be in a defensive posture.

Soloff has found encounters at the Focolare's international Jewish-Christian symposia enriching on several levels, including the way she experiences her own spiritual life. She describes a key encounter that made her see her prayer life in a new light:

At the Jewish-Christian symposium in Castelgandolfo, a *focolarina* sat beside me and followed in English as I said my prayer in Hebrew. With a simple gesture, she pointed out all of the references to love in one of the prayers. One of the challenges for many American Jews is that we learn the prayers in Hebrew without always having the full sense of what they mean. I realized that I had not been thinking about the meaning. This simple gesture turned on a light bulb, and worked a paradigm shift for me. It enlivened and changed my whole approach to prayer. This experience has also enhanced my ability to be comfortable sharing my Jewish spiritual life with others, not just people in the Focolare, and this has been a tremendous gift for my work. Their language about God, love, and unity has also helped me to have a more expansive way of looking at my own spiritual life and relationship with the community.

In 2009, the Focolare held its Jewish-Christian symposium in Jerusalem. Contacts at that encounter were important for Soloff's ongoing work. She explains:

American Jews do not have many opportunities to meet Arab Christians, and so our images and stereotypes are often quite negative. At the Focolare's international Jewish-Christian symposium in Israel, it was important for me to meet an Arab-Christian *focolarina*, who embodied that desire to be loving, that value of unity. It stripped away the layers of defensiveness, hostility, and anger, modeling a way of behavior from which we can all learn.

Building on "America's Grace"

In *American Grace*, their 2010 study of religion in the United States, Robert Putnam and David Campbell set out to resolve the "puzzle" of the American religious landscape — namely, the fairly peaceful and harmonious coexistence of people who are deeply devout and who come from vastly different religious traditions. The key, they conclude, is that the experience of religious pluralism is "personal" — "America's grace" is the tendency to create "a web of interlocking personal relationships among people of many different faiths."[29]

They recount how people's daily encounter with religious diversity influences their perception. Just about everyone has an "Aunt Susan" — "the sort of person who epitomizes what it means to be a saint, but whose religious background is different from our own."[30] "If you know that Aunt Susan is going to heaven, maybe other people who share her religion or lack of religion can go to heaven too."[31] Similarly, I may befriend Al because of our shared interest in beekeeping. "But if your pal Al is an avid beekeeper — just like you — and is also an evangelical, then perhaps evangelicals are not so bad after all."[32] Finally, Putnam and Campbell ask whether there might be a "spillover" effect. "In other words, can becoming friends with evangelical Al mean warmer feelings toward Mormons or people without religious faith at all?"[33] They claim "reasonably firm evidence that as people build more religious bridges they become warmer toward people of many different religions, not just those represented within their social network."[34]

Without doubt, this harmonious co-existence is a gift, a "grace" to be welcomed and treasured. The Focolare's spirituality as lived in daily life, and its organized projects to foster interreligious dialogue certainly typify such "American grace." Encounter between people of different faith traditions, however, often entails working through difficult obstacles to relationships that go beyond superficial differences. These include fears of proselytism or syncretism, prejudice, and partial or incorrect knowledge about each others' traditions. The Focolare experience of dialogue also leads to an actual healing of these wounds which opens people to deeper levels of trust and sharing.

Anant Rambachan, a Hindu, is chair and Professor of Religion, Philosophy and Asian Studies at Saint Olaf College, Minnesota. Having grown up in Trinidad and having studied in England and in India, a constant feature of his life has been contact with people who profess a religion different from his. He has found deep satisfaction in friendships with Christians and Muslims, in interreligious dialogue through the World Council of Churches, and in his academic work at a Lutheran college. Nevertheless, he recognizes the need for something more — for dialogue that generates "deep engagement."

> In my personal life and work, the influence of Christianity is like that of a close friend — subtle and overt, elusive and unmistakable. I have pondered its doctrines, learned from the wealth of its theological reflections and struggled with some of its claims and assumptions.
>
> I encounter Christianity most meaningfully through its embodiment in friends who express profoundly its meaning in their way of life. Among the friends most valuable to me, for over twenty-five years, are members of the Focolare Movement.
>
> Opportunities for interreligious learning and sharing, for enrichment, growth and challenge, are among the most precious gifts of our contemporary context of religious diversity. In the case of Hindus and Christians, such opportunities are often hindered by fears, real and imagined, that the principal motive of Christians is proselytism and not mutual learning. We will all be deprived if such fears are not addressed and if these lead to isolationism and not deep engagement.
>
> The way forward, I believe, is through cultivating interreligious relationships infused with humility, trust, hospitality, self-criticism and respect for religious freedom. I have found such relationships with Focolare friends here in the United States and in other parts of the world.
>
> In characterizing such friendships, Gandhi often used the example of a rose and called attention to the fact that a rose does not need to proclaim its fragrance. Its fragrance was its sermon. And the fragrance of our religious lives, said Gandhi, "is much finer and subtler than that of the rose."

Gil found that the "Focolare approach" to love of neighbor helped him to reconcile the tensions that emerged when his mother became an evangelical Christian.

> I am an observant Jew who was born and raised Jewish. When I was an adult, my mother re-married and became an evangelical Christian. Within my family it was pretty hard for us to know how to deal with this. On the one hand, she and my step-father were very loving toward me and my

whole family. On the other hand, it was hard to know how to respond to her new belief that non-Christians, including us, were going to hell. It was hard to know what to say when she wanted to share how her relationship with Jesus had helped her through difficult moments.

The Focolare approach to love of neighbor helped me to reconcile all of this within myself, and also learn how to have a deeper relationship with my mother and step-father. It helped me to fully accept and even embrace them, in spite of our different religious commitments and views about the afterlife. It helped me to see that what was most important was that we treated each other with love and respect in this world.

The Focolare spirituality informs an approach to building personal relationships that can help to heal misunderstanding and tensions. Kenneth Tanaka, a Buddhist who grew up in Northern California, is a professor of Buddhist Studies at Musashino University, Tokyo. He first encountered the Focolare at the January 2002 Day of Prayer for Peace in Assisi, where Pope John Paul II had invited the world's religious leaders to gather in the aftermath of the 9/11 attacks. Professor Tanaka served as the academic advisor to the Reverend Chiko Iwagami, head of the Japanese Buddhist Association. He explains what his encounter with the Focolare initiated for him:

In Assisi, the Focolare people greeted us and helped us get settled in our hotel and learn about the schedule of the upcoming activities. What struck me immediately about them was their bubbly demeanor and infectious smiles. I was impressed that a group of lay people would be inspired enough to spearhead dialogues with people of other faiths.

The existence of such a group within the Catholic Church made me more hopeful regarding the Church's relations with other religions. Like many Buddhists, I respected John Paul II in many ways but was quite disappointed with his assessment of Buddhist teachings in his 1994 book, *Crossing the Threshold of Hope*. The Pope's view appeared to be based on what I thought to be a superficial and stereotypical understanding of Buddhism and, perhaps, of Asian religions and cultures in general.

Against this backdrop, the Focolare people certainly sent a message of openness and reconciliation. It further impressed me that the Movement was founded by a woman,

Chiara Lubich. When I met her during the Assisi event, I could see how her unassuming and friendly demeanor served as the model for Focolare people.

Since that time, Kenneth Tanaka has maintained an ongoing friendship with one of the Focolare's scholars of Buddhism and has collaborated with him on different projects.

Those who live the Focolare spirituality establish a bonding-bridging dynamic not through mere habits of being together with other people but through the vision that permeates all of their relationships — the destiny of humanity to live as one family, as Jesus prayed, "That they may all be one" (Jn 17:21). This approach invites each person to delve into his or her own identity, while at the same time remaining open to discovering how, as Chiara puts it, "the person next to me" — no matter how different — "was created as a gift for me."[35] This approach strikes a deep chord of appreciation in those most concerned about building a future of loving respect for distinct religious and ethnic identities. Emily Soloff states:

> In the American experience of diversity, ideas get picked up and mushed around, and that can lead to misunderstandings about one's own identity and about one's neighbors. It is important to help people become comfortable in their own religious skin and develop the religious language which will enable them to ask religious questions in a much more sophisticated way of someone from a different faith. There is something in the Focolare Movement that engages people in an intellectual way, reaching their hearts and their minds, enabling them to ask these kinds of questions.

Rev. Dr. Sherman Hicks, of the Evangelical Lutheran Church, also finds that through the Focolare spirituality diverse people, without losing their identity, can engage each other so as to generate an authentic community. He explains:

> Where can we find a model that can help us accept the diversity and respect it, yet be united for the common good? This is where the Focolare spirituality of unity becomes so important, and can play a vital role in the life of this country. And not only those within the spiritual life, but also those who are not spiritually inclined can look and say unity in diversity is possible.

9

A Common Commitment to the Common Good — A Spirituality of Unity and the Future of Public Life

Ideological Polarization: Intractable Gridlock?

Whether in a metropolis or a small town, day-to-day interactions bring people into contact with those who are different — because of race, ethnicity, religion, social class and political perspective. In recent decades, however, two major cultural shifts have posed significant obstacles to engagement with cultural and political difference.

First, as Bill Bishop describes in *The Big Sort*, increasing physical and economic mobility has allowed Americans to "sort" themselves into like-minded communities. Able to "create" their own identity, many seek out "those who share their lifeworlds — made up of old, fundamental differences such as race, class, gender, and age, but also, now more than ever, personal tastes, beliefs, styles, opinions and values."[1]

Associations that people choose for themselves may be particularly susceptible to extremes. As Putnam explains in *Bowling Alone*:

> Voluntary organizations that are ideologically homogenous may reinforce members' views and isolate them from potentially enlightening alternative viewpoints. In some cases such parochialism may nurture paranoia and obstruction. In a polarized voluntary group universe, reasonable deliberation and bargaining toward a mutually acceptable compromise is well nigh impossible, as each side refuses "on principle" to give ground.[2]

In the later study, *American Grace*, Putnam and Campbell affirm that religious social networks tend to function as "echo chambers." "Social interaction among like-minded co-religionists reinforces and even hardens one's beliefs, even if the process is subtle."[3]

The shift toward identification with ever more homogeneous social and religious communities, which reinforces the ongoing "sort" in American culture, is amplified by a similar tendency in the use of media and computer technology. As Bishop observes, Americans increasingly live in a "giant feedback loop" that is reinforced by the television shows we watch, the newspapers and books we read, and the blogs we visit online.[4] As they watch and read the news that fits their political proclivities, they tend to "ignore the other side."[5]

Even presentations that claim to air speakers who represent "both sides" of a social issue tend to reinforce polarization. Political theorist Benjamin Barber recounts how he had engaged in a "thoughtful and civil on-screen conversation" during the taping of a public television debate with a colleague who represented a different political party. The producer asked for a reshoot, "this time with 'more agitation and hostility, please.'" They complied with the director's request. Barber notes that the reshoot "pushed us away from common ground and from the provisional understanding we had achieved through an appreciation of our differences. The simulated 'conflict' — more prosaic, less truthful, and much less productive — made for 'better television.' The reshoot, naturally, was the version that was eventually broadcast."[6]

These two cultural shifts have combined to exacerbate political segregation. As Bishop describes:

> We all live with the results: balkanized communities whose
> inhabitants find other Americans to be culturally incompre-
> hensible; a growing intolerance for political difference that has
> made national consensus impossible; and politics so polarized
> that Congress is stymied and elections are no longer contests
> over politics, but bitter choices between ways of life.[7]

How might such tendencies be tempered, or countered? In *Going to Extremes*, an analysis of group polarization, legal scholar Cass Sunstein points to the "architecture" of forums that allow people to express their views in public places so that shared space promotes "a set of exposures to diverse views and conditions."[8] What Sunstein describes might take a variety of forms — standing on a soapbox in a public park to oppose tax policy, protesting labor policies on the sidewalk in front of a department store, or joining fellow-citizens at a state legislator's office to register disagreement with health-care policy.

> When you go to work or visit a park, it is possible that you
> will have a range of unexpected encounters, however fleet-
> ing or seemingly inconsequential. On your way to the office
> or when eating lunch in the park, you cannot easily wall
> yourself off from the contentions or conditions that you

would not have sought out in advance or that you would have avoided if you could.[9]

Sunstein hopes that the possibility of encountering real people with real differences of opinion in public places will widen the range of individuals' consciousness. Bishop demonstrates, however, that mere contact with difference is not enough. In a society marked by strongly differing worldviews, even if both sides of an issue are presented, "people don't hear or don't remember arguments that counter their initial opinion."[10] Studies of group polarization reveal that simply putting two groups together does not lead to mutual respect — "It often had the opposite effect."[11]

Bridging the gap between homogeneous groups that hold opposing views requires changes not only in "architecture," but also in attitude. People have to *want* to engage the differences that would otherwise make them uncomfortable. They have to *want* to do the serious work of finding ways to communicate across these differences. What can bring about this needed shift in attitude? Studies by social psychologist Gordon Allport delineate some of the necessary conditions for bringing opposing groups together: first, seeing themselves as equals; second, meetings in "regular pursuit of an ordinary and shared goal"; and third, above all, avoiding "artificiality."[12] As Bishop summarizes, when groups are asked to pool their resources in order to resolve a common problem, "contact between the groups both reduced conflict and prejudice and increased tolerance and cooperation."[13]

Political Diversity within the Focolare Movement

Cultural and political polarization are fed by deep roots, and the Focolare in the United States is a relatively small group at the beginning of its efforts to engage these social divisions. Thus the ideas and examples that follow resemble the initial observations of a cellular experiment in a Petri dish. They are limited, tentative and subject to varying environmental factors, but nonetheless indicate patterns for more extensive study and research.

Generally, individuals are attracted to the Focolare by its spirituality of unity, through which, in the words of Rebecca, they discover the "depth and simplicity of God's love," and their potential for becoming "global persons" (p. 13). They stay involved because the spirituality gives, as Laurie put it, "dignity and purpose" to their daily lives, offering hope even in the face of difficult circumstances (p. 53). Traveling the paths of a spirituality of unity together with others offers staying power as well as accountability for choices. A structure like the Focolare may not seem to have the power to heal the social wounds of political polarization, but it does — in three ways.

First, without conscious or, as Allport cautioned, "artificial" effort, Focolare communities in the United States bring together people of different political leanings and convictions. In contrast to the problematic "like-minded clustering" according to the "lifeworlds" that Bishop describes, the Focolare attracts people from differing ethnic, religious, generational and social backgrounds, as well as from differing personal tastes, styles and opinions.[14] As a result, Focolare communities in the United States include people with a variety of perspectives regarding the role of government in a political system. Like that of any other citizen, their political stance emerges from their own history, education, profession and experience, as well as from geographical location. In the current cultural landscape of the United States, the Focolare Movement offers one example of Martin Marty's "town meeting place" where people with different political perspectives can still "meet and interact."[15]

Second, this diverse assortment of people within the Focolare Movement come together for what Allport describes as the "regular pursuit of an ordinary and shared goal."[16] Most broadly, Focolare communities pursue the "regular" goal of sustaining members in their efforts to build unity through relationships of dialogue and service. The power of such efforts to bridge political differences in the pursuit of a common end is demonstrated in the Focolare's annual North American Economy of Communion convention.[17] There, people who hold widely differing political convictions — those convinced of vitality of the free market as well as those passionate about sustainable and integral worldwide social development — Republicans and Democrats and Independents — work together, convinced that this small but flourishing business network can make a difference in alleviating global poverty.

Third, the Focolare has explored how a spirituality of unity might inform an approach to political life and activity. At this point in its history and development, the Focolare has relatively limited resources for direct engagement in local or national American politics. For this reason, more than in other parts of this book, the sections that follow refer to the Focolare's political experience in other countries to suggest what the future holds for the Movement in the United States.

Spiritual Resources for Engaging Political Difference

The Focolare Movement's "involvement" in politics consists first of all in encouraging a positive vision of political engagement. Chiara describes politics as "the possibility of loving our neighbor in a crescendo of charity: from interpersonal love to an ever greater love toward the *polis*."[18] Within this vision, she explains, "politics is the love of all loves, gathering the resources of people and groups into the unity of a common design so as to provide the means for each one to fulfill in complete freedom his or her specific vocation."[19] Chiara defines the choice to become politically active as "an act of love" through which a politician responds to "a genuine vocation, to a personal calling."[20]

Members of the Focolare line up along the entire political spectrum. Some have staunch partisan political views; others feel conflicted and ambivalent. Most do pick a place to stand, taking a cue from Chiara's encouraging words to her friends in Italy: "Don't be afraid of choices. Have before you Jesus who chose to be one gender and not another; to come during one historical time and not another; to be part of one people and not another, risking to exclude. He made particular choices, but he lived within this particularity in a universal way."[21]

For Focolare members who serve as elected officials, their conscience is their guide for their political activity. Shortly after Lucia Fronza Crepaz, a married *focolarina*, was elected to the Italian Parliament in 1987, she tried to open a conversation with others in her Focolare house about the general direction that she should take. The person responsible for the community told her, "I can sustain you spiritually, but for the rest, you need to turn to the leadership of your party and those who elected you."[22] Chiara offered Fronza similar advice before a meeting with a noted political figure: "Go and tell him what *you* want to say. Reach within yourself."[23]

What resources does the Focolare spirituality offer for engaging political difference? For those who live a spirituality of unity, *wanting* to engage the other who is different is not an added dimension, but the very core of their way of being. Such engagement is their particular path to union with God. Using the image of "a great garden full of flowers," Chiara cautions against the tendency to fix one's gaze on a single flower without noticing the others.[24] "Look at all the flowers," she suggests, because God "is in them all, and by observing them all we love him more than the individual flowers."[25]

To "look at all the flowers" is not a matter of personal effort or sacrifice, but a logical consequence of being attracted to God. "God who is in me, who has shaped my soul, who lives there as Trinity, is also in the heart of my brothers and sisters."[26] Therefore, "*it is not reasonable* that I love him only in me."[27] "Just as I love him in me, recollecting myself in this heaven — when I am alone — I love him in my brother or sister when he or she is close to me."[28] Looking at "all the flowers" opens human experience to the life of the Trinity flowing through human relationships. Where "two heavens meet, a single Trinity comes to be, where the two are like Father and Son and among them is the Holy Spirit."[29] The encounter with a brother or sister is an opportunity to "recollect" oneself in the "heaven" of the other, and to "recollect" the other into one's own.

Why would you *want* to engage and embrace someone who is different? Because, as Chiara explains, it is an opportunity to experience "the miracle of the Trinity and the beauty of God who is not alone because he is Love."[30] It is also a point to access the continuing power of the Incarnation, God's presence on earth. "Since this Trinity dwells in human bodies, Jesus is there: the God-Man."[31]

These spiritual thoughts touch on the deep foundations of Focolare members' attitude toward persons who are different in any way. How does this disposition translate into the political realm? How can persons with different partisan commitments live this approach in the rough and tumble of political life? For answers to these questions, we look to the work of Focolare co-founder, and member of the Italian Parliament, Igino Giordani.

In 1949, the newspaper *La Via* published an editorial by Giordani entitled "Communists and Catholics."[32] As an elected member of the Christian Democrats, he argued that the first step his party should take in response to communism was not to "slam the door in the face of our brothers because they are communists," but to build a more equal society, so that they might see how "true justice is fulfilled through the eternal revolution of the Gospel."[33] "Communion will resolve communism," he concluded, "and will bring back the communists."[34]

Amid growing cold-war tensions, many derided this proposal, as well as his advocacy for pacifism, as "naïve," "ambiguous" and "out of date."[35] In 1951, he responded to these critiques:

> The Bolsheviks ... are the persecutors of the Church. Their system includes concentration camps and secret police.... But it's exactly because they are so fallen that we should see

how they need to be redeemed, and they will be redeemed first of all with charity. This is the reason to offer a common meeting ground on which we can work together: conservatives and democrats, communists and anti-communists … this is the Christian democracy that works peace.[36]

Whether one agrees or disagrees with Giordani's political views, it is clear that he was striving to find the good in members of the opposing party, seeing them first of all as other human beings to be loved. What would it mean to take seriously the gospel message that God's love embraces every person, even adversaries? What would it mean to base all relationships in politics on the conviction that those who one believes fall short — even very short — "will be redeemed first of all with charity"?[37]

Giordani's challenge to the Christian Democrats suggests guidelines for political rapprochement. The first step is to recognize that the other has a valuable voice in the political conversation. When disagreement arises, one can still look for, as Giordani describes, "a common meeting ground." On this basis, people of different political parties can seek a vantage point for working together.

In 1946, shortly after his election to Parliament, Giordani wrote in his diary: "Can a politician be a saint? Can a saint be a politician? Test the answer to the question on yourself now that you are becoming a politician."[38] The answer seems to be "yes," given that on June 6, 2004, the Diocese of Frascati opened Giordani's process toward canonization.

Closer to our own times, another member of the Focolare, Josef Lux, like Giordani answered the call to politics as "the love of all loves" during a tumultuous time for his country. He served as the Vice-Prime Minister of the Czech Republic from 1992 to 1998. Service to members of all political parties characterized his career. He wrote: "For a Christian one cannot serve God without serving other people, and service to others is at the same time service to God."[39] For Lux, this attitude led him to stop often to help someone in need, even in the midst of a busy schedule. It meant being attentive enough to see when a sleepy colleague needed a cup of coffee, and then personally going to get it. Even journalists were touched by his capacity to bring people together. One wrote, "He tried to make relationships in political life more humane, even amidst ideological controversy…. He worked so that politicians could understand each other, and even love each other."[40] In this way, he enabled political leaders to find common ground and craft together policies for the common good.

In 1998, Lux resigned from his post as he battled leukemia. A year later, after Lux's death, Vaclav Havel, President of the Czech Republic, reflected: "Josef Lux held within himself something transcendent.... He was able to rise above partisan interests in order to put them in harmony with those of everyone. We will try to accept his death as a challenge in order to foster the most beautiful values that he embodied."[41] The head of the opposition, Prime Minister Milos Zeman confirmed: "It is said in politics that one does not have friends, especially among one's political adversaries. I would like to express my great esteem for Josef Lux, even though he was the president of another party, my adversary, whom I considered a friend."[42]

The Movement for Unity in Politics

Might these examples be limited to a few rare personalities, extraordinary leaders who grace a country's political scene every few decades? Since 1996, the Focolare's "Movement for Unity in Politics" has sought to sustain those involved in public life, helping them transform their approach to public service.[43]

In her meetings with these groups, Chiara challenged them to be receptive to the possibility that even political opponents, "may have also chosen politics as a vocation to love"[44] — and therefore to respect them, to try to understand their values, and to look past political labels to the substance of their proposals. She explains, "'Loving everyone' means being interested in bringing to fruition the good proposals of one's adversaries." Public servants who take this approach "seek to live out the apparent contradiction of loving the others' party as their own because they realize that the nation's well-being requires everyone's cooperation."[45]

In several countries, officials from different parties gather to encourage one another in their efforts to engage in politics in this way. A description from Brazil illustrates how this is done:

> Since the Brazilian Movement for Unity in Politics was founded in 2001, we have held periodic meetings in the federal parliament among politicians from different parties and of different religions and convictions. Our objective has been to build peace within national politics, and to foster dialogue by sharing how we have tried to live brotherhood with other representatives.[46]

At the Parliament in Seoul, Korea, representatives have been meeting regularly since September 2005. Representative Kim Nak-Sung reports that next to his telephone he keeps the points of "the art of loving in politics." He explains: "This way I remember to put them into practice in the course of my day-to-day work."[47] A Buddhist representative, Kim Sung-Gon, had intended to drop into a meeting of this group only briefly, but he ended up staying the whole time. "What I took away is the idea of seeing Jesus in my brothers. I would say to see Buddha in my brothers."[48] He would later report that this approach helped him to go beyond previous divisions with certain colleagues. He played a key role in preparing the next meeting together with a member of an adversary party.[49]

In June 2008, the "Permanent Political Forum for Unity" was registered with the Korean Parliament as an official group, with thirty-four representatives from four different parties, including the majority and the opposition.[50] In February 2010 the group's contributions to the Parliament were officially recognized by the Parliament with a monetary prize. The money has been donated to help support a "school of formation" for young people to explore the positive potential of politics.[51]

Throughout the world, many participate in the Movement for Unity in Politics because they are attracted by the global vision that Chiara set out:

> Those who respond to their political vocation by practicing brotherhood enter into a universal dimension that gives them a vision open to all humanity … each political act, not only that of a national government, but also the most local gesture … assumes a universal significance, because the politician who implements it is fully human and fully responsible.[52]

Sustaining Citizens in their Quest for the Common Good

How have Focolare communities in the United States dealt with political difference? During politically charged elections, they have to face and live with the same forces that tend to divide people along political lines. One Focolare member who had worked in local government for several years reflected, "We see how fragile we are and how difficult it is to step into political dialogue."

In response to the desire to explore how a spirituality of unity might inform ordinary citizens' discourse about public life, in September 2007 the New York area community gathered at Mariapolis Luminosa for a weekend workshop, "Citizens for a United World." They began their conversation as Focolare groups always do, with a "pact" to put love first — before political convictions — even if participants did not reach ultimate agreement. The group then began to explore Church documents and statements on political life, and how they apply to varying perspectives.[53] The program also included moments of recreation and working together, such as doing the dishes after meals, which provided opportunities to continue the exchange in non-confrontational settings.

As a result of the pact that they had made, their discussions were transformed. The atmosphere of mutual love allowed them to identify and develop the tools that they needed to communicate across political differences. As one participant reflected: "I realized that when differences come up, I don't need to run away from them, but listen and try to enter into that person's cares and concerns."

They also began to see how their individual perspectives could mature if they remained open. One person shared, "I was touched by the power of the framework of being open to all. This makes me a better citizen and a better person and also leaves me free to see the positive and negative of both sides, to embrace the other, and to be enriched by different points of view."

At the end of the weekend, many expressed a new sense of freedom in realizing that their perspectives could be enriched by other points of view. "It was amazing for me how I was able not to be affected negatively upon learning that the other person belonged to an opposing political party. I was able to drop all prejudices and preconceptions about that person that would have automatically taken over if I were not living for unity in diversity."

Observers of the American political landscape note a tension between robust and vibrant participation in political life and the kind of deliberation that could emerge from an encounter between different political perspectives. In her study, *Hearing the Other Side*, University of Pennsylvania political scientist Diana Mutz describes the problem:

> [W]hen people do talk about politics they are particularly likely to talk with those of like mind. Such interactions will tend to have more to do with rooting for the same candidate or political cause than with exploring political options or discussing differences of opinion. In short, these interactions do little to promote the cause of deliberation among members of the general public.[54]

Mutz applies to the political sphere the concern that Putnam raised in *Bowling Alone* — "strong in-group loyalty" may also create "strong out-group antagonism."[55] She explains, "Tight-knit networks of reciprocal obligation are unlikely to go hand in hand with high levels of cross-cutting political conversation."[56] Acknowledging that she can offer "no easy solution," Mutz indentifies the seemingly insoluble tension at the heart of political engagement:

> How do we conceptualize a framework within which a diverse array of ordinary people can live their lives both as active citizens in a competitive political system and as compassionate fellow human beings? In particular, how do we accomplish this when one of these tasks appears to require strong partisanship and confident judgments about which political choices are right and which are wrong, while the other requires a tolerant, open-minded, nonjudgmental nature, and an acceptance of people's worth on their own terms, however disagreeable we may find their political views?[57]

In the United States the Focolare Movement has just begun to explore how to apply, in the realm of political discourse, a vision in which active and engaged citizens welcome one another as "compassionate fellow human beings." Experiences here and throughout the world indicate, however, that Focolare communities are well-configured and well-poised both to "conceptualize" and to live within a "framework" that demonstrates their capacity to hear, understand, and open themselves to the position taken by "the other side."

Conclusion:
A Hearth for the Human Family

The story is familiar: On December 9, 1531, while Juan Diego was walking through the Tepeyac Hills from his village to Mexico City, Mary appeared to him.

Our Lady of Guadalupe, Patroness of the Americas, does not deliver warnings of divine retribution or chastisement. Nor does Mary give instructions about what to do or what to change. Instead, as theologian Maxwell Johnson observes, the Virgin of Guadalupe makes one simple request — build a "temple," or a "home" where "all people might find love, compassion, help, and protection and where the laments of all people would be heard."[1] Mary creates a space where each person might experience what it means to be loved. Whatever "conversion" follows is a consequence of being loved, and loving in return.

On Juan Diego's cloak, she is portrayed with both indigenous and Spanish features, as well as with symbols that the indigenous would recognize as their own. This image invites those who see it to immerse themselves in the beauty of being loved precisely in the concrete circumstances of their own ethnic, social, cultural and religious identity. Theologian Fr. Virgil Elizondo sums up Mary's purpose: "The method of the Guadalupe is based on beauty, recognition and respect for 'the other,' and friendly dialogue. It is based on the power of attraction, not on threats of any kind."[2]

Throughout the world the Focolare — the Work of Mary — does one thing. It builds a "home," a hearth where the entire human family can gather. Focolare communities aim to be places where everyone can experience God's unconditional love and welcome. This experience then becomes the basis for working together to build a more united and peaceful world.

Dr. Paul Crow, of the Disciples of Christ, describes the particular contribution that the Focolare makes to the United States:

> The gospel is universal. It should never be limited to any culture, any language, however you want to divide people up. Those who receive the Christian faith should under-

stand that they have been transposed into a new community that is worldwide, that goes beyond all of the human divisions. Once the gospel comes to a person, their whole understanding of life in the world is transformed, we break the bonds of our parochialism, the scales are removed from our eyes, and we see the whole world again — it is that dramatic. This sense of the universal is the gift that Focolare brings to the United States.

Bibliographical Note

This note indicates recent primary sources in English on the Focolare Movement. With few exceptions, it does not include the voluminous secondary sources in Italian, English, and other languages.

Part I: Origins and Brief History of the Focolare Movement

1. General Information about the Focolare Movement and Chiara Lubich

The Focolare's websites, international (focolare.org) and national (focolare.us), include information about the Movement's origin and goals, news about international and local events, and contact information for international offices, regional headquarters, and local communities.

Chiara Lubich, *Essential Writings: Spirituality, Dialogue, Culture* (New City Press, 2007), is the most complete thematically arranged collection of her talks, meditations, poems, and other writings. *Essential Writings* includes a bibliography of Lubich's original works and of secondary literature in various languages.

Works by Chiara Lubich published after the *Essential Writings* bibliography was compiled include:

The Art of Loving, New City Press, 2010.
God Loves You Immensely, New City Press, 2010.
Living Dialogue: Steps on the Way to Communion among Christians, New City Press, 2010.
No Thorn without a Rose, New City Press, 2008 (Julian Ciabattini, ed.).
Rays: Short Reflections on Living God's Will, New City Press, 2011.

Shortly after Chiara Lubich's death in 2008, the Movement established the "Chiara Lubich Center" (www.centrochiaralubich.org), which conserves her legacy and makes it available in document and multimedia formats. The website includes a bibliography of Lubich's original works and English translations of some documents.

The most complete biography of Chiara Lubich in English is Jim Gallagher, *A Woman's Work: The Story of the Focolare Movement and its Founder* (New City Press, 1998).

The best primary source concerning the life and activities of the Focolare in the United States is the Movement's monthly magazine, *Living City* (livingcitymagazine.com), established in 1961. An online archive includes back issues through 2003.

Part II: Living a Spirituality of Unity in the United States

2: How Focolare Members Live

Essential Writings, Part II, "A New Look at Faith," includes Lubich's writings, meditations and poems ordered according to the points of the spirituality.

The Art of Loving (New City Press, 2010) includes writings and reflections on each aspect of this practice.

A New Way: The Spirituality of Unity (New City Press, 2006) collects a series of reflections on the "collective" dimensions of the points, aspects and instruments of the spirituality.

3: Walking the Path to Unity Together

Essential Writings, Part III, "Reflections of Light upon the World," includes Lubich's addresses to particular groups: "The Family, Treasure Chest of Love" (179–194); "To the Youth" (360–368). She describes the vocation of the *focolarini* in "And the Focolare Was Born" (49–52).

4: A Spirituality of Unity and the Renewal of Social Life and Culture

Essential Writings, Part III, includes Lubich's addresses concerning particular sectors of professional life: "Persons in Communion" (215–229); "The Charism of Unity and Politics" (230–268); "The Charism of Unity and Economy" (269–289); "The Charism of Unity and the Media" (290–303); "The Charism of Unity and the Arts" (304–319).

An Introduction to the Abba School: Conversations from the Focolare's Interdisciplinary Study Center (New City Press, 2002) includes translations of initial scholarship in theology and philosophy.

The Focolare international and local websites include links to pages dedicated to specific areas of social life and cultural renewal.

"The Cube of Love" teacher's kit includes a book with examples of children living the points of loving, an instructional guide, and a detachable inscribed cube. Materials are available through the *Living City* website (livingcitymagazine.com).

Information about Sophia University Institute is available at www.iu-sophia.org/public/documents/folder_iglese.pdf. The website, iu-sophia.org, has not yet been translated into English.

5: The Focolare Movement and the Church

Essential Writings, Part II, includes Lubich's reflections on "The Church as Communion" (110–119), "The Word that Gives Life" (120–128), and "Jesus in the Eucharist" (129–134).

The Cry (New City Press, 2001) includes Lubich's account of the Church approval process.

Living Dialogue: Steps on the Way to Communion among Churches (New City Press, 2009) includes an introduction by Rowan Williams and Lubich's principal themes on ecumenism.

Part III: The Focolare Spirituality and Contemporary Culture in the United States

6: The Focolare Spirituality and "The Pursuit of Happiness"

Essential Writings, Part III, includes Lubich's "The Charism of Unity and Economy" (269–289).

The international Economy of Communion website (edc-online.org) includes news about EOC developments and references to scholarly and popular articles. The "Business to Business" Economy of Communion website (edc-info.org) includes a map of the businesses throughout the world.

Lorna Gold, *New Financial Horizons: The Emergence of an Economy of Communion* (New City Press, 2010) provides the most complete guide to the EOC.

Other recent scholarship on the EOC and the "culture of giving" includes:

Luigino Bruni, "Economy of Communion: Between Market and Solidarity," in *Catholic Social Thought: Twilight or Renaissance*, Leuven University Press, Leuven 2000, 238–248.

Luigino Bruni, ed., *The Economy of Communion: Toward a Multi-Dimensional Economic Culture*, New City Press, 2002.

Luigino Bruni & Amelia J. Uelmen, "Religious Values and Corporate Decision Making: The Economy of Communion Project," *Fordham Journal of Corporate and Financial Law* 11 (2006) 645–80.

Lorna Gold, *The Sharing Economy*, Ashgate, Burlington VT, 2004.

Thomas J. Norris, "The New Sociality: An Economy of Communion," in *The Trinity: Life of God, Hope for Humanity*, New City Press, 2009, 113–130.

Amelia J. Uelmen, "*Caritas in veritate* and Chiara Lubich: Human Development from the Vantage Point of Unity," 71 *Theological Studies* (2010/1) 26–45.

7: The Focolare Spirituality, the Moral Life and the Quest for Freedom

Essential Writings, Part II, includes Lubich's reflections on death and the afterlife, "The Final Hour" (157–165).

Further reflections on family life include:

Chiara Lubich, *The Love that Comes from God: Reflections on the Family*, New City Press, 1995.

Igino Giordani, *The Family, a Community of Love*, New City Press, 1989.

John Olsen and Thomas Masters, eds., *The Family and Education*, New City Press, 1989.

John Olsen and Thomas Masters, eds., *The Family and Prayer*, New City Press, 1991.

For further information on Chiara Luce Badano: Michele Zanzucchi, *Chiara Luce: A Life Lived to the Full*, New City (London) 2007. The official "Chiara Luce Badano" website: chiaralucebadano.it.

8: *E Pluribus Unum*: The Focolare Spirituality and the Quest for Community in a Pluralistic Society

Essential Writings, Part III, "360° Dialogue" (320–359), describes the Focolare's approach to ecumenical, interreligious and intercultural dialogue.

Donald W. Mitchell, "Founders Nikkyo Niwano and Chiara Lubich: An Interreligious Dialogue for Peace," *Dharma World*, 34 (2007/10–11) 31–33, presents the work of the Rissho Kosei-kai and the Focolare to promote world peace.

Amelia J. Uelmen, "Reconciling Evangelization and Dialogue through Love of Neighbor," *Villanova Law Review*, 52 (2007/2) 303–329, discusses how the Focolare's approach to dialogue has been applied.

9: A Common Commitment to the Common Good — A Spirituality of Unity and the Future of Public Life

Essential Writings, Part III, includes Lubich's "The Charism of Unity and Politics" (230–268).

The official Igino Giordani website, iginogiordani.info, includes biographical and bibliographical information and news about the cause for his beatification.

The website for the Movement for Unity in Politics, "Movimento Politico per l'unità," mppu.org, has not yet been translated into English.

Acknowledgments

M any thanks to all who opened their hearts and their lives to share what have become the precious tiles that compose the mosaic of this book.

The comments of numerous friends within the Focolare Movement have served to correct and refine the manuscript. Particular thanks to the board members and editorial staff of New City Press/ *Living City* Magazine, whose assistance, research and critique have been invaluable.

Our gratitude also to Howard Lesnick, Elizabeth McKeown, Vincent J. Miller, Donald W. Mitchell, Olivier Sylvain, and Robert K. Vischer for their insightful feedback on the manuscript.

Some of the material included in this book has been previously published in *Living City*, often in longer form. To protect the privacy of those who may not have anticipated an audience as broad as this book's when they granted their permission for publication in the magazine, many of their names have been changed.

Where sources noted are in Italian, the translations are our own.

Notes

Authors' Preface

[1] Recounted in Chiara Lubich, *Diary 64/65*, New City Press, New York 1987, 93.

[2] The Bibliographical Note (pp. 205–208) describes the Chiara Lubich Center's effort to conserve this legacy and make it accessible and available to scholars and the public.

Introduction

[1] Eternal Word Television Network provides Catholic programming and news coverage from around the world (ewtn.com).

[2] There are 35 of these "little cities" of the Focolare spread across the five continents (pp. 107–108). Mariapolis Luminosa is named after Luminosa Bavosi, an Argentinian *focolarina* who showed particular courage in living for unity as she succumbed to a pulmonary disease. She died in 1985, shortly before the little city in Hyde Park was established; Chiara Lubich suggested that it be named after her.

Part I: Origins and Brief History of the Focolare Movement

1. Chiara Lubich: A Life for Unity

[1] Ian Fisher, "Chiara Lubich, Who Founded Catholic Lay Group, Dies at 88," *New York Times*, March 15, 2008.

[2] Franca Zambonini, *Chiara Lubich: A Life for Unity*, New City Press, New York 1991, 31.

[3] Ibid., 36–38.

[4] Chiara Lubich, *Essential Writings: Spirituality, Dialogue, Culture*, New City Press, New York 2007, 4.

[5] Piero Damosso, *Il Mondo Unito di Chiara Lubich*, April 15, 2001 (Interview with Chiara Lubich on Italian television TG7) .

[6] *Essential Writings*, 5.

[7] Chiara Lubich, *Unity and Jesus Forsaken*, New City Press, New York 1985, 45–46. See Chiara Lubich, *The Cry: of Jesus Crucified and Forsaken in the History and Life of the Focolare Movement*, New City Press, New York 2001, 38; Jim Gallagher, *A Woman's Work: The Story of the Focolare Movement and its Founder*, New City Press, New York 1998, 37.

[8] Doriana Zamboni, "Stars and Tears," *Living City*, 42 (2003/5) 10.

[9] Ibid., 11.

[10] Ibid., 10–12. See Gallagher, 35–39; Zambonini 1991, 43–47.

[11] *Essential Writings*, 6.

[12] Ibid.

[13] Ibid.

[14] Ibid., 4.

[15] Ibid., 17.

[16] For a history of the Mariapolis in the 1950s, see Chiara Lubich and Igino Giordani, *Erano i tempi di guerra*, Città Nuova, Rome 2007, 193–228.

[17] Igino Giordani, *Memorie d'un cristiano ingenuo*, Città Nuova, Rome 1994, 149. See Gallagher, 71.

[18] Giordani 1994, 149–50.

[19] See Adriana Maria Avellaneda Torres, *Il giornalismo di Igino Giordani*, (unpublished thesis, 2000) 112, *available online at* www.netone.flars.net/testiPDF/tesi_AdrianaA.pdf.

[20]*Erano i tempi di guerra*, 149.

[21]Enzo Maria Fondi and Michele Zanzucchi, *Un popolo nato dal vangelo*, Edizioni San Paolo, Cinisello Balsamo 2003, 95 (source reference hereinafter, "Fondi").

[22]Zambonini 1991, 58.

[23]Tommaso Sorgi, *Un'anima di fuoco: Profilo di Igino Giordani*, Città Nuova, Rome 2003, 94–95. See *Erano i tempi di guerra,* 154; Gallagher, 72–73.

[24]Michele Zanzucchi, *Chiara Lubich: il cielo e l'umanità*, Città Nuova, Rome 2009, 33–34.

[25]*Essential Writings*, 175–76.

[26]*Erano i tempi di guerra*, 154–55.

[27]*Essential Writings*, 95.

[28]Pasquale Foresi, *Colloqui: Domande e risposte sulla spiritualità dell'unità*, Città Nuova, Rome 2009, 14.

[29]Ibid., 15. See Fondi, 71–73.

[30]Zambonini 1991, 59.

[31]*Essential Writings*, 17–18.

[32]Ibid., 4.

[33]*Erano i tempi di guerra*, 200.

[34]Fondi, 194.

[35]Franca Zambonini, *Chiara Lubich: La sua eredità*, Paoline, Milan 2009, 7.

[36]See Zambonini 1991, 72.

[37]John Paul II, Discorso ai Giovani Riuniti nel Palaeur di Roma per il Genfest 1990, March 31, 1990.

[38]John Paul II, Message to Ms. Chiara Lubich on the Occasion of the 60th Anniversary of the Birth of the "Work of Mary" (Focolare Movement), December 5, 2003.

[39]*Essential Writings*, 18.

[40]Chiara Lubich, "Engaging in Fruitful Dialogue," *Living City*, 35 (1996/10) 10–11.

[41]Chiara Lubich, *Incontri con l'Oriente*, Città Nuova, Rome 1986, 25.

[42]Chiara Lubich, "A Spirituality of Unity for the Harmonious Living of the Human Family," *Living City*, 40 (2001/1) 22–24, 24.

[43]Ibid., 24.

[44]Piero Coda, *Viaggio in Asia: con Chiara Lubich in Thailandia e Filippine*, Città Nuova, Rome 1997, 54.

[45]Focolare Information Service, "Defender of Peace Award Citation," <http://www.focolare.org/En/sif/2001/20010111e_c.html> (November 20, 2010); quoted in Amelia J. Uelmen, "Chiara Lubich: A Life for Unity," *Logos*, 8 (2005/1) 52–64, 58.

[46]Cardinal Tarcisio Bertone, "A Song to the Love of God," *Living City*, 47 (2008/5–6) 19–21, 20–21.

[47]*Work of Mary (Focolare Movement) General Statutes*, New York 2008, 13 (provisional translation from the Italian, *Opera di Maria — Statuti Generali*, on file with the authors). The official name under which the Focolare was approved in 1961 is *Opera di Maria* (Work of Mary).

[48]For a more detailed account of the 2008 General Assembly which elected Maria Voce, see Michele Zanzucchi and Paolo Loriga, "Consensus After Chiara," *Living City*, 47 (2008/8–9) 15–16; Amy Uelmen, "In Gratitude for the Life and Legacy of Chiara Lubich (1920–2008)," *Church*, 25 (2009/3) 14–17.

Part II: Living a Spirituality of Unity in the United States

2. How Focolare Members Live

[1]John Paul II, Discourse to the Focolare Movement, Rocca di Papa, Rome, August 19, 1984. See *L'Osservatore Romano*, August 20–21, 1984, 5; "Your Radicalism of Love," *Living City*, 23 (1984/11) 6–11. See also *The Cry*, 119.

[2]Walter Kasper, *An Introduction to Christian Faith*, Paulist Press, New York 1972, 193.

[3]*Essential Writings*, 18.

[4]Ibid., 65.

[5]*Incontro con l'Oriente*, 25. See Zambonini 2009, 75.

[6]Chiara Lubich, *The Art of Loving*, New City Press, New York 2010, 98.

[7]*Essential Writings*, 87.

[8]Ibid., 102.

[9]*General Statutes*, 13.

[10]Judith Povilus, *United in His Name: Jesus in the Midst in the Experience and Thought of Chiara Lubich*, New City Press, New York 1992, 65–66 (quoting Lubich).

[11]See Lorna Gold, *New Financial Horizons: The Emergence of the Economy of Communion*, New City Press, New York 2010, 55–59. See generally Thomas J. Norris, *The Trinity: Life of God, Hope for Humanity — Towards a Theology of Communion*, New City Press, New York 2009.

[12]*Essential Writings*, 211.

[13]Ibid., 14.

[14]Ibid., 169.

[15]Chiara Lubich, *A New Way: The Spirituality of Unity*, New City Press, New York 2006, 40.

[16]Chiara Lubich, *Colloqui con i gen 1970–74*, Città Nuova, Rome 1999, 18.

[17]Ibid.

[18]*A New Way*, 76.

[19]Ibid., 77.

[20]*Fondi*, 87.

[21]Gerard Rossé, "Aspetti dell'etica cristiana nella luce dell'ideale dell'unità," *Nuova Umanità*, 19 (1997/109) 53–60, 56 (quoting Lubich).

[22]Ibid., 55.

[23]Fabio Ciardi, "Come vivere il 'nulla-tutto' dell'amore," *Nuova Umanità*, 32 (2010/188) 185–215 (quoting Lubich).

[24]Chiara Lubich, "L'amore al prossimo," *Nuova Umanità*, 24 (2002/144) 709–719, 718.

[25]Chiara Lubich, *Santità di popolo*, Città Nuova, Rome 2001, 22–24.

[26]*Santità di popolo*, 25–27.

[27]Ibid., 28–30.

[28]Ibid., 34–37.

[29]Ibid.

[30]*Colloqui con i gen 1970–74*, 59.

[31]*Santità di popolo*, 31–33.

[32]Ibid., 42–43.

3. Walking the Path to Unity Together

[1]A rough translation from the Italian would be "carriers of fire."

[2]Gallagher, 12–13.

[3]Ibid., 13.

[4]Ibid.

[5]Ibid., 15–17.

214

Notes

[6]Zambonini 1991, 60. See Edwin Robertson, *Chiara*, Christian Journals, Ireland 1978, 15–16.

[7]Fondi, 212.

[8]*A New Way*, 136.

[9]Ibid. (probably referring to Antonio Petrilli, who understood his vocation when struck by the love with which Marco Tecilla, the first *focolarino*, was chopping the vegetables for lunch).

[10]*Essential Writings*, 50.

[11]*A New Way*, 134.

[12]Ibid., 144.

[13]Ibid., 142.

[14]*Essential Writings*, 49–50.

[15]Ibid., 108.

[16]Fondi, 214.

[17]Zambonini 1991, 153–54.

[18]Chiara Lubich, *Lettere dei primi tempi*, Città Nuova, Rome 2010, 31 (letter of January 30, 1944, to Chiara's sister Liliana). See Fondi, 244.

[19]Edwin Robinson, *The Fire of Love: A Life of Igino Giordani*, New City, London 1989, 148.

[20]Fondi, 226.

[21]Ibid., 227.

[22]Chiara Lubich, "I volontari di Dio," *Città Nuova*, 2 (1957/1) 1 (January 15, 1957). See *L'unità è la nostra avventura* (S. Veronesi, G. Boselli, G. Marchesi, eds.), Città Nuova, Rome 1986, 20.

[23]Ibid.

[24]Michele Zanzucchi, "The Incisive Idealists: The Volunteers of God Turn 50," *Living City*, 45 (2006/12) 10–13, 12.

[25]Fondi, 244.

[26]Ibid., 247.

[27]Chiara Lubich, *Colloqui con i gen 1966–69*, Città Nuova, Rome 1998, 9.

[28]Ibid., 11.

[29]Fondi, 255.

[30]Ibid.

[31]Ibid.

[32]Ibid., 261.

[33]Ibid.

[34]Ibid., 279–80.

[35]Ibid., 282–83.

[36]Ibid., 287.

[37]Ibid., 290.

[38]John Paul II, Message to the Sisters Adherents of the Focolare Movement, *L'Osservatore Romano*, April 18, 1996.

[39]Fondi, 296.

[40]Ibid.

[41]Opera di Maria, *Regolamento della branca dei presbíteri e dei diaconi permanenti*, 1990, Article 4.

[42]Fondi, 307.

[43]John Paul II, Greeting to Seminarians, December 30, 1994, reprinted in *Gen's*, 25 (1995/2) 70. See Lino D'Armi, "Priests for the Future," *Living City*, 34 (1995/4) 13–15, 14.

[44]Fondi, 320–321.

4. A Spirituality of Unity and the Renewal of Social Life and Culture

[1]Chiara Lubich, *Colloqui con i gen, 1975–2000*, Città Nuova, Rome 2001, 44.

[2]Ibid., 43.

[3]Ignio Giordani, *La famiglia: ricordi, pensieri*, Città Nuova, Rome 2005 (2d ed.) 101.

[4]See Carole Spale, "The Village with a Caring Heart — North Riverside, Illinois" *Living City*, 46 (2007/5) 24–26, 24.

[5]See Jim Webber, "Christmas at the Village with a Caring Heart," *Living City*, 47 (2008/12) 18–19, 18.

[6]Ibid., 18–19.

[7]See Spale, 26. See also North Riverside Mayor's Committee of Neighborhood Services, *Neighbors All: Creating Community One Block at a Time* (forthcoming) (describing applications of the "Art of Caring").

[8]*Essential Writings*, 365.

[9]See www.mondounito.net.

[10]See www.run4unity.net.

[11]The Cube of Love has been adopted by many schools as part of their educational program. See the bibliographical note for information about materials for students and teachers' guides. See also Michael James, Thomas Masters, Amy Uelmen, *Education's Highest Aim: Teaching and Learning Through a Spirituality of Communion,* New City Press, New York 2010, 48–53. See page 41 for a discussion of the "art of loving."

[12]Emily Christie, "Cubed Love: resources for conflict resolution and character building," 49 *Living City* (2010/4) 11.

[13]Ibid.

[14]Ibid.

[15]Ibid.

[16]Maria Dalgarno, "Cube-inspired Creations," 48 *Living City* (2009/12) 8. For further resources describing how the Cube of Love reduces bullying, see Maria Dalgarno and Tom Sherrard, "What a Small Cube Can Do," 46 *Living City* (2007/2) 16–17.

[17]See azionemondounito.org/english/pvs/index.asp.

[18]Ibid.

[19]See www.new-humanity.org.

[20]*Essential Writings*, 242.

[21]Ibid., 175–76.

[22]Ibid., 242.

[23]Fondi, 471.

[24]David Schindler, "Introduction," in *Introduction to the Abba School*, New City Press, New York 2002, 14.

[25]*Essential Writings*, 243.

[26]Fondi, 35.

[27]Fondi, 499.

[28]*Essential Writings*, 219–224.

[29]Michael James, Thomas Masters, Amy Uelmen, *Education's Highest Aim: Teaching and Learning through a Spirituality of Communion*, New City Press, New York 2010.

[30]Donald W. Mitchell, *Spirituality and Emptiness: The Dynamics of Spiritual Life in Buddhism and Christianity*, Paulist Press, New York 1991.

[31]See also Donald W. Mitchell, "New Forms of Lay Spirituality, Buddhist and Christian," *Buddhist-Christian Studies*, 15 (1995) 249–256; "The Christian Notion of Kenosis," *Pro Dialogo: Bulletin of the Vatican Pontifical Council for Interreligious Dialogue*, 100 (1991/1) 139–156; "The Church and the Laity," *Pro Dialogo*, 113 (2003/2) 277–289; "Re-Creating Christian Community," *Buddhist-Christian Studies*, 23 (2003) 21–32; "Founders Nikkyo Niwano and Chiara Lubich: An Interreligious Dialogue for Peace," *Dharma World*, 34 (2007/Oct-Nov) 31–33; "A Phenomenological Answer to the Question 'What is the Lotus Sutra,'" *Dharma World*, 37 (2010/Jul–Sept) 9–14.

[32]Judith Povilus, *United in His Name*, New City Press, New York 1992.

[33]Paul O'Hara, "Interpretations of Reality," in *Interpretazioni del Reale: Teologia, Filosofia e Scienze in Dialogo* (Piero Coda and Roberto Priscilla, eds.), Pontificia Università Lateranese, 2000. O'Hara also applies a spirituality of unity to his research in mathematics. See "Rotation Invariance and the Spin-Statistics Theorem," *Foundations of Physics* 33 (2003/9). "Minkowski Space and Quantum Mechanics," in *Space, Time and Spacetime – Physical and Philosophical Implications of Minkowski's Unification of Space and Time* (Vesselin Petkov, ed.), Springer, New York 2010; and "Quantum Mechanics and the Metrics of General Relativity," *Foundations of Physics* 35 (2005/9).

[34]*Faith and the Media: Reflections by Christian Communicators* (Dennis D. Cali, ed.), Paulist Press, New Jersey 2010.

[35]See Amelia J. Uelmen, "Reconciling Evangelization and Dialogue through Love of Neighbor," *Villanova Law Review* 57 (2007/2) 303–329 (applications in law, politics and interreligious dialogue); "Toward a Trinitarian Theory of Products Liability," *Journal of Catholic Social Thought* 1 (2004) 603–645 (application to tort law); "Can a Religious Person Be a Big Firm Litigator?" *Fordham Urban Law Journal*, 26 (1999) 1069–1110 (application to legal ethics).

[36]Amy Uelmen, "University Education — Seeking a New Model: The Sophia Summer School for a Culture of Unity," *Living City*, 45 (2006/4) 8–11.

[37]"University Aims to Build Culture of Unity," *Zenit*, January 23, 2008.

[38]*Essential Writings*, 309.

[39]Ibid., 310.

[40]Maria Hartmann Kastan, "An Open Studio Mentality," *Living City*, 48 (2009/2) 13.

[41]Ed Roy, "A Filmmaker's Inner Focus," *Living City*, 49 (2010/6) 7–8, 8. For more information about the film "Hidden in Time," see www.J6Entertainment.com.

[42]Roy, 8.

[43]Interview with Ron Austin, God Who is Beauty Arts Congress, April 25, 1999, available at www.focolare.org/articolo.php?codart=4443.

[44]Ibid.

[45]Emily Christie, "Hard Earned Wisdom in Hollywood," *Living City*, 46 (2007/11) 20–21. See Ron Austin, *In a New Light: Spirituality and the Media Arts*, New City Press, New York 2007 (published jointly with Wm. B. Eerdmans Publishing Co.).

[46]Fondi, 435.

[47]Ibid.

[48]Recipients represent a spectrum of religious and cultural backgrounds. They include Norma Levitt, past president of the World Conference on Religions and Peace; Donald Mitchell, professor of Eastern Religions at Purdue University; Dawud Assad, of the Muslim World League; Professor Masao Abe, leader in Christian-Buddhist dialogue; Rabbi Jack Bemporad, leader in Jewish-Christian dialogue; Vivian Juan, representative of the Tekakwitha Conference, a Catholic

Native American/Aboriginal Organization; Rev. Diane Kessler, Executive Director of the Massachusetts Council of Churches; Reverend Nichiko Niwano, president of the Japanese Buddhist Rissho Kosei-kai Movement; Pat and Jack Shea, screenwriter and motion picture director; Cardinal Pio Laghi, former papal nuncio to the United States; Cardinal William Keeler of Baltimore; Cardinal John O'Connor of New York; Cardinal Theodore McCarrick of Washington D.C.; Mother Mary Rose Schulte, founder of the Servant Sisters of Christ the King; Imam W. Deen Mohammed, leader of the American Muslim Society; Hon. Douglas Roche, O.C., Canadian diplomat and specialist in peace and human security issues; His Royal Highness Lukas Njifua Fontem, the Fon of Fontem, Cameroun; Bishop Henrik Svenungsson, pioneer of ecumenical dialogue between the Swedish Lutheran Church and the Catholic Church; Dr. Shantilal Somaiya, proponent of unity in diversity through education; Dr. Tony Cernera, president of Sacred Heart University; and Howard and Rose Belcher, one of the founding families of Mariapolis Luminosa.

5. The Focolare Movement and the Church

[1] *Essential Writings*, 30.

[2] See Carlo Maria Martini, *La parola di Dio alle origine della Chiesa*, Università Gregoriana, Rome 1980, 14 (citing Paul Claudel, *La Vie intelletuelle*, May 1948).

[3] Zambonini 2009, 40–42.

[4] Ibid., 42–43. See Zambonini 1991, 62.

[5] Zambonini 2009, 43–46 (quoting *La Libertà nella Chiesa*, EDB, Bologna, 1992, which includes discussion of the investigations of the Focolare Movement from 1957–1959).

[6] *The Cry*, 68.

[7] Ibid., 66.

[8] Ibid., 72.

[9] Ibid., 66.

[10] Ibid.

[11] Ibid., 69.

[12] Ibid., 74.

[13] Ibid., 79.

[14] Ibid., 85.

[15] Ibid., 90.

[16] Ibid., 91.

[17] *Diary 64/65*, 80.

[18] Joseph Cardinal Ratzinger, *New Outpourings of the Spirit: Movements in the Church*, Ignatius Press, San Francisco 2007, 38–50. See Joseph Ratzinger, "The Theological Locus of Ecclesial Movements," in *Communio* 25 (1988/3) 480–500.

[19] Ratzinger, *New Outpourings*, 42.

[20] Ibid., 52.

[21] John Paul II, Speech for the World Congress of Ecclesial Movements and New Communities, May 27, 1998.

[22] Ratzinger, *New Outpourings*, 21.

[23] Tom Hoopes, "Groundswell: The Pope, the New Movements and the Church," 22 *Crisis* (2004/11) 32–38.

[24] Renée M. LaReau, "SuperCatholics? Sizing up the new lay movements," *U.S. Catholic*, 71 (2006/2) 12–17.

[25] *Essential Writings*, 33.

[26]Leonor Maria Salierno, *Maria negli scritti di Chiara Lubich*, Città Nuova, Rome 1993, 96.

[27]Sharry Silvi, "Pentecost '98: The Movements and the Pope for an Unprecedented Event," *Living City*, 37 (1998/8–9) 6–10, 9 (quoting Lubich's address).

[28]*The Parish Community: A Path to Communion* (Fr. Adolfo Raggio, ed.), New City Press, New York 2000, 111.

[29]John Paul II, *Novo Millennio Ineunte* (2001) 43.

[30]Fondi, 365.

[31]*Essential Writings*, 37.

Part III: The Focolare Spirituality and Contemporary Culture in the United States

[1]David Brooks, "The Summoned Life," *New York Times*, August 2, 2010.

[2]Ibid.

6. The Focolare Spirituality and "The Pursuit of Happiness"

[1]United States Declaration of Independence, July 4, 1776.

[2]J. Hector St. Jean de Crèvecoeur, *Letters from an American Farmer* (1782), Applewood Books, Carlisle, Massachusetts 2007, Letter III, 56–57.

[3]Crèvecoeur was obviously not speaking for the experience of Africans held in the bonds of slavery; nor did he comment on the fact that much of the occupied farmland had previously provided sustenance for Native American tribes.

[4]Alexis de Tocqueville, *Democracy in America* (Harvey C. Mansfield & Delba Winthrop, eds.), University of Chicago Press, Chicago 2000, 484.

[5]Ibid.

[6]Ibid., 482.

[7]John Winthrop, "Model of Christian Charity," in *Classics of American Political and Constitutional Thought* (Scott J. Hammond et al.), Hackett Publishing, Indianapolis 2007, 17–18.

[8]Robert Bellah, Richard Madsen, William M. Sullivan, Ann Swidler, Steven M. Tipton, *Habits of the Heart*, Univ. California Press, Berkeley 1985, 276.

[9]Ibid., 23.

[10]Ibid.

[11]Ibid., 148. See Tocqueville, 403–410.

[12]Bellah, 149 (quoting Schneider and Smith).

[13]Ibid., 51.

[14]Tocqueville, 504–505. See Bellah, 223.

[15]Bellah, 143.

[16]Charles Taylor, *Sources of the Self*, Cambridge Univ. Press, New York 1989, 509–510.

[17]Taylor, 509–510.

[18]Marisa Cerini, *God Who is Love in the Experience and Thought of Chiara Lubich*, New City Press, New York 1992, 12. See *A New Way*, 39, note 3. See also Lucia Bellaspiga, "Instrumental Friar," *Living City*, 49 (2010/5) 20–21 (interview with Fr. Casimiro Bonetti, the unknowing "spark that lit the fire in the soul of Chiara Lubich.")

[19]*A New Way*, 40.

[20]Cerini, 12, 17.

[21]*A New Way*, 40.

[22] Ibid., 41.

[23] Cerini, 13.

[24] *Essential Writings*, 58–59.

[25] Cerini, 18.

[26] *A New Way*, 81.

[27] Ibid.

[28] Ibid., 113.

[29] Bellah, 149.

[30] See Gold, *New Financial Horizons*, 65–80 (discussing the Focolare's "alternative economic vision").

[31] *Essential Writings*, 281.

[32] Chiara Lubich, *Journey to Heaven: Spiritual Thoughts to Live*, New City Press, New York 1991, 122.

[33] See Chiara Lubich, Response to "What can we Gen 3 do to limit consumerism?," Marino Ice Arena (Rome), June 12, 1991, transcript and video available at http://centrochiaralubich.org/index.php/en/component/rokdownloads/downloads/pdf/146-chi19920612en.html?ItemId=48.

[34] John Allen, "Benedict in Cameroon: A tale of two trips," *National Catholic Reporter* ("All Things Catholic" Blog) March 20, 2009.

[35] *Essential Writings*, 281. For the most extensive and in-depth English-language analysis of the Economy of Communion to date, see Gold, *New Financial Horizons*.

[36] Benedict XVI, *Caritas in veritate* ("Charity in Truth") (2009) 46.

[37] Ibid. See John Allen, "Indiana Firm Can Claim a Papal Thumbs-up from New Social Encyclical" and "Pope proposes a 'Christian Humanism' for the global economy," *National Catholic Reporter* ("All Things Catholic" Blog) July 7, 2009. See Austen Ivereigh, "The Hidden Hand in 'Caritas' of Focolare," *America Magazine* ("In All Things" Blog) July 8, 2009; Jim Graves, "Economy of Communion: A Radical Business Makeover," *Our Sunday Visitor Newsweekly*, May 23, 2010, 6–8.

[38] George Weigel, "Charity in Truth: The Vatican, the United States, and the issues, after the week that was," *National Review*, July 13, 2009.

[39] Graves, 6.

[40] Ibid.

[41] See Stefano Zamagni, "On the Foundation and Meaning of the 'Economy of Communion' Experience," in *The Economy of Communion: Toward a Multidimensional Economic Culture* (Luigino Bruni, ed.), New City Press, New York 2002, 130–140, 132.

[42] Caterina Mulatero, "The Needy are Full Participants in This Initiative," *Living City* 40 (2001/5) 14–15, 15.

[43] Tocqueville, 502.

[44] Ibid., 501. The editors of the *Democracy in America* note that of "American moralists," Benjamin Franklin would have been foremost in Tocqueville's mind.

[45] Brian Danoff, "Asking Freedom Something Other than Itself: Tocqueville, Putnam, and the Vocation of the Democratic Moralist," *Politics & Policy* 35 (2007) 165–190, 176.

[46] *Caritas in veritate*, 53.

[47] *Essential Writings*, 211.

7. The Focolare Spirituality, the Moral Life, and the Quest for Freedom

[1] Bellah, 23.

[2] Planned Parenthood v. Casey, 505 U.S. 833, 852 (1992) (plurality).

[3]Bellah, 75–76.

[4]Ibid., 79.

[5]Ibid., 76.

[6]Ibid., 148.

[7]Ibid., 77.

[8]Ibid.

[9]See Taylor, 509–510.

[10]*Essential Writings*, 5.

[11]Chiara Lubich, *On the Holy Journey*, New City Press, New York 1988, 109.

[12]Bellah, 23–24.

[13]Robert Wuthnow, *Sharing the Journey: Support Groups and America's New Quest for Community*, The Free Press, New York 1994, 6. See Putnam 2000, 152.

[14]Angela Clara, "Sheri Schiltz," in *Verso la vita* (Arnoldo Diana, ed.), Città Nuova, Rome 1991, 109.

[15]Ibid., 110.

[16]Ibid., 112.

[17]Ibid., 116.

[18]Ibid., 118.

[19]For the complete account from which excerpts were drawn, see T. M. Hartmann, "You Must Have Loved Very Much," *Living City*, 45 (2006/11) 20–23; Sharry Silvi, "Living Together, Dying Together," *Living City*, 45 (2006/11) 22; T. M. Hartmann, "The Spiritual Bouquet," *Living City*, 45 (2006/11) 24–25.

[20]Michele Zanzucchi, *Io ho tutto: i diciotto anni di Chiara Luce*, Città Nuova, Rome 2010, 33. See Michele Zanzucchi, *Chiara Luce: A Life Lived to the Full*, New City, London 2007, 36–37.

[21]Zanzucchi, *A Life Lived to the Full*, 39.

[22]Ibid.

[23]Ibid., 40.

[24]Ibid., 49.

[25]Ibid.

[26]Benedict XVI, Angelus, Castelgandolfo, September 26, 2010. See "On Love with a Capital 'L'" *Zenit*, September 26, 2010.

8. *E Pluribus Unum* — The Focolare Spirituality and the Quest for Community in a Pluralistic Society

[1]Tocqueville, 489.

[2]Ibid., 491.

[3]Ibid., 492.

[4]Robert D. Putnam, *Bowling Alone: The Collapse and Revival of American Community*, Simon & Schuster, New York 2000, 18–19. As may be evident from the discussion in Chapter 5, we are ambivalent about the term "social capital" for its tendency to overemphasize the utilitarian and economistic nature of social change and cohesion. As one critique put it, "the tension, conflict, and contradiction between capital and community are obscured by the term social capital because it strongly suggests that it, financial capital, and human capital are merely different species of the same genus, capital." Stephen Samuel Smith and Jessica Kulynych, "Liberty, Equality and… Social Capital?" in *Social Capital: Critical Perspectives on Community and "Bowling Alone"* (S. McLean, D. Schultz, M. Stegers, eds.), New York Univ. Press, New York 2002, 129.

[5]Putnam 2000, 22.

[6]Ibid., 23.

[7]Ibid.

[8]Ibid.

[9]Ibid., 337.

[10]Ibid., 340.

[11]Ibid., 358.

[12]Ibid.

[13]Ibid., 361.

[14]Bill Bishop, *The Big Sort: Why the Clustering of Like-Minded America is Tearing Us Apart*, Houghton Mifflin Harcourt, New York 2008 (Mariner Books Paperback, 2009), 12.

[15]Ibid., 14 (quoting marketing analyst J. Walker Smith).

[16]Ibid., 6.

[17]Ibid., 173 (recounting conversation with Marty).

[18]Putnam 2000, 78 (quoting Wuthnow).

[19]Robert D. Putnam and David E. Campbell, *American Grace*, Simon & Schuster, New York 2010, 550.

[20]*Colloqui con i gen 1970–74*, 77.

[21]Ibid., 80.

[22]*Unity and Jesus Forsaken*, 34–35. For further reflections on the art of "making ourselves one," see *The Art of Loving*, 69–88.

[23]Brenda Balli, "Bonding Correspondence," *Living City*, 47 (2008/11) 16–17.

[24]"From Harlem, to Washington, to the World: the Seeds are Sprouting," *Living City*, 49 (2010/5) 10–11, 10.

[25]Chiara Lubich, "A Spirituality of Unity for the Harmonious Living of the Human Family," *Living City*, 40 (2001/1) 22–24. See Piero Coda, *Nella Moschea di Malcom X*, Città Nuova, Rome 1997, 13–23.

[26]Ibid., *Living City*, 24.

[27]Sharry Silvi, "Toward Universal Brotherhood," *Living City*, 40 (2001/4) 10–13, 11.

[28]See ibid.; Clare Zanzucchi, "Thursdays at Shapiro's," *Living City*, 43 (2004/5) 14–17.

[29]Putnam and Campbell 2010, 550. See also ibid., 36.

[30]Ibid., 526.

[31]Ibid.

[32]Ibid., 531.

[33]Ibid., 532.

[34]Ibid., 533.

[35]*Essential Writings*, 87.

9. A Common Commitment to the Common Good — A Spirituality of Unity and the Future of Public Life

[1]Bishop, 255.

[2]Putnam 2000, 341.

[3]Putnam and Campbell 2010, 437.

[4]Bishop, 39.

[5] Ibid., 36.

[6] Benjamin R. Barber, *A Place for Us*, Hill and Wang, New York 1998, 115.

[7] Bishop, 14.

[8] Cass R. Sunstein, *Going to Extremes*, Oxford Univ. Press, New York 2009, 157.

[9] Ibid.

[10] Bishop, 75.

[11] Ibid., 284.

[12] Ibid., 285 (summarizing the mid-1950s research results of social psychologist Gordon Allport).

[13] Ibid.

[14] See ibid., 255.

[15] See ibid., 173.

[16] See ibid., 285.

[17] See Gold, 162–179 (describing Economy of Communion networks and gatherings).

[18] *Essential Writings*, 236.

[19] Ibid., 254.

[20] Ibid., 263.

[21] Zambonini 2009, 126.

[22] Ibid., 124.

[23] Ibid., 123.

[24] See pages 115–16 for a discussion of the same text applied to the diverse gifts in the life of the Church.

[25] *Essential Writings*, 33.

[26] Ibid.

[27] Piero Coda, "Una mistica per il terzo millennio," *Nuova Umanità*, 24 (2002/5) 577–590, 587.

[28] *Essential Writings*, 33.

[29] Ibid.

[30] Ibid., 34.

[31] Ibid.

[32] See Igino Giordani, *Dare un'anima alla democrazia* (Francesco D'Alessandro, ed.) Edizione Giuseppe Latzerza, Bari, Italy 2003 (selected articles from *La Via* between 1949–1953).

[33] Ibid., 156–57.

[34] Ibid., 157.

[35] Torres, *Il giornalismo di Igino Giordani*, 100.

[36] Ibid. (quoting Giordani, "Riarmo o Reazione," *La Via*, February 10, 1951).

[37] See Second Vatican Council, *Gaudium et spes* (1965) 21 ("This faith should show its fruitfulness by penetrating the whole life, even the worldly activities, of those who believe, and by urging them to be loving and just especially towards those in need. Lastly, what does most to show God's presence clearly is the brotherly love of the faithful who, being all of one mind and spirit, work together for the faith of the Gospel and present themselves as a sign of unity.").

[38] Igino Giordani, *Diary of Fire*, New City Press, New York 1982, 25.

[39] "50 anni di Josef Lux," *MPPU News* (Newsletter of the Movimento politico per l'unità) (April 2006, n.2) 7, available at www.mppu.org/downloads/newsletter.html.

[40] "Josef Lux," Movimento politico per l'unità website, www.mppu.org/chi-siamo/figure-storiche/28-josef-lux.html.

[41]"50 anni di Josef Lux," 7.

[42]Ibid. See also Veronika Hankusova, Ondrej Maly/Ondrej Maly, "Josef Lux Died," *Carolina* (Students' E-mail News from the Czech Republic, Charles University in Prague) no.353, Nov. 26, 1999, available at http://carolina.cuni.cz/archive-en/Carolina-E-No-353.txt.

[43]See *Meditazioni per la vita pubblica: il carisma dell'unità e la politica* (Antonio Maria Baggio, ed.), Città Nuova, Rome 2005 (reflections offered by the Movement for Unity in Politics during gatherings at the Italian Parliament from 2001–2003).

[44]*Essential Writings*, 263.

[45]Ibid., 264.

[46]Sergio Previdi, "Incontri nazionali del MPPU in Brasile," *MPPU News* (April 2006, n.2) 10–11, 11, available at www.mppu.org/downloads/newsletter.html.

[47]"In Parlamento a Seoul: un anno di incontri del MPPU," *MPPU News* (November 2005, n.1) 8, available at www.mppu.org/downloads/newsletter.html. See also "Chi siamo / un'amore politico," MPPU Website, www.mppu.org/chi-siamo/un-amore-politico.html.

[48]Ibid., 8.

[49]Ibid.

[50]Angela Joo Synk Yung, "Il Movimento politico per l'unità in Corea," MPPU website, www.mppu.org/notizie/in-corea.html.

[51]Daniela Ropelato, "Corea del Sud. Un premio al forum del MPPU," MPPU website, www.mppu.org/notizie/in-corea.html. See also Michele Zanzucchi, "In the Land of Morning Calm," *New City Magazine* (Philippines) 45 (2010/4–5) 10–12, available at www.newcityph.com/archive/1004/event.htm (describing meetings between members of the Forum and Focolare president Maria Voce).

[52]*Essential Writings*, 256.

[53]Study materials for the 2007 workshop included United States Conference of Catholic Bishops, *Forming Consciences for Faithful Citizenship* (2007); Congregation for the Doctrine of the Faith, *Doctrinal Note on Some Questions Regarding the Participation of Catholics in Public Life* (2002).

[54]Diana C. Mutz, *Hearing the Other Side: Deliberative versus Participatory Democracy*, Cambridge University Press, New York 2006, 53–54. See Bishop, 292 (discussing Mutz's research).

[55]Putnam 2000, 23.

[56]Mutz, 34.

[57]Mutz, 126.

Conclusion: A Hearth for the Human Family

[1]Maxwell E. Johnson, *The Virgin of Guadalupe: Theological Reflections of an Anglo-Lutheran Liturgist*, Rowman & Littlefield, Maryland 2002, 74.

[2]Virgil P. Elizondo, *Guadalupe: Mother of the New Creation*, Orbis Books, Maryknoll, New York 1997, 119.

About the Authors

Thomas Masters holds a bachelor's degree in English and Philosophy from Lewis University, a master's in English Literature from DePaul University, and a Ph.D. in Language, Literacy, and Rhetoric from the University of Illinois Chicago. After nearly forty years in secondary schools and in college, he retired from teaching and works as an author and as editorial director for the Focolare's North American publishing house, New City Press. He met the Focolare Movement in 1973 in Chicago, and since 1984 has been a married *focolarino*. He lives outside of Chicago with his wife Kathleen. They have three adult children.

Amy Uelmen holds a bachelor's degree in American Studies and a J.D. from Georgetown University, and a master's in Theology from Fordham University. She currently serves as the director of the Institute on Religion, Law & Lawyer's Work at Fordham Law School. She has lectured and published widely on how religious values might inform the practice of law and how principles of dialogue might inform debates about religion in the public square. Amy met the Focolare Movement in 1977 when her family attended a Mariapolis. Throughout her childhood and youth she participated in the Movement's activities. Since 1996 she has been living in a women's Focolare house in New York City.